Strategy → execution

BEYOND GOVERNANCE

BEYOND

GOVERNANCE

Creating Corporate Value through Performance, Conformance and Responsibility

MARTIN FAHY

JEREMY ROCHE

ANASTASIA WEINER

John Wiley & Sons, Ltd

Published in 2005 by John Wiley & Sons Ltd, The Atrium, Southern Gate, Chichester, West Sussex PO19 8SQ, England

Telephone (+44) 1243 779777

Email (for orders and customer service enquiries): cs-books@wiley.co.uk
Visit our Home Page on www.wiley.com

Other Wiley Editorial Offices

John Wiley & Sons Inc., 111 River Street, Hoboken, NJ 07030, USA

Jossey-Bass, 989 Market Street, San Francisco, CA 94103-1741, USA

Wiley-VCH Verlag GmbH, Boschstr. 12, D-69469 Weinheim, Germany

John Wiley & Sons Australia Ltd, 33 Park Road, Milton, Queensland 4064, Australia

John Wiley & Sons (Asia) Pte Ltd, 2 Clementi Loop #02-01, Jin Xing Distripark, Singapore 129809

John Wiley & Sons Canada Ltd, 22 Worcester Road, Etobicoke, Ontario, Canada M9W 1L1

Wiley also publishes its books in a variety of electronic formats. Some content that appears in print may not be available in electronic books.

British Library Cataloguing in Publication Data

A catalogue record for this book is available from the British Library

ISBN 0-470-01151-3

Typeset by Dobbie Typesetting Ltd, Tavistock, Devon
Printed and bound in Great Britain by Antony Rowe Ltd, Chippenham, Wiltshire
This book is printed on acid-free paper responsibly manufactured from sustainable forestry in which at least two trees are planted for each one used for paper production.

CONTENTS

FOREWORD

··························

*I*t was the slightly eccentric biologist Charles Darwin whose theories on natural selection bore that famous phrase 'survival of the fittest'. Admittedly, Enterprise Governance is not evolution in its truest sense, but market legislation and stakeholder pressure are forcing organisations worldwide to face the facts of life – adapt to your environment or become extinct.

Organisations that fail to evolve culturally *will* find themselves operating in an increasingly hostile environment. The 'greed is good' days of Hollywood creation Gordon Gecko are gone; along sadly with the bright red braces and power shoulder pads, to be replaced by a more holistic 'quality of life' approach to business that extends to who we work for, who we invest in, and ultimately in whom we trust.

Globalisation, accelerated by advances in information technology, has led to more and more companies choosing to operate multinational business units. Each of those overseas units or subsidiaries will in turn be forced to adapt to their own 'local' environment, adding yet another strand of compliance to the corporate DNA. International Financial Reporting Standards, the Operating and Financial Review in the UK, the Sarbanes–Oxley Act in the USA and the King Report II in South Africa, are but a few legislative issues which will have to be taken into consideration by an increasing number of organisations.

However tempting it is to condemn these legislative acts as financial shackles pinning down the entrepreneurial spirit, governance must be seen as a value-added function, and not just a box-ticking exercise. Conformance will not only help drive financial success, but will create sustainable corporate value, if adopted as part of a triple-bottom line culture. The increase in ethical investment and corporate benchmarking indices, and the growth of stakeholder activism, all reflect the importance of delivering long-term shareholder value. Institutional investors are also increasingly exercising their shareholder rights to forcibly push organisations to adopt transparent corporate responsibility and governance policies, or remove failing senior executives, with the threat of withdrawing their millions.

In order to meet stakeholders' demands for unequivocal assurances on numbers, ethical behaviour and value, the finance function will have to undergo fundamental change. Senior finance professionals will be expected to contribute to strategy development, delivering analysis from data collected in 'real-time' terms. Sustainable conformance and performance will be driven by a new species of CFO, who will view compliance as a value-added function, and not just a 'box-ticking' exercise. A few enlightened senior finance professionals have already embraced this approach, but many still question it.

Accountants, for years isolated in their function from other business operations, will no longer solely focus on transactional processes or historical reporting, but help position organisations for market success, by combining their traditional services with technology consulting and assurance services. The new economy accountant will be expected to perform a range of essential services, e.g., due diligence, organise shareholder meetings, supervise cash management, and handle the payroll. Initial public offering, acquisition and merger skills will also be required, especially in the new regulatory environment. Senior finance professionals therefore need clear information to help them

operate in this rapidly evolving and highly challenging environment. Because people are behind the execution of systems and
processes, training and culture are as important as strategy.

It is important to remember, however, that although bad
governance can destroy an organisation, good governance on its
own cannot ensure success. Organisations need to balance
conformance with performance and corporate responsibility to
successfully evolve into sustainable enterprises that do not lurch
from feast to famine.

The importance of getting it right is not just in the costs of
failure. The benefits of a well-suited, well-implemented set of
business applications can bring real benefits both in terms of low
operating costs and ability to exploit opportunity. But creating
the perfect strategy is not enough. Only flawless execution will
push an organisation to the top of the corporate food chain.

David Kappler
CFO Cadbury Schweppes from 1995 to 2004,
non-executive director of Shire Pharmaceutical Group plc,
Chairman of Premier Foods, and
Fellow of the Chartered Institute of Management Accountants

PREFACE

· · · · · · · · · · · · · · · · · · · ·

*T*oday's finance professionals face a very different world to their predecessors. The steady, planned and predictable world of the accountant has been changed beyond measure, by a number of pressures including:

- corporate scandals and the consequent intense focus on corporate governance and risk management;
- changing expectations of the finance function – from number crunching and rear-view reporting to involvement in strategy setting, execution and monitoring;
- the rising significance of responsible business practice;
- business information technology.

In writing *Beyond Governance*, we wanted to examine how these changes were impacting organisations and, in particular, the business and finance personnel who have to cope with them. We particularly wanted to help them respond positively to the pressures of corporate governance – to realise that by improving systems and processes to address compliance, they could also position themselves to deliver better performance and thereby enhance the value of themselves and their organisations.

In the book we show how embracing Enterprise Governance can help organisations to meet emerging demands and growing market regulation. Many executives, advisors and journalists that we have spoken to feel that corporate governance and compliance stifle creativity and innovation in business. Here we argue that focusing on corporate governance, performance management, and corporate responsibility actually *drives* business performance. We seek to discuss the issues involved and show how organisations that embrace these disciplines can outperform others and create greater shareholder value.

As many firms rethink their finance activities in the light of e-commerce, shared service centres, business intelligence technology, cost cutting, and so on, this book explores the issues and highlights the people, processes and systems necessary to build a finance function capable of supporting today's organisations. We look at the challenges facing finance professionals in the coming decade and suggest that there is a need to shift from the current finance skills-based approach to one based on broader organisational and management competencies. We highlight the emerging role of the new CFO, how the career path of finance professionals has dramatically altered and describe the new technology that needs to be employed to tackle today's issues and future challenges.

This book draws on the diverse experience of the authors – an academic with broad practical experience drawn from advising organisations around the world in improving their people, processes and systems; the CEO of a global financial software organisation, who spends much of his time helping clients of all sizes and industries to deal with the complexities of financial control and strategy; and a business journalist who has interviewed entrepreneurs, business leaders and regulators from every imaginable sector in the course of her writing.

We have endeavoured to take a global view and draw on the experiences of leading analysts, finance experts, technologists and organisations around the world. We have included case studies and interviews with influential businesses and business leaders to illustrate how management theory, new business practices and leading edge technology can help companies achieve competitive excellence.

Most importantly, we have tried to take a pragmatic and real-life approach to these subjects. The book aims to provide a practical and useful guide for business and finance professionals to help you address the issues of today and the future. We hope you find it both enlightening and useful, and look forward to featuring some of your organisations in future success stories!

ACKNOWLEDGEMENTS

T he authors would like to thank the following people and organisations for their contribution and help with this book: Peter Hill, operations director Bellis-Jones Hill Group; Mark Adams, CFO STA Travel; CIMA (Chartered Institute of Management Accountants), Nick Jarman, ATOS Consulting; Tim Tribe; Judy Rowson; Steve Newton and Debbie Ashton from CODA; and the patient editorial staff at John Wiley & Sons, particularly Jo Golesworthy, Claire Plimmer and Francesca Warren.

Martin Fahy would like to offer particular thanks to his wife Sophie for her love, support, and patience in this and all their endeavours, and to Yves and Maryse Cacciaguidi for giving up their home to the Cacciaguidi-Fahy family every summer.

Special thanks go to David Turner, CODA's international marketing director, for his invaluable support and advice without which this book would have remained just a good idea.

CHAPTER 1

INTRODUCTION: ENTERPRISE GOVERNANCE

*I*t is almost impossible to write about the dramatic changes currently sweeping the world's financial markets without mentioning Enron. Never before has a corporate collapse caused so much public anger, resentment and distrust, nor created as much market turmoil. Enron was, after all, one of the most successful, responsible, and above all profitable organisations operating within the strict corporate governance parameters of one of the world's most highly regulated capital markets; and yet it disappeared amidst a puff of accounting scandal overnight. With investor pockets and confidence stripped to the bone, the performance and ethical behaviour of publicly listed organisations were put under forensic investigation. How had this happened, and, more importantly, what could be done to prevent such a collapse from happening in the future?

Unfortunately Enron proved only the first bad apple to fall. Just as the first public reports into corporate governance standards had been commissioned by governments, a similar 'corporate rot' was exposed at WorldCom, Tyco, Xerox, Global Crossing, and HIH, to name but a few. And the list of corporate casualties has continued to grow, with Italian dairy giant Parmalat one of the more recent to fall foul of alleged widespread accounting irregularities and fraud. The full effect of new regulations born out of those reports, such as the Sarbanes–Oxley Act in the USA, remains to be seen. What can be said is that the traditional view of stock market investment has changed irreversibly. Investors want to see the inside workings of the organisation they are putting their money into; they want explanations of every material issue that affects or could affect their investment; and, above all, they want long-term shareholder value.

Although studies of corporate scandals involving companies such as Enron, Vivendi, Cable and Wireless, and Royal Ahold show a lack of ethical culture and tone from the top,[1] poor corporate governance alone will not necessarily bring a company to its knees. Corporate strategy is of equal, if not greater, importance. There is plenty of evidence to show that companies with poor strategies commonly suffer ineffective risk management, weak strategy execution, and an inability to respond to fast-changing market conditions. But while there have been lengthy discussions on how to achieve effective compliance and improved strategic performance, the two disciplines rarely collide, despite considerable evidence that adopting good conformance as well as effective strategic management is essential to achieving sustainability.

Enterprise Governance – a New Framework

Enterprise Governance is based on the principle that good governance alone cannot make an organisation successful. The emerging framework, under the three dimensions of *Performance*, *Conformance* and *Corporate Responsibility*, addresses the primary concerns that boards and senior executives must effectively manage to ensure the delivery of long-term value to stakeholders (Figure 1.1). Unlike most current management thinking, which is based on the premise that conformance links directly to accountability, and performance to value creation,[2] Enterprise Governance clearly shows that these two disciplines are interchangeable; in other words performance can lead to

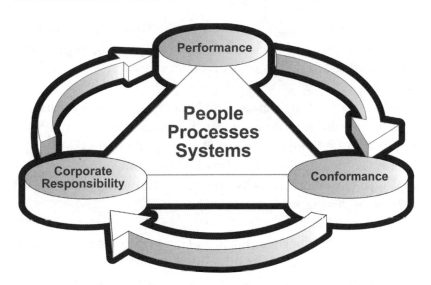

Figure 1.1. Enterprise Governance.

assurance and conformance to value creation.[3] Furthermore, it provides evidence that this is not only desirable, but essential in returning stability to the capital markets.

Neatly bridging the two established principles is Corporate Responsibility (CR). Inextricably linked to corporate governance and risk management, as well as 'ethical' environmental and social stewardship, on which its origins are founded, CR has fast gained considerable significance for stakeholders and the corporate community. Although the emerging concept of Enterprise Governance originally focused on the conformance and performance dimensions, we believe that CR is of sufficient importance to create a third element within the framework. Furthermore, evidence shows that sustainable value can only be successfully achieved with the adoption of all three disciplines; as Dell, Microsoft, Tesco, GE and Alcoa, to name but a few, can testify.

The Performance Dimension

The performance dimension of Enterprise Governance is concerned with developing and deploying effective strategic management processes to ensure that the firm creates value for shareholders. As such, it encompasses the systems, people and processes that enable the firm to determine:

- Which parts of the business are creating shareholder value?
- What are the real drivers of our performance?
- What do these figures mean? How important are they?
- How are we performing relative to the competition?
- Which customers are delivering the bulk of our profit?
- What is driving cash generation?

US-based technology consultancy Gartner[4] coined the phrase Corporate Performance Management (CPM) as 'an umbrella term for the methodologies, processes, metrics, and systems that enterprises use to monitor and manage business performance'. Research suggests that more effective CPM capability may in the long term be the only sustainable form of competitive advantage. Firms that have embraced CPM are able to make effective strategic choices, which deliver the superior financial outcomes ultimately reflected in long-term shareholder value.

In more tangible terms, CPM involves deploying systems across the enterprise including analytical applications such as:

- scorecards;
- planning and budgeting;
- business intelligence.

Decision-makers are then given access to these applications, ensuring that that they are all working from the same data, thereby guaranteeing that management analysis is consistent and up-to-the-minute.

A key feature of this decision support approach is the recognition that technology needs to be combined with management intuition and 'gut feel' for the most effective outcome. This, in turn, attempts to address what has become known as 'strategic drift' or oversight, whereby organisations that have failed to keep pace with change adopt aggressive or overly-ambitious strategies to survive. As such, objectivity and transparency are often substantially compromised, and risk assessment is rendered ineffectual. Although the creation of strategy committees has been suggested as a possible solution to this particular problem, it is seen as a somewhat militant and unpopular prospect. Having the appropriate systems and culture in place to create efficient performance-orientated 'checks and balances' is a more plausible and sustainable solution.

The Conformance Dimension

The conformance aspect of Enterprise Governance is concerned with corporate accountability, which is governed by regulatory codes, corporate legislation and accounting standards. Conformance concerns the effectiveness of management structures (including the role of directors), the sufficiency and reliability of corporate reporting, and the effectiveness of risk management systems.

Corporate governance typically addresses the following:

- risk management and internal controls;
- corporate culture;
- stewardship and accountability;
- board operations and composition;
- monitoring and evaluation of activities.

Corporate governance, or its apparent failure, has received a lot of attention in recent years with market meltdown and high profile scandals. Often regarded as a mandatory box-ticking exercise, corporate governance has rarely been counted as an activity that can create sustainable shareholder value. However, as the recent corporate collapses go to show, focusing solely on profit and aggressive earnings targets often fosters an environment of unethical corner cutting, and risks commercial failure. Traditionally, financial performance was the main concern of

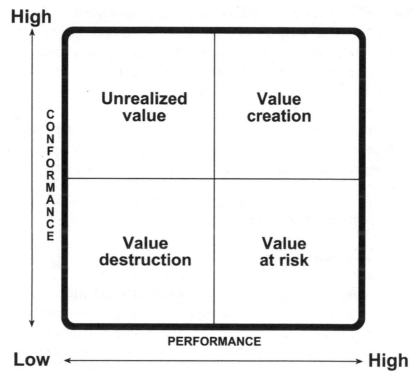

Figure 1.2. The relationship between value and conformance.

shareholders, but increasingly performance and corporate accountability have become the domain of a wider audience of stakeholders (such as employees, strategic partners, customers and non-governmental organisations).

These stakeholders are now more interested in long-term value rather than short-term gains, as reflected in the growth of ethical investment and corporate benchmarking indices (Figure 1.2). With the growth of communication technologies such as the Internet, compounded by regulatory changes allowing shareholders to communicate with each other without prior screening, previously isolated shareholders have become a force to be reckoned with. Companies must now cope with share-holder coalitions and cyber-campaigns run to force organisational change.[5] Financial institutions are also flexing their shareholder muscles; forcing organisations to adopt transparent ethical policies, or remove failing senior executives with the threat of withdrawing their investment.

However, the rise of shareholder activism is not solely connected with a desire to take back corporate control and ownership. The wider public is fully aware that the world's capital markets, and economies, cannot continue to weather such dramatic financial losses. But in order to meet stakeholders' demands for unequivocal assurances on numbers, ethical behaviour and value, the finance function will have to undergo fundamental change. Sustainable conformance and performance will be driven by a new species of Chief Financial Officer (CFO), who will view compliance as a value-added function and not just a 'box-ticking' exercise. Finance professionals, for years isolated in their function from other business operations, will no longer solely focus on transactional processes or historical reporting, but will help position organisations for market success, combining their traditional services with technology consulting and assurance services. The next generation finance professional will be expected to perform a range of duties, including due diligence, shareholder relationship management, and business process outsourcing (BPO). They will also be expected to have merger and acquisition skills, especially in the new regulatory environment, and deliver value-added strategic decision support.

The Corporate Responsibility Dimension

The third dimension of Enterprise Governance is Corporate Responsibility (CR). Despite having previously been regarded as a 'philanthropic' business practice preached by non-governmental organisations (NGOs), CR is fast becoming the latest value-added platform for organisations seeking long-term shareholder value and brand protection (Figure 1.3).

CR typically addresses the following areas:

• managing/reducing environmental, societal, and cultural impact;

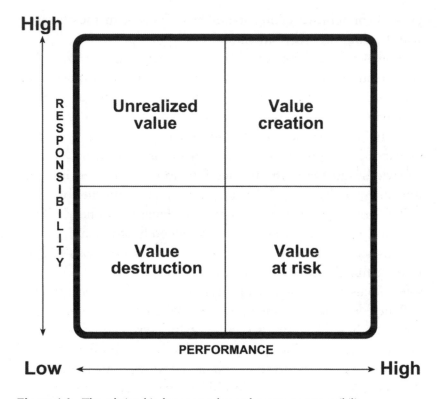

Figure 1.3. The relationship between value and corporate responsibility.

- the protection of intangible assets such as reputation;
- the promotion of corporate ethics and governance best practice;
- risk management, including mega risks such as climate change;
- traceability in supply chain management and procurement;
- employee motivation and productivity.

Although the moral reasons for practising CR lend themselves to easily identifiable benchmarks such as the reduction of environmental impact or the adoption of human rights policies, the financial motives have until now been more difficult to measure. However, research supporting the business case is mounting. Companies with embedded CR policies, such as Cadbury Schweppes or beverages giant Diageo can boast superior brand protection, consumer loyalty, and greater access to available capital.[6] Ethical investment funds, previously associated with shareholders less concerned with financial return than company ethics, have reported significant growth across the UK, Europe and the USA, having attracted capital from a wider investment base. Mainstream institutional investors, such as insurance companies and pension funds, have also recognised the need to offer members access to ethical investment, or have chosen to invest in companies with proven governance and CR records. These investors wield substantial power and influence – even acting as catalysts for boardroom change, having adopted a more 'hands on' approach to fund management.[7] After all, fewer people today want to keep their investment in companies with poor environmental or human rights records. The risks to brand, reputation and ultimately the creation of long-term value are just too high.

However, CR is not just about protecting intangibles and avoiding unpleasant and controversial exchanges with NGOs. Adopting an ethical corporate culture also has other significant business and societal benefits. It is well documented that CR can help attract, motivate and retain talent, especially in a fast-moving employment market, can stimulate departmental and organisational innovation, and can provide organisational flexibility, thus allowing a company to take advantage of opportunities, react to market fluctuations and manage risk effectively. It is also inextricably linked to governance and performance. As such, organisations that fail to implement sustainable development strategies will be unable to develop the culture vital to the creation of long-term value. Nor does CR mark the end of the chemicals, oil, and mining sectors. Corporate responsibility also translates as the recognition of impact, and what can be done to minimise its effect. Companies such as ChevronTexaco, Alcoa, and BP have made considerable efforts to improve the quality of life in countries where they operate. Whereas companies such as ExxonMobil still refuse to recognise the Kyoto Treaty, BP has invested heavily in renewable energy, giving other large manufacturers the choice and the ability to reduce their emission rates. Such development is a catalyst for innovation, which in turn helps create value and long-term sustainability.

The Importance of People and Culture

Developing and maintaining a performance-orientated entrepreneurial culture are essential ingredients of Enterprise Governance. Companies that champion high level performance and ethical behaviour will not only meet and exceed shareholder expectations by adding value, but will also generate loyalty from their employees. Innovation, leadership, internal and external communication are therefore vital in achieving best practice. Bureaucracy and hierarchical management structures, for example, often hinder innovation and entrepreneurship. Employees feel they are unable to exercise initiative – not only damaging morale but also affecting organisational efficiency. It is not by chance that Tesco, Microsoft, and Dell, all highly successful companies that strive for long-term shareholder value, regularly come top in the 'best places to work' surveys. Each has developed a supportive employee culture that focuses on career development, equality, ethnic diversity, as well as community involvement. Some companies, such as coffee chain Starbucks, have even stopped referring to staff members as employees, but call them partners, emphasising their wider value as stakeholders within the enterprise. The company supports and encourages local community-based CR initiatives as well as national projects, including the education programme Right to Read. It has developed a series of pilot funding schemes to help coffee farmers in developing countries such as Colombia. The company's firm belief in the development of an ethical culture has resulted not only in low staff turnover, but also in market success, brand loyalty and a sustainable supply chain, even if its high street domination has become food for satirists and the target of anti-globalisation protestors.

People and culture are just as significant, if not more so, for small organisations, especially in highly competitive low-margin industry sectors where quality of service can act as an effective market differential. Mid-market organisations can qualify for many of the benchmarks and awards now being used for ethical measurement by financial institutions and venture capitalists, such as ISO 14001. Larger organisations also want assurances that their smaller partners are adopting an ethical culture. But while it is important to allow employees to sustain an inspirational environment, evidence shows that the development of an ethical culture should be fostered from the 'boardroom to the mail-room'. A CEO's ability to communicate with all levels of employees is therefore essential, even if it does mean donning an overall and working on the shop floor sometimes.

It is all about Flawless Execution

According to 'What Really Works'[8] – a comprehensive study of what makes an organisation a corporate 'winner or loser', published in the *Harvard Business Review* – organisations that excel at four primary management practices: strategy, execution, culture and structure, supplemented by any two of the following secondary disciplines: talent, innovation, leadership, mergers and partnerships, deliver sustainable value. Their study, which led to the development of the 4+2 success formula, showed that corporate 'winners' such as FedEx demonstrated innovation, commitment to strategy, organisational excellence, clear communication, and a commitment to meet customer expectations. The losers were companies that offered poor technical support, delivered inconsistent messages and had a poor 'ethical' culture.

What the study really highlighted, however, is that developing the best corporate strategy alone is not enough. To produce the anticipated results, strategy needs to be executed flawlessly.

Flawless execution is about having the right systems and processes, culture and people.

How this Book Supports Flawless Execution

Successful firms have long recognised that excelling at Enterprise Governance is about creating an environment in which executives have the time and capability to design and configure an effective business model which delivers value to shareholders but which does so at an acceptable level of risk and in a manner which is socially responsible.

Our research shows that the biggest constraint on more effective Enterprise Governance is not a shortage of technology or techniques but a lack of time to think about the challenges facing the firm. In recent years the demands on an executive's time and resources have grown exponentially. The Enterprise Governance concepts discussed in this book are designed to support executives to leverage information and insights to provide better decision support. As such, it uses a range of approaches to help executives manage the enterprise better. In this respect, Enterprise Governance may finally fulfil our expectations and provide useful information for senior managers.

But it is important to appreciate that Enterprise Governance is not a magic wand that will completely transform an organisation overnight. In fact, this book will argue that Enterprise Governance as a management activity has been around for decades ever since firms began to recognise the need for better strategy formulation and execution. Finance professionals such as management accountants and others have been struggling for decades to address Enterprise Governance issues using calculators, spreadsheets and old-fashioned elbow grease. For years we have seen a continuous stream of management innovations such as TQM, BPR, and Six Sigma, many of which were sold as a panacea for all corporate shortcomings. In this book we put forward a framework for Enterprise Governance, which draws valuable lessons from our less-than-successful experiences with these earlier approaches by recognising the primacy of the executive.

The book is divided into three parts, each focusing on a dimension. Chapters 2 to 6 look at performance, Chapters 7, 8 and 9 focus on conformance, and Chapters 10 and 11 on corporate responsibility. Chapter 12, in conclusion, offers insights into actionable knowledge to allow finance professionals to respond to the challenges of Enterprise Governance.

Resources

A website with web links to many of the professional organisations, studies and reports used in this book has been created to allow further investigation of any chosen area. Visit www.beyondgovernance.com.

Notes

1   CIMA and IFAC (2004) *Enterprise Governance: Getting the Balance Right*, IFAC, Feb. Available online at: www.ifac.org
2   Ibid.
3   Ibid.
4   Gartner Group (2002) *Introducing the CPM Suites Magic Quadrant*, Gartner Group Research Note 2, Oct. 2002, Ref: Markets, M-17-4718.
5   Rosie Lombardi (ed.) (2000) *PwC Risky Business*, December.
6   The Equator Principles. Available online at: www.equator-principles.com
7   Examples include Michael Green, former CEO of UK broadcasting network Carlton, who was forced to quit after a shareholder revolt led by investment group Fidelity following the announcement that Carlton and rival broadcaster Granada were to merge. In 2004, Sir Peter Davis, former

chairman of UK supermarket chain J Sainsbury resigned after shareholders threatened to vote against a proposed £2.5m bonus despite falling profits.

8   N. Nohria, W. Joyce and B. Roberson (2003) 'What really works', *Harvard Business Review*, July, vol. 81, no. 7, pp. 43–52.

PART I
··········

Performance

CHAPTER 2

DEVELOPING STRATEGY

The Importance of Strategy

Strategy enables organisations to achieve long-term and sustainable competitive advantage in every business in which they participate. Shareholder value is therefore based on how confident stakeholders feel with an organisation's chosen strategy, and how confident they are in the competency of the board responsible for carrying it out. The end objective is the successful development of corporate values, managerial capabilities, organisational responsibilities and decision-making, at all levels across the business. As such, it lies at the heart of the performance dimension.

The complexity of modern business has led to strategic management becoming the responsibility of everyone in the organisation. As a consequence, they require an awareness of the techniques, processes and technologies needed to successfully execute business strategy.

Understanding Strategy

Like most business functions, strategy has many definitions. According to leading Harvard academic, Michael Porter,[1] success comes from being different. Porter points out that strategy is about competitive position, differentiation in the eyes of the customer, and adding value through a mix of activities different from those used by competitors.

Meanwhile, Henry Mintzberg,[2] in his 1994 book *The Rise and Fall of Strategic Planning* suggests that strategy emerges over time in response to changing market conditions. Thus, a perfectly crafted plan will evolve as a strategy reflecting decisions and actions made over time. Mintzberg defines this pattern as 'realised' or emergent strategy.

Regardless of the definitions or the many factors affecting the choice of corporate or competitive strategy, there are fundamental questions to be asked and answered. Strategic decisions are those that normally fall within the remit of top management. We can view the pattern of strategic decisions made by top management as constituting the strategy of the total organisation. This strategy is aimed at effectively matching or aligning organisational capabilities with environmental opportunities and threats. Strategic decisions are therefore highly complex and involve a host of dynamic variables.

Managing for Value: Strategies for Results

Boards and senior managers have been concerned with value creation ever since the ownership structure of organisations moved from the individual to wider ownership. The increasing power and influence of financial markets have driven many company boards to regard the creation of 'shareholder value' as their primary strategic business focus.

The concept of managing for value has been at the forefront of much of the contemporary literature concerning strategy and strategic management. The interest in managing for value is gaining momentum as a result of several recent developments:

- the threat of corporate take-overs by those seeking under-valued, under-managed assets;
- impressive endorsements by corporate leaders who have adopted the approach;
- the growing recognition that traditional accounting measures such as earnings per share and return on investment are not reliably linked to increasing the value of the company's shares;
- reporting of returns to shareholders along with other measures of performance in the business press such as *Fortune Magazine*'s annual ranking of the 500 leading industrial firms;
- a growing recognition that employees' long-term compensation needs to be more closely tied to shareholder returns.

A series of studies suggests that institutional investors and analysts no longer rate companies by mere financial criteria alone. They now derive their company ratings from shareholder value-based valuation models that are built on quantitative forecasts of the most important value drivers. The studies also indicate that forecasts of operating results of companies are better when non-financial information is also taken into account.[3] Of the 38 identifiable influencing factors, the following topped the list:

- ability to implement the enterprise strategy;
- credibility/ability to manage;
- quality of the enterprise strategy;
- ability to innovate;
- ability to hire talented new staff;
- market position.

Accenture Consulting,[4] in a recent study, suggests that in the past, high expectations of investors and analysts have forced many companies to focus on quarterly earnings almost to the point of obsession. This short-term focus can be detrimental as companies focus on the very things that run contrary to the creation of

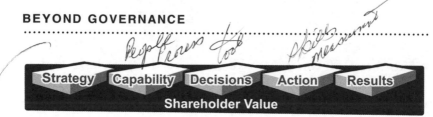

Figure 2.1. Elements of value creation.

long-term shareholder value. The group argues that successful companies focus on both the short-term and long-term results. Therefore, they develop and articulate long-term strategies and the roadmap(s) for getting there, and at the same time set short-term 'milestone' goals or targets aligned with the longer-term direction.

Accenture believes that sustainable value creation requires strategy, capability, decisions, actions and results to be aligned and focused on the key drivers of value for an organisation (Figure 2.1). The management of an organisation must understand where value is created and destroyed, whether its business model is operating effectively and how this can be improved. This is done by defining and evaluating the strategy, setting targets, measuring performance, forecasting and then re-evaluating the strategy.[5]

The 'Managing for Value'-Based Approach to the Strategy Process

Corporations often find that their strategic decisions are not converted into the operational objectives of the business and that the strategic decisions are not understood or optimised at all levels. Strategy has to move out of the executive office and be integrated into the day-to-day work of each employee. The employee can then contribute to making strategy happen and can provide feedback for further optimisation of the strategy. Only then can an enterprise really align its entire activities with the value expectations of the shareholders and other stakeholders, (such as employees, business partners, customers, or public

Table 2.1. The 'Managing for Value'-based approach to strategy

Strategic assessment	A strategic assessment entails the analysis of the operating environment, both current and future. Details include competitive assessments; pricing and volume trends; supplier assessments; analysis of pending legislation and other legal matters; market analysis and consumer trends; and assessment of threats and opportunities. Identification of *value* drivers, what drives success, and key performance indicators that reflect the *value* drivers.
Long-term planning	Senior managers formulate the best response to the environment described in the strategic assessment. Start by setting targets with the business units, having formed a shared understanding of the anticipated operating environment. These targets relate to financials and the key performance measures as defined in the strategic assessment, and are set for a five-year period. Incentive compensation for senior level executives gets drafted at this point, based on achievement of these key targets.
Operational planning	After defining high-level targets, business units determine how these goals will be met. Each leader needs to work with his or her managers to build a plan to achieve the high level goals of the operating plan. Plan elements such as capital expenditures, headcount, advertising and promotional spending, and departmental expenses are developed at this stage. When the detail is completed and approved, then incentive compensation for managers gets drafted, based on achievement of key targets.
Performance measurement and management	In a 'managing for value' approach, a company identifies key performance measures as part of its strategic assessment, defines these measures when it completes long-term and operating plans, and uses it as the basis of its incentive compensation. These key measures are the ones used to run the business and to make decisions.
Incentive compensation	Companies often shy away from asking people to put money on the line to deliver what they say they will deliver. Without carefully crafted incentive compensation tied to achievement of plan goals, the plan becomes a paper tiger.

interest groups), and thus ensure long-term profitability (Table 2.1).

In his study of managing for value, Lawrence Serven identified what he called 'Value Killers'.[6]

The Value Killers

The fire-fighting trap – management focuses on making immediate fixes instead of building long-term capabilities. Efforts like total quality and re-engineering are designed to get more out of current resources, but do little to seize new opportunities. Assessing and planning are often over-shadowed by urgencies.

Management lacks the incentive – if incentives (raises, promotions, bonuses) are simply based on making the best of current resources and circumstances, little else will be accomplished.

Absence of a value management system – most companies recognise the need to do strategic planning, to develop an annual plan, to forecast results to measure and manage performance, and to develop individual incentive compensation plans. Yet in many companies these processes are run as separate, distinct, and uncoordinated activities. Value management requires that all of these processes be integrated and focused on building shareholder wealth.

So What Really Works?

It is far too easy for management to embrace the newest 'management fad' to secure a quick fix solution without addressing the cause. Experience shows that these management fads often only address the symptoms, not the cause. Rather than becoming fad addicts, managers need to focus on developing a clear vision of where the organisation is going and to flawlessly execute its business model in pursuit of that objective.

While the past ten years have seen the rise (and fall) of numerous business luminaries and gurus, a recent seminal *Harvard Business Review* article suggests that a return to basic business principles may be the best route to successful long-term value creation. In 2003, a group of researchers published the results of a comprehensive five-year study of large US firms. The article, 'What Really Works',[7] described the essential management practices important for business enterprises. Besides identifying those practices that can significantly affect a company's performance, the researchers developed a list of behaviours that can support excellence in each practice.

Primary Management Practices

- *Strategy.* Whatever your strategy, whether it is low prices or innovative products, it will work if it is sharply defined, clearly communicated, and well understood by employees, customers, partners, and investors. Firms should build a strategy around a clear value proposition for the customer. In other words, develop strategy from the outside in, based on what your customers, partners, and investors have to say and how they behave – not on gut feel or instinct. Continually fine-tune your strategy based on changes in the marketplace, for example, a new technology, a social trend, a government regulation, or even a competitor's breakaway product. Clearly communicate your strategy within the organisation and to customers and other external stakeholders.
- *Execution.* Develop and maintain flawless operational execution. You might not always delight your customers, but make sure never to disappoint them. Deliver products and services that consistently meet customers' expectations. Put decision-making authority close to the front lines so employees can react quickly to changing market conditions. Constantly strive to eliminate all forms of excess and waste; improve productivity at a rate that is roughly twice the industry average.

- *Culture.* Corporate culture advocates sometimes argue that if you can make the work fun, all else will follow. Our results suggest that holding high expectations about performance matters a lot more. Inspire all managers and employees to do their best. Empower employees and managers to make independent decisions and to find ways to improve operations – including their own. Reward achievement with pay based on performance, but keep raising the performance bar. Pay psychological rewards in addition to financial ones. Create a challenging, satisfying work environment. Establish and abide by clear company values.

- *Structure.* Managers spend hours agonising over how to structure their organisations (by product, geography, customer, and so on). Winners show that what really counts is whether structure reduces bureaucracy and simplifies work. Simplify. Make your organisation easy to work in and work with. Promote cooperation and the exchange of information across the whole company. Put your best people closest to the action. Establish systems for the seamless sharing of knowledge.

CFOs and Shareholder Value – the Reality Gap

In the past, finance professionals' fundamental understanding of the performance environment was often based on a linear view of business and economic behaviour. The destructive technologies of recent years have revealed signs of subsidence in the cornerstones of management practices based on the linear, mechanistic, and deterministic paradigm.

At a more general level, significant changes in management structures, strategy and decision-making have occurred. The traditional passive management philosophy and approaches, which had served CFOs and others well for decades, are being questioned. Increased competition and cost reduction requirements have led to a significant restructuring of organisations.

These changes have involved redundancies, major investments in new IT equipment and increased consumer awareness.

Given these complex and bewildering environments, finance professionals and the executives they support are increasingly concerned with identifying key business drivers and internal performance measures. Senior managers require information systems, which help them to manage the 'key control variables' for their organisation, i.e., the set of factors which are at least partially controllable by the organisation and are likely to affect its medium- or long-term success. Thus, they are looking to move to finance information systems which reflect a more strategic view of the organisation.

As the volume of information from processes grows, so too does the complexity associated with managing organisational performance. In many cases, the pressure this puts on finance professionals means that they end up using the tools they know and understand to manage the complexity. As a result, vital processes like consolidation, budgeting, and reporting and analysis end up being managed and controlled on ever-more complex spreadsheet based systems – a role for which the common spreadsheet was never designed. In effect, the finance function is failing to keep up with advances in the business strategy.

The ability to 'sense and respond' based on the right information at the right time within the strategic planning process is crucial. Today, spreadsheets dominate the planning process in over 80 per cent of organisations. Yet technology is now available to support much more sophisticated, responsive and enterprise-wide applications in the form of corporate performance management systems.

Research shows that significant change is planned, with many CFOs indicating that they expect to make some form of technology investment to enhance planning data and processes. In a recent CFO Survey by IBM Business Consulting Services[8] more than two-thirds of those interviewed cited supporting shareholder value creation as their highest priority, followed

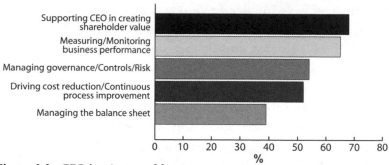

Figure 2.2. CFOs' main area of focus.
IBM Business Consulting Services, 'CFO Survey: Current State and Future Direction', The IBM Institute for Business Value, 2003. Copyright © IBM. Reproduced by permission of IBM.

closely by measuring/monitoring business performance (Figure 2.2). These are clear indications that CFOs are positioned for the role of driving shareholder value.

The report also confirmed that there were significant gaps in a CFO's ability to deliver on the business partnering role needed to deliver shareholder value creation. Specifically in a section examining what information they need versus what they are getting, CFOs identified a number of shortcomings (Figure 2.3). Areas such as customer and product management are obviously critical to managing a dynamic business, yet the quality of such information is severely lacking and will require significant attention.

Corporate Performance Management Systems: Bridging the Gap

In order to bridge the gap between intention and delivery of shareholder value it is important to view CPM as an activity and process and not just a technology. CPM is a process that is made up of a number of key elements. The first being the visioning phase, where management creates the intention and surfaces the governing objective – in most cases, maximising shareholder value. A key part of delivering this vision is designing and configuring a successful business model where everybody in the

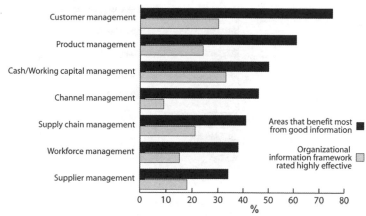

Figure 2.3. CFOs' information needs and effectiveness.
IBM Business Consulting Services, 'CFO Survey: Current State and Future Direction', The IBM Institute for Business Value, 2003. Copyright © IBM. Reproduced by permission of IBM.

organisation understands the levers that drive value. The next phase involves operationalising the business model into an integrated performance management capability, which allows the measurement reporting and evaluation of performance against targets. The final phase involves creating a bias-for-action by explicitly linking rewards and incentives to performance measures.

By avoiding the confusion and complexity of spreadsheet-based systems, CPM allows finance professionals to streamline their decision support activities and accomplish more in less time, with considerably less effort. As such, CPM provides management accountants with a solution that enables them to provide information to senior executives in an organised and inter-connected manner. Firms can collect information at multiple levels and roll it into an integrated model. Executives can assess their strategies using the business models to see changes and their impacts, helping to solidify the all important 'buy-in' from those ultimately responsible for delivering shareholder value. The majority of organisations use a combination of best practices to obtain information and plan their strategies (Figure 2.4).

We shall investigate this area further in Chapter 4. Before then, we will look at the importance of achieving excellence in

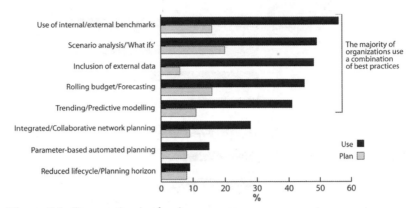

Figure 2.4. Best practices in planning processes.
IBM Business Consulting Services, 'CFO Survey: Current State and Future Direction', The IBM Institute for Business Value, 2003. Copyright © IBM. Reproduced by permission of IBM.

transactional systems in order to form the foundations necessary for Performance Management.

Notes

1 M. E. Porter (1998) *Competitive Strategy: Techniques For Analyzing Industries and Competitors*, New York: Free Press.
2 H. Mintzberg (1994) *Rise and Fall of Strategic Planning*, New York: Free Press.
3 Series of studies by Ernst and Young, 1998.
4 Accenture (2001) 'A holistic approach to creating sustainable shareholder value', Accenture Finance and Performance Management Practice, *Point of View*.
5 Ibid.
6 L. Serven (1999) 'Shareholder value', *Executive Excellence*, Dec., pp. 13, 14.
7 N. Nohria, W. Joyce and B. Roberson (2003), 'What really works', *Harvard Business Review*, July, vol. 81, no. 7, pp. 43–52.
8 IBM Business Consulting Services (2003) *CFO Survey: Current State and Future Direction*, The IBM Institute for Business Value.

CHAPTER 3

TRANSACTIONAL EXCELLENCE

The Emerging E-enabled Finance Environment

New technologies play a key role in the delivery of effective Enterprise Governance. One of the most influential revolutions in the finance function today has been the automation of finance transaction processing. Most of the finance transaction processing that companies need involves recurring activities that are well suited to automation and management by a software platform. The bedrock of most finance transaction processing consists of a small number of key processes: order-to-cash, purchase-to-pay and account-to-report, and so on.

In the early days of Enterprise Resource Planning (ERP) the focus was on cost reduction and internal integration. Although a significant number of major organisations decided to revamp their global supply chains, many focused on stock management, ordering or distribution within the organisation or along traditional distribution channels.

Under the emerging e-business approach, firms are using the Internet to create a seamless and fully automated electronic network to link buyers, suppliers, capital markets and other stakeholders. As a result, transaction processing is becoming largely automated and the traditional supply chain relationships

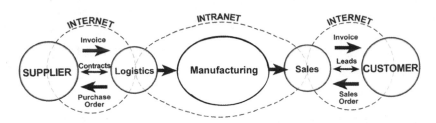

Figure 3.1. E-business across the supply chain.

are moving to a closed loop virtual model. The benefits to organisations are impressive and take many forms; service levels have improved; significant transaction processing costs have been eliminated and processes move from being cost-focused to revenue enhancing (Figure 3.1).

To date, three core e–business activities have emerged:

- *e-procurement* involves firms in a particular industry or sector creating virtual market places where they conduct their purchasing with business counterparts over the web. However, as this approach is still in development, firms have chosen to create direct links as an alternative.
- *e-fulfilment* which involves the on-line seller presenting their products or services over the web. A key part of the e-fulfilment model is the use of experience gained from previous transactions to form a one-to-one relationship with each customer.
- *e-self-service* which uses the web to facilitate transactions with the workforce, customers or suppliers. In the case of employees, typical applications include expenses, remuneration, and HR data collection.

The aim of this approach is to establish an e-finance capability that intends to have 95 per cent of transactions going through an integrated suite of applications including e-procurement, e-fulfilment and web-enabled e-self-service applications integrated with the core financial and accounting applications.

Purchase-to-pay is a classic example of a process that can be fully automated. Under a collaborative finance approach the vendors and suppliers can literally carry out transactions on a virtual basis without the need for manual intervention.

Case Study: Wallenius Wilhelmsen[1]

Wallenius Wilhelmsen was founded in 1999, following the merger of Wallenius Lines of Sweden and Wilhelmsen Lines of Norway. It is a global leader in ocean transportation for vehicles and machinery that can be rolled on and off uniquely designed ships. It specialises in the transportation of cars, agricultural and construction machinery, boats, and project cargo. In addition to ocean transportation, the Scandinavian-owned carrier offers logistics management, vehicle processing, terminal management and land transportation services.

The company operates a global logistics network of offices and agents in five continents and has worldwide trade routes. With approximately 60 modern vessels and 600 transporters in its fleet, the company carried 1.6 million vehicles by sea and 1.5 million by road in 2002.

Hans-Tore Brekke, Wallenius Wilhelmsen's Head of Financial Systems, explains the company's approach to systems following the merger of the two companies: 'With a dedicated staff of 3,000 across five continents (in regional headquarters, terminals, vehicle processing centres and local offices), Wallenius Wilhelmsen is a truly global company and with this comes a complex financial management operation. We have offices and agents in Europe, North and South America, Asia and Oceania. We have to collate and deliver information about our cargo to whomever might require it, in the form that is of most use to them. However, preferences vary from region to region.

'We identified the financial accounting element of our operations as the backbone for us to deliver this information across our organisation more effectively – providing the driving element of our "bigger and broader" IT strategy. We outlined our key requirements for updating this element as: "A more front-office oriented approach to financials – employing thin client technologies to make crucial financial information available to much broader audiences: agents; customers; suppliers; and a much larger population of the company's internal people".'

Secure, Immediate Online Access

Wallenius Wilhelmsen implemented CODA e-Finance (part of an e-suite of web browser-architected products). e-Finance enhances information visibility, intercompany working relationships, speed and quality of service, as well as control and decision-making capabilities. The e-Finance application lets the company enjoy the power and flexibility of the financials over the Internet, intranets, extranets, and so forth, with the ability to deliver information to PCs, palmtop computers and even mobile telephones. 'e-Finance enables us to get financial data directly and immediately to where it is needed most – external departments, remote offices, homeworkers, field staff or travelling executives. It brings corporate financials to the whole enterprise and beyond, as well as providing a framework for us to implement a more proactive approach to the opportunities of collaborative commerce,' explains Hans-Tore Brekke.

Global Control

The company's next step was to implement e-Billing – a web-browser architected sales invoicing solution to support their global billing process. The solution is scalable, with global accessibility and low bandwidth requirements to increase access, making it ideal for a globally operating organisation.

And it is not just finance processes which are moving on line. Hewitt, a provider of web-enabled integrated services designed to manage the human resources function for Global 500 corporations, uses the latest Internet-enabled interactive technology at its Glasgow-based client service centre. One of the primary roles of the eHR services centre is the support of Hewitt's 'myHR' – a browser-based, personalised web portal that promotes and enables employee self-service for key HR functions.

Transforming the Supply Chain with Collaborative Planning[2]

Delivering finance transaction processing requires close co-ordination between suppliers, customers and other stakeholders. With a dedicated software platform, companies are able to improve co-ordination on many different levels. Co-ordination goes far beyond pure inter-personal communication and e-mail. It involves the structuring, sequencing and synchronising of activities for efficient service delivery. Collaborative planning allows buyers and sellers throughout the supply chain to develop the following:

- a single shared view of inventory;
- a forecast of demand;
- a plan of supply to support this demand.

Key supply chain partners would all have real-time access to point-of-sale or order information, inventory and forecasts and provide changes as necessary. They would share forecasts so all parties could work to a schedule aligned to a common view. Schedule, order, or product changes trigger immediate adjustments to all schedules. Surprises and emergency actions are minimised. Pricing decisions do not create surprises for suppliers and 'end-of-range' pricing decisions are made on the basis of the whole supply chain, not just the immediately visible inventory.

Collaborative planning is designed to synchronise plans and product flows, optimise resource utilisation over an expanded capacity base, increase customer responsiveness and reduce inventories.

The same principles are now being applied in industries where the supply chain has not always been viewed holistically. For example, most large building contractors now operate an extranet for each project. They grant sub-contractors access to the extranet so that information on quality, plans and scheduling can be communicated and shared between all parties. This means that the communication chain becomes much shorter and the supply chain is both controlled and visible to all parties.

There are now strong signs that the whole concept of doing business is changing. Customers have far more access to a range of suppliers. Suppliers are gaining direct access to customers. Market communities are springing up that could transform existing supply chains and alter the buying balance of power. Organisations must find how to operate effectively in the new market places and must find a resilient niche for medium- to long-term business.

E-procurement and e-fulfilment technology are also instigating other transformations. They are allowing the creation of markets 'owned' by customers or suppliers. Everyone who wants to supply must integrate their systems into the marketplace or the marketplace catalogue. The marketplace must be able to respond to a request for a product from a customer and indicate the price and delivery date from each supplier. The customer is able to choose manually or automatically the combination that meets their need. The order and payment can be processed automatically. The supplier can tune the price according to supply and demand. The owners of the marketplace can value all orders placed with each supplier over the period and expect a commission or volume discount that could be passed onto the customers. Suppliers who decide not to integrate into the market lose the chance to sell.

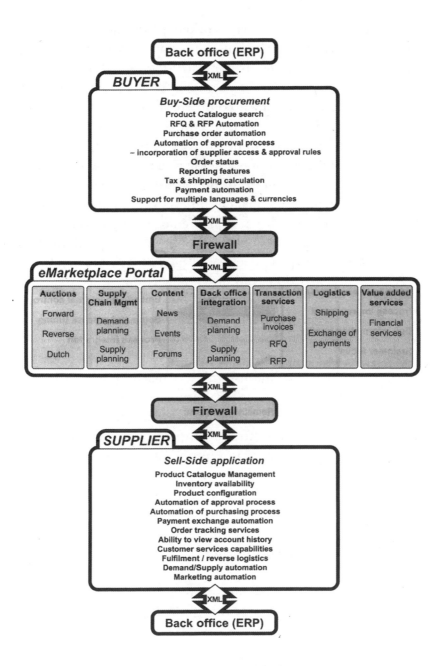

Figure 3.2. The e-Procurement and electronic marketplaces. *Source:* From a KPMG presentation by Peter Kurtz. Reproduced by permission of Atos Consulting.

This electronic market has worked particularly well where either the buyer or the seller is dominant and can force the supply chain to comply with the marketplace (Figure 3.2 on page 35). However, the marketplace is secondary to the main business of buyers and sellers. In normal commercial operations often both buyer and supplier resist the marketplace, generally because the marketplace is set up by a third party that tries to force people to join because of the threat of not being able to sell, and then wants to take a commission on every transaction. Suppliers may resist because they do not want their customers to be exposed to bidding from other suppliers – this may just remove margin. Buyers may resist because they do not want their supply chain exposed to other buyers who may push up negotiated prices by outbidding them.

A great deal has been said about 'lights-out processing' and how it will shape the future of the finance function. Both the concept and the terminology are seductive, but the real question is, how will it benefit organisations? In essence, 'lights-out' processing is a nirvana state – a vision that back-offices are aiming towards. It actually means that transaction processing is automated to such an extent that firms can process transactions, generally overnight, with no (or virtually no) human intervention! In reality, however, no one is quite there yet because we will still have transactions that require human intervention, e.g. when invoices come in and do not match the orders (either because the quantity is different or the price has changed).

E-Procurement Technology[3]

Companies large and small are jumping on the e-procurement bandwagon. Most report savings in time, paper and postage. But few are enjoying the really large savings promised from creating a true end-to-end e-procurement system. E-procurement involves the application of information or electronic technology to streamline and enable the procurement activities of an organisation. It typically refers to Business-to-Business (B2B) activities sourcing and purchasing goods and services via electronic or Internet channels. The 'end-to-end' procurement process would include searching or sourcing the product or service, selecting the appropriate supplier, generating a purchase requisition, obtaining the required approval(s), issuing the purchase order, fulfilment (order receipt, accounting for the transaction in the back office, connecting to the supplier in relation to order tracking) and payment (invoice payment and reporting).

Generally e-procurement involves some element of self-service; a secure personal login to the relevant website would give the ability to browse an online catalogue, select the goods, get quotes and availability, create an online purchase order, get approval online, send the PO electronically to the supplier. All this can then be tracked online. The final stage relates to receipt of goods, and the reporting on procurement activities including supplier performance.

This technology is typically used in dispersed or multinational environments, including regional or global shared services operations, as a web-based tool to handle the purchase of indirect goods. Through these buy-side Internet applications, the procurement group organises, expedites and monitors the purchasing process, facilitating communication within the company as well as with the company's suppliers.

Case Study: DIY Retail

Like all retailers this European home improvement retailer deals with many invoices, in this case around 15 million per annum. Its process for matching these invoices before an automation project was to deliver goods to each of their 400 or so stores, enter goods received data into their ERP application from the store, have the supplier send the invoice for the goods to the store (typically on paper), and finally have the store match the invoice to the goods received and approve it for passing to their accounts payable application.

One full-time equivalent (FTE) person was generally required for this for every two stores, resulting in 200 FTEs matching invoices and dealing with suppliers. Apart from the cost of 200 people performing this function, it was inefficient because any discrepancies were followed up with the supplier by each store. So a supplier with a faulty batch could receive 200 telephone calls from different stores. The invoice was also entered many times since it was on paper, and in addition for every two stores that opened, an additional FTE was required in store operations as well as support staff in Head Office.

When the retailer took the decision to automate this process:

- It implemented an automatic invoice matching system. Supplier invoices that correctly entered the transactional applications would be matched to the delivery documentation and passed to accounts payable ready for payment. There was no need to re-enter and no manual intervention for an invoice that was correctly received for goods correctly delivered.
- All suppliers were asked to transmit their invoices electronically so that there was no need to enter them manually. A second benefit of this is that each line on the invoice can be matched to each line on the delivery, allowing very precise control of under-deliveries and overcharging.
- An invoice-matching shared service centre was established where initially 32 central FTEs could complete the work of 200 FTEs in the stores.

Apart from the cost savings, the retailer achieved a faster turnaround on processing the invoices, producing a much more accurate view of accounts payable and cash flow. A further benefit was tighter control over supplier performance and margins.

The most popular form of e-procurement involves the use of software acquired from a third party vendor. In the classic case the buyer negotiates a contract with each of its suppliers, agreeing to purchase certain indirect goods at discounted prices, then loads digital versions of the suppliers' product catalogues alongside an e-procurement application such as Ariba Buyer or Commerce One Buysite. Employees use their browsers to search the catalogues, choose what they need and create requisitions. When a manager approves a requisition through a browser, the e-procurement system creates a purchase order, which is streamed directly into a supplier's inventory application for processing. A third party can also host the e-procurement application for the buyer. Sometimes the application is purchased and operated by an e-marketplace, a website serving as middleman between multiple buyers and suppliers.

Whatever the scenario, the benefits are twofold:

- Automated contract settlement, consolidation of suppliers, optimised prices and increased supplier collaboration together with better information to make more informed purchasing decisions.
- The end-to-end procurement process becomes much more efficient when requisitions and orders move around electronically instead of on paper, notes or faxes, circumventing the time-consuming processes that drain firms' corporate assets.

Table 3.1 illustrates several of the deficiencies of traditional, paper-based purchasing and the benefits of e-procurement. In sourcing the goods or services, templates and personalised views of options replace the need to browse through large supplier catalogues. Also, most good websites will include search facilities, thus sparing the effort of searching through lists, menus or (in the case of manual systems) catalogues. The several levels of manual approvals may be replaced by systematic, automated approval based on business rules. Time-consuming and error-prone retyping of order details by suppliers may no longer be necessary

Table 3.1. Benefits of e-procurement

	Purchases today: managed per transaction	e-procurement: managed by exception
Online product selection	Search large paper catalogues	Personalised views – templates and shopping lists
Requisition approval	Multiple levels of manual approval	Transactions automatically approved based on business rules
PO transmission	Fax, email, EDI direct to the supplier, who retypes the order	Order sent through central hub
Payment authorisation	Dependent on three-way match of PO with invoice and receipts	Immediate – based on receipt notice
Analysis	Ad hoc; not linked to supplier performance	Continuous – linked to supplier performance

Source: Andrew Kris, SBPOA, web article
Reproduced by permission of Shared Services and Business Process Outsourcing Association (SBPOA).

as orders are transmitted electronically (and no longer by paper or fax) through a central hub. Analysis of supplier performance is also facilitated by e-procurement, as are payment authorisations. The automation of some elements of traditional order processing should free up time for the procurement person to do more analysis of supplier performance. Excessive focus on time-consuming manual order processing may mean that very little time is spent on supplier selection and evaluation.

How the Web is Transforming 'Bean Counting'

The days of 'bean counting' – spending the majority of time processing transactions and deriving numerical analysis – are over for many finance professionals. According to KPMG (now ATOS Consulting),[4] the concept of e-finance is closer to reality than anyone could have predicted. In 1998, the firm controversially said that due to changing business and operational models driven by Internet technologies, 'accountants could go the way of coal miners if they did not adapt to the new environment within ten years'. Since then, developments in e-business have been so rapid that these predictions have already been realised and companies need to make immediate changes to their finance departments to avoid the role of finance becoming sidelined.

Manual tasks, such as processing expense forms, are being automated and replaced with web-enabled systems. This can reduce processing costs by 20 per cent, although some companies achieve much more. As companies automate their processes and link directly with customers and suppliers, there will no longer be a need for large accounting 'factories' in a single location (Figure 3.3).

Just as increased access to information delivers greater decision-making power across an organisation, the potential risks for the organisation also increase in the form of potential disclosure of sensitive information. However, new technology allows consistent procedures, tools and templates to be easily implemented. Chief executives have always wanted finance directors to deliver the 'Holy Grail' of finance: making the finance function a strategic business partner. The Internet facilitates this role by allowing real-time, customised management information to be delivered through a web browser to employees on an anytime, anywhere basis. The performance management portal effectively provides a single and instant version of the truth, provided it is built on a single data platform or data mart (see page 53), allowing the whole organisation to manage performance against clear strategic priorities.

The specialist skills typically found in finance, tax, treasury, investor relations and corporate finance departments are being profoundly affected by the Internet. This is having an impact both on the way these skills are delivered (common tax and treasury questions can now be answered over an intranet or Internet), and on the skills that are required, for example, in co-ordinating a cross-border transaction. Finance will become much more project-based and finance professionals must develop and update their skills to meet this challenge.

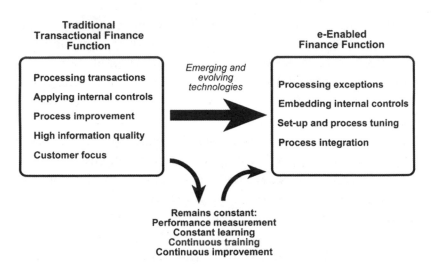

Figure 3.3. Transforming finance.
Peter Kurtz and Nick Jarman, 'E-Finance @ Work', KPMG Consulting, June 2000. Reproduced by permission of Atos Consulting.

In the past three years a more consistent finance systems architecture has emerged to support the growing need for collaboration between supply chain participants and between different functional areas within organisations. This architecture combines the emerging open standards of the Internet with the established enterprise systems which have been widely deployed in organisations (Figure 3.4).

The key elements of this approach are as follows:

1. A well-developed communications infrastructure. A corner-stone in the deployment of effective systems is an enterprise-wide data communications infrastructure. This allows not just workflow applications such as email and word processing but more importantly provides the communication backbone for all the transactional and analytical applications.

2. A web-based front end. Increasingly users access applications through a single organisational web front end, as a one-stop shop for self-service requirements, such as time and expenses entry, account and budget queries, payroll and HR queries, supplier payment chasing, etc. This will often be a portal

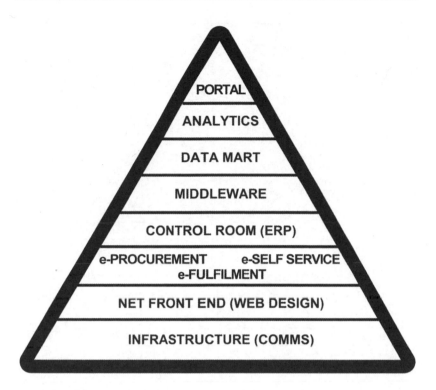

Figure 3.4. The emerging collaborative systems architecture.
Peter Kurtz and Nick Jarman, 'E-Finance @ Work', KPMG Consulting, June 2000. Reproduced by permission of Atos Consulting.

linking users transparently to multiple back-end systems, as well as to the performance management reporting infrastructure (data mart) described in Chapter 3.

3. e-business applications. As described above, these would include e-procurement and e-fulfilment applications, delivering core business functionality on-line to employees, customers and suppliers.

4. Core enterprise systems. Core systems might include the finance accounting ledgers, customer relationship management (CRM), supply chain and manufacturing systems.

5. Middleware. The communication and transfer of data between systems and technology platforms across (and even beyond) an enterprise are managed by specialist software known as middleware.

Case Study: Lin TV[5]

LIN TV is a leading US TV and broadcasting corporation operating 26 television stations, including two under local marketing agreements, one under a management services agreement and one low-power network. In 2002 the company undertook an IPO (Initial Public Offering) on the New York Stock Exchange, and also decided to extend its services by offering high-definition TV. To support this, it needed to track the performance of its profit centres and television channels, and monitor the financial status in an instant through accurate forecasting and analysis.

LIN TV was using CODA-Financials and upgraded to v9e, CODA's web browser-based version which exploits the latest Web and XML (eXtensible Mark-up Language) integration technologies, to provide online accounting for LIN TV's 26 stations. The new e-finance application allowed LIN TV to consolidate hundreds of spreadsheets centrally, eliminating manual re-keying and helping to speed up period close by up to 50 per cent; the web-browser capability enabled the company to dispense with its dedicated Wide Area Network (WAN) to produce savings of several hundred thousand dollars a year.

'For accounting and budgeting purposes, Excel spreadsheets are an effective tool but they are typically static and provide fragmented data,' says William Cunningham, Vice President and Controller, LIN TV. 'The CODA XML-Link has allowed us to revolutionise this and produce what would normally be a contradiction in terms – "real-time spreadsheets". With browser-based accounting we will save millions of dollars previously spent on maintaining our WAN and will also be able to add more users quickly and at little cost as LIN TV continues to grow and acquire more stations.'

> Cunningham adds: 'LIN TV is a successful company that is growing rapidly. To support this, we need to track the performance of our profit centres and television channels, and monitor our financial status in an instant through accurate forecasting and analysis. Our e-Finance application provides us with a solid foundation for growth. It allows our stations across the country to operate their own accounts at a local level and process their own payment runs at the touch of a button. At the same time, it ensures that this information is updated centrally for real-time month-end reports, forecasting and market intelligence reports.'

Organisations can adopt two different approaches to the implementation of the necessary applications – single source or best of class. In the late 1990s many companies chose the single source route (the traditional ERP-style of implementation) where business applications are sourced from a single supplier.

- Advantages:
  - If sourced from a single supplier, the various applications should be integrated 'off the shelf' thus reducing the time and cost needed to integrate the applications.
  - When a new version of the applications is made available, the user can decide whether to implement this and upgrading should be simpler since it is a single application set.
  - Some organisations consider that managing a single supplier of applications is better from a supply and support perspective (only one set of contracts, one support desk) for example.
- Disadvantages:
  - Most applications suites are compiled from a number of software modules, written by different teams within the supplier (and increasingly from software that the supplier has acquired and integrated rather than written). This means

that the integration of the modules will still require work and is rarely as 'seamless' as promised.

— Most organisations cannot upgrade all their business systems in one go, often resulting in different versions of the applications being in use in different departments. Initial implementation and significant upgrades represent major projects generally measured in years and many millions of pounds, which can be daunting to all but the largest organisations.

— The initial negotiation with a single supplier may be easier, but managing that supplier once the contract is signed is more difficult, since the supplier has an effective monopoly. Downstream contract and upgrade negotiations will probably reflect the fact that the supplier has this relative monopoly, often making attractive initial negotiations less attractive.

— In the increasingly complex and diversifying world of applications and technologies, it is unlikely that a single software vendor will meet all the business application requirements of a firm. As a result many organisations find themselves running a number of different applications. While this can present integration challenges, new technologies and emerging standards, particularly in the area of web services and XML, are helping to simplify integration challenges and make best-of-class a viable route for many.

Naturally, by taking on the integration challenge, companies face a number of hurdles. Consider, for example, when a telecommunications company integrates and consolidates its customer information. In a simplified example, customer information usually resides in at least five different places:

● a customer relationship management system, which contains sales history and customer background information;
● a billing system, in which resides tariff information related to billing;

- a service management system, which contains the customer's service history;
- a network management and provisioning system that provides details about the customer's physical service on the network;
- a financial system that essentially maintains payment history and credit information on the customer.

So, currently, when employees create new customer records or update existing records, they probably have to access more than one of the five systems unless the applications are properly integrated. The key lies in picking the applications that support this integration and selecting an appropriate mechanism to complete the integration.

Selecting Applications

Suppliers who expect their applications to co-exist with others typically provide more sophisticated integration facilities than the traditional ERP suppliers who would rather exclude third party applications. It is therefore important to select an application with a strong API (Application Programming Interface) that allows it to be manipulated by outside applications. In addition, applications that play strongly in integration provide well-defined XML and web service interfaces to facilitate data movement. Applications that provide weak interfacing capabilities require an understanding of their file layout and expect data to be passed directly into the files. This method is both weak and dangerous since control of data entering and leaving the application is lost.

The only way to establish software vendors' claims in this area is to do the following:

- Examine the integration claims in detail.
- Expect to see integration in operation.
- Take references from organisations who have integrated with the application and see how they achieved it and how the integration is affected when the applications are upgraded.

Vendors such as CODA (which specialises in finance applications) and Siebel (which specialises in CRM applications) expect their software to co-exist with others (since they do not provide the other line-of-business applications) and so will spend more on their integration capabilities than their ERP competition.

Selecting the Integration Methodology

Applications traditionally have been *interfaced* with programs that pass data from one application to another. This can often be achieved relatively cheaply, but can result in increasing complexity over time and higher long-term costs of maintenance (Figure 3.5).

Increasingly organisations are selecting a more strategic route to integration, both internally and externally: the use of an EAI (enterprise application integration) or AIC (application integration component) structure. Using this method, an additional application is implemented as a controlling hub. An example of this is Microsoft's BizTalk server. This approach has a number of key advantages:

- The AIC performs a postbox role, translating and forwarding data in the format that applications require.
- Each piece of data that enters can be forwarded to those applications that actually need it.
- In the event that any of the business applications becomes unavailable (e.g. when it is being upgraded), the AIC will queue the data ready for forwarding when the application becomes available again.
- Provided the business applications have a suitable API (see above), the interface to the AIC should be version independent and need no changes when the application is upgraded.
- Applications can be chosen as master or slave with the integration occurring through the central hub. Either

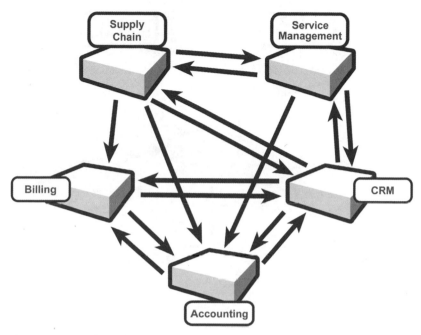

Figure 3.5. Interfacing between applications can build complexity.

alternatively or in addition to this, single points of data entry can be constructed that control through a single point the data that all applications require – this is often achieved through browser-based input to multiple applications at once.

The other benefit this demonstrates is that the integration server is communicating not just with the internal applications, but also acting as a gateway to supplier, customer and other external third party applications (Figure 3.6).

In order for the EAI solution to be effective in this scenario – to provide a 'single customer view' – the integration team must define and construct business rules to specify how the different elements of customer information in different systems will relate to one another. For example, when the same customer record resides in more than one system, a decision must be made about which system will become the 'master' and which the 'slave'. Any changes made to that piece of customer information must be

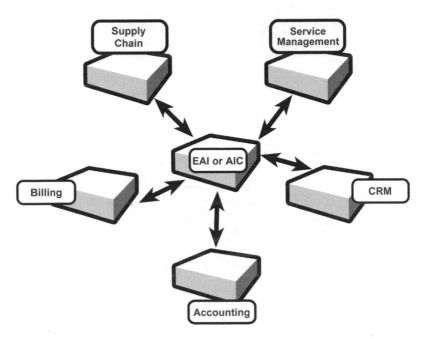

Figure 3.6. A more strategic route to integration.

made to the master system, which then drives the change to the slave systems.

Making this determination requires the integration team to identify what business processes are being driven by the particular piece of customer information and, based on that, which data source would logically become the master. Who is responsible for the ultimate decision? Typically the project sponsor should be the decision-maker. But that person should empower a cross-functional team of all affected parties to provide recommendations on what makes the best business sense. Thus, the integration issue becomes a change management problem, in which one functional area of the business must be convinced to agree that this piece of information on their system will actually be populated and driven by information from another functional area.

As a result of the increased availability of e-technology, firms are faced with a number of challenges with respect to their systems:

- Requirement for higher levels of data integrity.
- Data will become externalised with open systems.
- High volumes of detailed data are captured automatically, exceptions still occur.
- Higher percentages of transactions are automated, exceptions still occur.
- Difficult to predict future work and growth.
- Process and data consistency and standardisation.
- Continuous flow of new or modified e-applications.

Through EAI, a company can align its organisation with its technical environment, regardless of the technology platform. EAI tools enable truly seamless operation of business processes across a wide variety of legacy, ERP and specialised applications. Core functions of an EAI tool set include data transport, routing, translation and mapping, as well as workflow management and specific business processes.

Reporting and Business Intelligence

Having a well-integrated set of transactional applications provides the basic foundation for producing good reporting or business intelligence information. This introduces two further challenges:

- How to create the foundation for reporting.
- How to disseminate that information to interested parties.

Creating a Reporting Infrastructure

Many organisations that have integrated their transactional applications fail to integrate their reporting environment. There are two types of reports and they can be addressed in different ways:

- A transactional report (e.g. a debtors list), which can be obtained from the application containing that data.
- A business intelligence report (for example, a debt analysis, which is broken down by customer profile and the products that the debt relates to). This is a more complicated report since it contains more analytic information and will probably be obtained from more than one application, in this case the production system, the CRM system and the accounting system.

It is at this point that most organisations fail. They select a 'Business Intelligence' tool, create a data dictionary (a 'map' of the underlying data structure) and then obtain the information directly from the transactional applications. This creates issues such as:

- The data that the report is created from is stored for internal application use and not reporting.
- If two employees tried to create the same report, would they get the same answer?
- The information the report is based on is likely to change while the report is being used.

Smart organisations that understand these issues will typically extract reporting data from their transaction applications and create a data mart, data warehouse, or reporting data that provides information to employees in a well-defined, multi-dimensional format. Consumers of that data are then able to select it and combine it with other relevant data (see Chapter 4, on Performance Management).

The whole process can be likened to a supermarket, which has a stockroom and a shop floor. Essentially, the stockroom and the shop floor contain the same items but in a different format. The stockroom is designed for the efficiency of getting the goods in and stacked and is designed for just a few people with fork lifts to operate in. The pallets of goods are stacked high and are located by computer.

The shop floor is for customers to find the same goods in an enticing and well-presented manner. They need to be able to locate the goods that they want without the use of location barcodes and while they are looking, the store will show them other items they may be interested in.

Now customers could go into the stockroom to find the goods they want, but with more than a few shoppers, chaos would ensue and the throughput and stores sales would fall as customers failed to find what they were looking for and bottlenecks slowed their progress down.

In this example the stockroom can be likened to the transactional systems – optimised for fast input but not for complex output or reporting. The shop floor is akin to a data mart, where data is optimised for reporting and analysis, where many users want simultaneous access and seek to associate different pieces of data and manipulate data in different ways.

Delivering Data – Portals and Browser-Based Distribution

Organisations are becoming increasingly aware that the use to which their employees can put data depends on how it is delivered to them: 'Pushed' data is data that organisations determine their employees should receive, based on their function. 'Pulled' data is data that employees mine for themselves based on a specific task, project or interest.

In order to deliver the pushed data and to allow the employee to search for pulled data, the most effective mechanism is the portal. This is simply a delivery mechanism, a portal being a gateway to the information. Increasingly organisations have placed a common, browser-based delivery mechanism across all their applications, including the data mart or reporting repository.

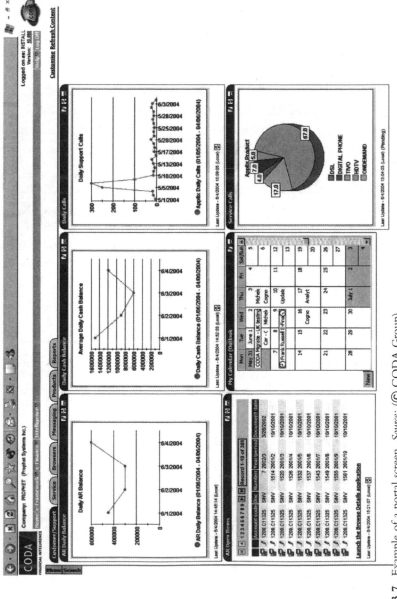

Figure 3.7. Example of a portal screen. *Source:* (© CODA Group).

This allows employees to navigate data in a common format, irrespective of the structure or style of the underlying applications. In this example, a series of applications have been used to provide the information that is delivered in a cohesive format to the employee. Smart organisations provide multiple portal views of the information, tailored to the determined requirements of functions within the organisation or individual employees.

In Figure 3.7 we see information gathered from Finance, CRM and Service Management. Some of the content comes from a single application and some has been combined from multiple sources. In addition to the pages displayed in this figure, note the tabs at the top of the page that provide further views and that each of the displays can be 'clicked on' to reveal the underlying information or more detail.

This display shows daily accounts receivable balances are increasing and that we have seen a fall in the cash we are collecting. At the same time, daily support calls have dramatically increased and that service calls relating to our 'DSL' product have created by far the highest proportion of support requirements. This information can now be 'mined' or examined to determine if the information is linked. If a meeting is required to discuss these findings, the Microsoft Outlook content provider in the centre can be used to set this up without leaving the portal. If a group of employees has access to identical portal presentations, this can be used as the basis for discussion, rather than the common scenario where the first half of the meeting is spent establishing whose data is correct.

In Chapter 4 we shall look at how technologies such as data marts and portals are being used as the foundation for extending traditional reporting and business intelligence techniques to create a much more extensive and strategic view of organisational performance.

Notes

1 From CODA Group Case Study CS0016, 'Delivering the goods for Wallenius Wilhelmsen'.

2 Martin Fahy (ed.) (2001) *ERP Systems: Leveraging the Benefits for Business*, London: CIMA Publishing, p. 170.

3 Martin Fahy and Andrew Kris (2003) *Shared Service Centres: Delivering Value from Effective Finance Processes*, London: FT Prentice Hall, p. 188.

4 *Transforming Finance*, taken from KPMG E-Finance report, 2000, KPMG Consulting, on file with authors.

5 CODA paper (2002) 'Leading TV corporation saves US$ hundreds of thousands annually with browser-based financial accounting', CODA Group.

CHAPTER 4

CORPORATE PERFORMANCE MANAGEMENT

What Are We Doing Wrong Today?

An organisation's ability to evaluate the value of its products and customers, in terms of their contribution to the overall stakeholder and shareholder value of the business, is critical to its competitiveness and long-term success. But as the volume and value of information from these processes grow, so too does the complexity associated with managing company performance. Yet all too often, we see finance professionals resorting to self-built spreadsheet-based systems for consolidation, budgeting, and reporting and analysis, which do not deliver real-time analysis or the flexibility needed by organisations in today's economic and political climates. In effect, the finance function is failing to effectively support strategy.

Historically, financial information has been extracted from different legacy systems and spreadsheets, and then presented neatly summarised to senior executives. To achieve this, the finance function at corporate or business unit level often spends a large part of the monthly close manually cleaning the data from different operating sites and systems, invariably creating multiple versions of the truth (Figure 4.1). The information produced,

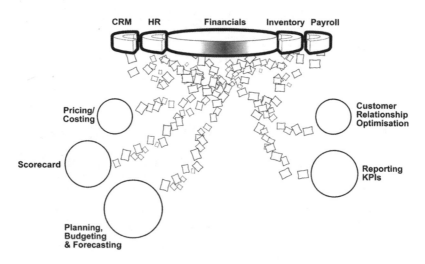

Figure 4.1. The problems associated with the current approach to decision support and reporting. *Source:* (© CODA Group).

which is often of poor quality and plagued by inconsistent data from different sources, is then supplemented with yet more information and forecast data from other sources, often outside of the organisation (Figure 4.2). Tight reporting deadlines typically lead to a situation where there is very little time for value-added analysis of business performance.

The problem is exacerbated when the executive committee requests one-off or *ad hoc* analysis of a particular issue such as declining sales in a particular market. This inevitably leads to additional extract programmes and spreadsheet analysis. As a result, the staff in such decision-support roles often complain about the burden of manual, menial work which incompatible systems place on them.

For an organisation to successfully achieve its objectives, management must understand where value is created and destroyed and whether its business model is operating effectively and how this can be improved. This is done by defining and evaluating the strategy, setting targets, measuring performance, forecasting and then re-evaluating the strategy. All of this requires

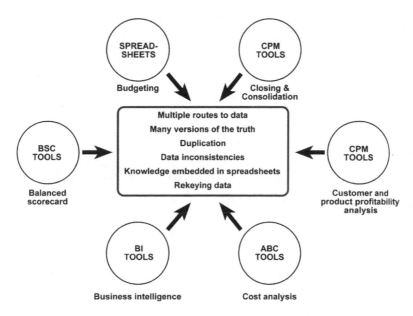

Figure 4.2. The reality of reporting in many organisations. *Source:* (© CODA Group).

a vital ingredient – information. Crucially, that information must be timely, accurate and consistent across the organisation.

Unfortunately many organisations' reporting systems and decision-support capability are rooted in the 1980s. Our work with organisations around the world has highlighted a large number of shortcomings in existing approaches and confirms that finance professionals continually struggle to provide the value-added strategic decision support which senior executives require. These shortcomings include the following:

- There is a lack of strategic focus on competitors, customers and products and the failure to address the information needs of the wider stakeholder groups.
- There is an absence of a 'balanced scorecard' or related approach for linking strategy to operational activities. This results in a focus on mainly historical financial measures of performance.
- Reporting under traditional legacy systems is cyclical in nature and often restricted to month-end reporting.

- In many cases, IT is a constraint on the firm's ability to implement new reporting processes and measures.
- Important business knowledge and understanding of the underlying processes are often embedded in poorly documented, stand-alone spreadsheets.
- With business models and corporate strategies continually changing, many firms find that their reporting systems do not reflect the changing corporate strategy.
- There is too much focus on information for tracking and control purposes; poor support for planning, direction setting and forecasting.
- The strong financial accounting bias in many management reporting systems often leads to a lack of focus on the drivers of performance and in particular the customer-facing revenue creation processes.

Traditional performance measures also try to quantify performance and other improvement efforts in financial terms. However, most improvement efforts are difficult to quantify in currency (i.e. lead time reduction, adherence to delivery schedule, customer satisfaction and product quality). As a result, traditional performance measures are often ignored in practice at the 'sharp end' of the business – the factory shop floor or client-facing levels. Traditional financial reports are also incredibly inflexible in that they have a pre-determined format which is used across all departments. This ignores the fact that even departments within the same company have their own characteristics and priorities. Thus, performance measures that are used in one department may not be relevant for others.

As a result, corporations often find that their strategic decisions are not converted into the operational objectives of the business, and that the strategic decisions are not understood or optimised at all levels. Strategy, therefore, has to move out of the executive office and be integrated into the day-to-day work of each employee. The employee can then contribute to making strategy happen and can provide feedback for further optimisation of the strategy. Only then can an enterprise really align its entire activities with the value expectations of the shareholders and other stakeholders (employees, business partners, customers, public interest groups), and thus ensure long-term profitability.

Corporate Performance Management – a New Methodology for Finance

According to technology consultancy Gartner,[1] Corporate Performance Management (CPM) can be defined as 'an umbrella term for the methodologies, processes, metrics, and systems that enterprises use to monitor and manage business performance'. Also known as business, enterprise, or even integrated performance management, CPM essentially encompasses a range of core financial activities including month-end close and reporting, planning and budgeting, activity-based costing management (ABC/M) techniques and scorecarding (Figure 4.3). Broader frameworks such as the Performance Prism and the European

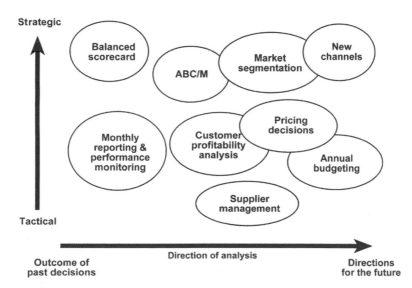

Figure 4.3. The range of activities covered by the CPM space. *Source:* (© CODA Group).

Foundation for Quality Management are also included within the definition.

Admittedly, there has been a never-ending stream of methodologies, frameworks, and software over the years offering businesses the ultimate performance measurement. In fact, many of CPM's elements have been around ever since organisations began producing monthly reporting packs and using spreadsheets for analysis. Management accountants have provided CPM-type support for years using spreadsheets, extract programs and OLAP (on-line analytical processing) tools like Cognos PowerPlay, combined with commitment and hard work. The real benefit of implementing a CPM framework is that it frees finance professionals and others from the drudgery of monthly corporate monitoring and allows them to concentrate on more valuable analysis such as solving specific business problems concerning profitability management and long-term direction setting. It is not lack of technology but a lack of time to think that is the biggest constraint on most analysis and planning groups. Successful businesses have long recognised that excelling at tasks such as analysis, business intelligence and decision-making is a competitive advantage in itself. To gain competitive advantage companies need to be able move through the decision-making cycle quickly and iteratively.

Admittedly, one of the major criticisms surrounding recent performance improvement initiatives is that they require organisations to abandon previous performance improvement techniques and systems and replace them with the 'latest solution'. However, this is generally not the case with CPM as it can often lead to existing systems and 'shelfware' (software bought but never used) being used more effectively.

The aim of CPM is to improve the quality and effectiveness of the strategic management processes by doing the following:

- providing consistent data from internal and external sources as well as knowledge and insights created from simulation and scenario modelling;

- giving managers the capability to deconstruct value into its components;
- establishing a flexible modelling and analysis environment to support problem solving and direction setting;
- making relevant information easily available at the point of decision-making;
- connecting top-down communication of strategic targets with bottom-up reporting of performance;
- meeting the changing information requirements arising from dynamics of the organisational structures and processes;
- combining both historic and predictive views to support the entire value management cycle;
- enabling strategic feedback to support learning;
- keeping managers informed of changes in the extended value chain.

The Case for Corporate Performance Management

Senior managers require information systems, which help them to manage the 'key control variables' for their organisation, i.e., a set of factors that are at least partially controllable by the organisation and are likely to affect its medium- or long-term success. As such, they are adopting finance information systems that reflect a more strategic view of the organisation. These information systems typically provide:

- analysis of costs and business drivers;
- indicators of progress towards achievement of a 'total quality' environment in the organisation;
- information relevant to strategic planning and forecasting.

In addition, senior management will generally require information that is from external as well as internal sources, and is both financial and non-financial in nature. As a result, they need:

- substantial flexibility in the type and format of information which they can obtain from their information systems, since the type of information which managers require for strategic planning purposes is likely to vary over time;
- flexible modelling capabilities to let them analyse data and information in whatever manner they consider appropriate in given circumstances.

Business executives are continually evaluating the outcomes of past decisions. A good CPM framework helps them link performance measurement and internal controls to strategic objectives, thereby ensuring that operational decision-making is fully focused on delivering strategic objectives. As part of this approach, the drivers of stakeholder value are the key performance evaluation criteria. The traditional approaches to performance measurement and control should be extended to include competitors, customers, products and relative market position.

To support this activity effectively, finance professionals must:

- support decision-makers' information needs, providing seamless integration of strategic, financial and operational information;
- provide transparency across the enterprise to ensure continuity of information from strategy through to business execution.

Support for Forward-Looking Modelling and Analysis

Senior managers are faced with a continuous stream of complex and often unique organisational business challenges. But to provide effective business support to executives, the finance function must recognise that providing information processing and analysis capabilities is only a small part of improving decision-making. Finance staff need to recognise that even sophisticated modelling and statistical techniques are of limited value when managers are faced with unique situations where their ability to specify the variables involved is constrained.

To improve management's ability to leverage insights and share tacit knowledge, managers must be provided with specific tools for improving problem definition, analysis and alternative evaluation and given access to the technology and data. Doing this provides managers with a flexible environment in which to explore ideas and eliminates irrelevant information that could threaten the process. Therefore, a key role for finance staff is helping managers to articulate and make more explicit their understanding of the environment they face and to develop complex mental models of their problem space.

Driving Managers' Understanding of Value Creation

A successful organisation is capable of charting a course that maximises stakeholder value in the face of a hostile environment. One of the most effective strategic management tools of recent years has been shareholder value management (SVM). SVM seeks to effectively link strategic objectives to resource allocation and performance management to ensure that operational decision-making is fully focused on delivering strategic objectives. This can only be achieved if firms have systems in place to give full transparency to the decision-making process, therefore enabling managers to see the likely impact of specific decisions on the value of the business. Thus, CPM has a key role to play by helping executives do the following:

- understand what factors drive value;
- find where value is created or destroyed;
- establish value as the criterion for decision-making;
- embed value into the firm's performance and compensation systems.

Systems to Support CPM

Corporate Performance Management (CPM) attempts to improve the strategic management of an organisation by giving managers better tools and approaches designed to meet the continuous stream of demands for analysis and information. CPM tools are therefore specifically designed to help staff retrieve and exploit data buried within an organisation's systems to enable better decision support. It essentially encompasses a range of core financial activities including month-end close and reporting, planning and budgeting, ABC and ABM techniques, the balanced scorecard, plus other frameworks such as the Performance Prism and EFQM (European Foundation for Quality Management).

To implement a CPM framework, the key element is the introduction of a data mart (as discussed in Chapter 3) to act as a common repository for key data, which may originate in different operational systems across the enterprise. This gives a platform for performance management tools that support analysis, ABC or whatever the technique, and ensures everyone uses a common set of data for their analysis. This contrasts with traditional reporting and analysis environments, where tools are run against operational systems where the transactional data is constantly changing and can often be defined differently in different systems.

Robust data links are established from the data mart back to the source operational systems, ensuring the analytical applications are dynamically tied to the operational data (Figure 4.4). This eliminates the costly, cumbersome and manually intensive exchanges of data between different applications, which characterise the spreadsheet-driven approach to data access common in many organisations. Using the data mart approach, cross-functional data is made available for CPM purposes thus allowing managers greater insight into the value-creating process. With less time spent on data extraction and cleansing, more time can be devoted to understanding and interpreting the outputs of the analysis.

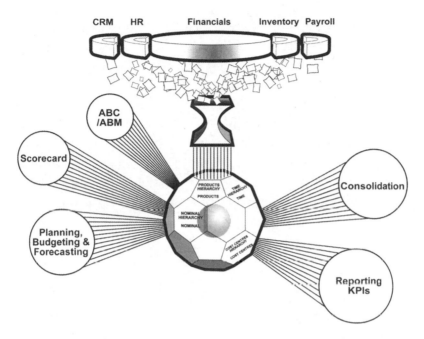

Figure 4.4. The emerging CPM approach. *Source:* (© CODA Group).

Case Study: CPM in Action[2]

Simunovich Fisheries is a privately owned New Zealand-based fishing company established in 1960 with one small boat. Today the company has a fleet of 17 inshore and deep-water trawlers[3] and also owns comprehensive onshore processing, freezing and storage facilities. The company is recognised as the 'pioneering developer' of the commercial New Zealand scampi resource and today operates the largest fleet of fishing vessels in the fishery. But expert crews and state-of-the-art fishing vessels are only part of the success of Simunovich. Its long-term success has been built on the ability to respond to the changing demands of the marketplace and its success in configuring its business model to deliver real value to customers.

As a fast-growing company in a highly competitive global market Simunovich is faced with the dual challenge of meeting increasing customer expectations and delivering value to stakeholders. In the past it had relied heavily on complex spreadsheet-based approaches to help deliver information for decision-makers. For group accountant, Mark Taplin, this approach restricted the analysis which his group could carry out. 'The manual-intensive nature of the process meant that by the time the data was scrubbed we had little opportunity for thinking about the numbers.'

So what prompted Simunovich to re-examine this approach to decision support? Many managers within Simunovich did not have enough time to address the more important strategic issues facing the firm: decisions such as what type of vessels to acquire, which markets to pursue and what type of value-added processing to carry out on the various catches. In many cases the important information was locked away in spreadsheets and in people's heads, while inefficient reporting and analysis processes led to delays in delivering information.

In the 1990s Simunovich made a substantial investment in IT solutions. This meant it had strong control over its core transactional processes. The next step was to leverage this investment to achieve greater insight into its market. Like many other organisations, Simunovich's managers needed to answer some very important questions:

- Which parts of the business (vessels, products, markets, customer and channels) are creating value?
- What are the real drivers of our performance (type of catch, processing, brand)?
- Which customers, species and vessels are delivering the bulk of our profit?
- What is driving cash generation?

Simunovich implemented a data mart solution which draws data not only from the company's finance system but from other business systems. The data are transformed and optimised for reporting and analysis, and made available to managers across the business. They can then use business intelligence tools to carry out tailored analysis on the same source data, ensuring consistent results.

For Simunovich the implementation of a CPM solution dramatically reduced the amount of time finance staff spent extracting data and left them free to spend more time interpreting the numbers. Examples of the types of analysis which the CPM environment supports include the following.

Business Unit Reporting and Consolidation

Simunovich's supply chain activities stretch from the ocean floor to the supermarket shelf. In order to effectively exploit its value chain it has established a presence in a number of different countries. Each month the performance of these different business units must be analysed and managed. A key motivation in implementing its CPM infrastructure was to speed up monthly reporting and free the finance staff to concentrate on analysing the numbers. As a result, monthly closing has moved from a time-consuming 'necessary evil' to providing a value-added insight into the relative value contribution of the different high-level business units.

Sophisticated Modelling of Vessel Performance

With its large fleet of vessels Simunovich must optimise deployment of these valuable resources to the best effect. Using the data mart capability staff can determine relative vessel performance and make important fact-based decisions about deployment of crews, vessels and on-board processing facilities.

Product Profitability Analysis

John Dory, hoki, snapper, orange roughy, . . . the list seems endless but for Simunovich each species has its own unique profile. Using statistical modelling managers are able to take species data, vessel data, historical catch patterns, relative processing yields and market forecasts to accurately predict the likely return from fishing for different species at different times of the year. This 'product' mix optimisation was traditionally the domain of experienced vessel skippers but they now have the help of up to six years of historical price and yield data to make these important decisions. This move to more data-driven decisions allows both crews and on-shore staff to develop a shared insight and understanding of the business model, where everyone can agree what the different drivers of the business model do – in this case, what impact different species can have on the bottom line.

Customer and Market Segment Optimisation

As Simunovich has grown beyond its home markets of New Zealand and Australia, it has learned to compete on a global stage. With vessels fishing as far away as Namibia Simunovich's managers are part of a 24×7 global market for fish. The morning prices for tuna in Tokyo are just as important as the AUS$:Yen exchange rate. With increasing regulation of the industry driven by both environmental and economic forces, the company's long-term survival depends on optimising its customer and market segment positioning. As part of this process Simunovich is using its CPM infrastructure to understand the buying patterns and value creation cycle of its major markets and customers. Customer rankings, segment profitability analysis and channel profitability assessment have become institutionalised as part of the CPM process.

Key Lessons from Successful Adopters of CPM

Research by the authors has shown that organisations that succeed with CPM are able to piece together many different capabilities to make CPM work. As Figure 4.5 on page 72 illustrates, success with CPM involves combining:

- the right technology
- the right modelling and analysis approaches
- knowledge of the data
- a good business understanding
- effective communication skills.

Knowledge of the Data – the Analysis is Only as Good as the Data Available

Many organisations approach CPM technology decisions on a piecemeal basis. As a result, they end up deploying point solutions across the key areas of closing and reporting, budgeting, balanced scorecard and business intelligence. This point solution approach will typically involve one-to-one extractions of data from the underlying systems, creating islands of data. A key concept underpinning CPM is the existence of a single underlying source that can be used for each of the analytical applications. The reality of most organisations is a multitude of different operational systems. Although some information will always be input manually, the aim should be to automate the collection of routine information. The challenge is to extract this data from diverse sources, transform it, correct it and load it into the data mart with as little manual intervention as possible. Previous work in this area by the CIMA (Chartered Institute of Management Accountants)[4] has highlighted a number of issues, which need to be addressed when putting CPM systems in place.

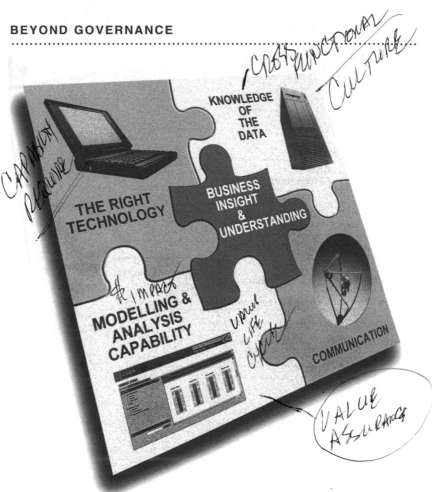

Figure 4.5. The CPM jigsaw. *Source:* (© CODA Group).

- Data delivery to the analytical applications must be fully automated and based on a single data-flow for closing and reporting.
- Integrate and store information within a central repository.
- Synchronise management reporting across multiple dimensions.
- Capture and consolidate linked data from multiple sources by developing a repeatable, end-to-end process for transforming data into information.
- The interfaces to the analytical applications need to be designed in a way which allows them to be changed quickly by users. If

these changes cannot be done easily, staff are likely to slip back in to the habit of using unofficial spreadsheet-based systems.

● The detailed information required at the lowest levels should be compatible with the summarised requirements needed higher up the organisation.

Case Study: ACC

Associated Co-operative Creameries (ACC), formerly part of the Co-operative Group, is one of the UK's main dairy operators and runs three divisions, Milk, Manufacturing and Distribution. These operate creameries, milk distribution outlets, manufacturing dairies and distribution centres across the UK. Several non-food manufacturing operations also report through ACC.[5]

Background

In 1999, ACC had implemented a leading finance package to address Y2K related issues. While the application handled the high data volumes well, users found that sophisticated reporting was slow due to technical restrictions and not ideal against a transactional system. ACC decided to address the situation to enhance reporting and analysis, give managers better access to information from across the organisation and increase the number of decision-makers with access to such reports. They wanted to develop and monitor key performance indicators (KPIs) to help in managing the business. That meant providing access to multiple data sources including manufacturing and operational applications as well as CODA-Financials.

Implementing CPM

ACC concluded that they needed a data mart solution, which would bring data together from multiple sources and make it accessible for managers to analyse and report against. ACC went live with its packaged data mart solution, CODA-Intelligence. They quickly had around 100 managers and finance staff across the UK accessing the data mart either via standard reports or creating their own reports and analyses.

The fundamental change the new system brought about was that users feel they can trust the data – they have just one version of the truth. This is a key goal for most organisations, since many waste too much time discussing whose data are correct rather than analysing the information it can reveal. From early on, ACC's users were enjoying reduced report times and increased amounts of data at their fingertips. They were able to identify and deal with business issues faster, and the data mart was already driving improvements in pricing and distribution decisions, and the analysis of day-to-day operations in the various business units. Examples of improvements include the ability to monitor the value of stock and trends in wastage across the business.

Develop Critical Skills and Experience

CPM activities are different from other types of initiative. Firms need to make the investment in training staff and managers in the key techniques, technologies and modelling approaches that make up the CPM 'space'. In particular, business managers need to be educated about data access and data modelling, since they must be able to locate and clearly define the appropriate source data for their analysis. Managers should be encouraged to explore more sophisticated approaches to modelling and make use of data mining possibilities such as regression analysis and correlations.

While the analysis and modelling aspects of CPM are important, being able to communicate analytic insights effectively to other managers is equally crucial. The best analysis in the world is worthless unless we can meaningfully share our insights with decision-makers and others in the organisation. Similarly, if executives are not comfortable with CPM principles, they will have difficulty articulating their needs to support staff. Success requires that organisations make CPM capability a key management and organisational competence. In this way it becomes part of the organisational culture and embedded in everyday decision support. It is only by doing this that we can create what has been called the 'fact-based culture' where decisions are based on objective realities rather than incomplete information.

Business Understanding – Give CPM Tools to the Decision-Makers

Those who report most success with CPM give those who are making the decisions the tools and data they need to make the decision. The focus is on putting in place the data mart and other business intelligence infrastructure needed for managers to carry out modelling and analysis. Effort is put into helping users understand their requirements and developing efficient routes to the data. Staff and managers are trained in the key techniques, technologies and modelling approaches and understand how to access data, thus presenting them with the appropriate source data for their analysis. In addition, managers use their knowledge to develop more sophisticated approaches to modelling and make use of data mining techniques.

As successful CPM practitioners, staff combine detailed knowledge of the firm's underlying business processes with a strong knowledge of their markets and customers. This organisational knowledge is critical to achieving meaningful insight from the data. CPM is highly context-specific and generalisations from one organisation to another in terms of model design are rarely successful. When it comes to developing models and achieving insights, the 'learning is in the doing' and managers need to understand the principles behind the modelling approaches.

Looking Forward

Translating information into effective business decisions requires CPM-based solutions that provide timely and accurate access to information to support the key decisions on products and services, channels and markets. CPM capability needs to be focused on improving the effectiveness of decision-makers by providing managers with business performance monitoring, modelling and business intelligence capability. As the custodians of a company's performance measurement and control systems, finance professionals have traditionally taken a mainly functional, internal perspective on CPM systems. In future, the challenge is for them to move beyond their traditional role as scorekeepers to one in which they are actively participating in the design and deployment of new business models. A key role in this business model redesign and deployment will be ensuring that the organisation's information and transaction processing systems are aligned with and support the evolving business model. So what should organisations be doing to achieve better coverage in their CPM efforts?

They should begin by setting up a project group to review the current approach to reporting and performance measurement. This team should undertake an organisation-wide review of the CPM activities in order to do the following:

- assess the level of strategic alignment between CPM priorities/ capability and the needs of managers;
- identify the key performance drivers for the organisation, and the owners of these measures;
- measure relative performance across the key CPM activities against best practice;
- identify opportunities for improvement;

- deploy problem-solving teams to begin addressing short-comings.

Success will come to those organisations that can deploy CPM systems that will provide clean, consistent data to executives and managers across the business, supporting decision-making at all levels, backed up by comprehensive forward-looking as well as historical analysis.

In examining CPM directions organisations should be mindful of the need to extend their CPM capability to cover analysis of external and more forward-looking areas. Non-finance staff should also be involved in CPM activities. In particular, marketing and supply chain managers have important information and analysis needs, which the CPM capability should support. It is also important to be aware of who the customers for CPM are and to consider using web-based portals (see Chapter 3) to improve information dissemination.

Notes

1 L. Geishecker and F. Buytendijk, the Gartner Group (2002) *Introducing the CPM Suites Magic Quadrant,* Gartner Group Research Note 2 Oct 2002 Ref: Markets, M-17-4718.
2 CODA Group (2003) 'Simunovich Fisheries maximises "net" profits with CPM', CODA Ref: CS0007.
3 Since this case study was written, Simunovich has sold off its fishing fleet. However, this remains a useful study of CPM in action in an SME.
4 CIMA (2003) *Improving Decision Making in your Organization,* The CIMA Strategic Enterprise Management (SEM) Initiative, London: CIMA.
5 Since writing this case study, ACC has been bought by Dairy Farmers of Britain.

CHAPTER 5

DRIVING PERFORMANCE THROUGH BETTER COST MANAGEMENT

Activity-Based Costing – a Historical Perspective

In 1901, an engineer called Hamilton Church recognised the need to identify what drove company activities, and to use that information to work out what those activities cost. Perceived as radical, the methodology was never widely accepted, and when Church died so did the practice. This methodology was activity-based costing (ABC).

It was not until the introduction of production line technology and automation in the manufacturing industry that life was breathed into Church's forgotten methodology. Its timely resurrection can be linked to a dramatic rise in overheads despite automation, which many blamed on the old 'labour rate to overhead' ratio method that manufacturing companies tradition-ally used to work out costs. Although the need to have an alternative methodology that would provide a realistic costing framework was apparent, it took the collaboration of Harvard academics, big five accounting firm consultants and engineers to make ABC an attractive proposition. Some reference material attributes ABC's 1970s' revival to manufacturers John Deere and Hewlett-Packard, but many believe that its real protagonists were the Texas-based Consortium for Advanced Manufacturing-International (Cam-I) and authors Johnson and Kaplan who wrote the ABC bible – *Relevance Lost*.[1]

Until that book's publication in the 1980s, few serious attempts to analyse and understand the importance of performance measurement, management accounting and control systems had been made (other than Church's little-known pioneer efforts). Kaplan and Johnson not only identified that existing management accounting systems were inadequate for modern business environments, but that they failed to provide the relevant set of measures that appropriately reflected the technology, the products, the processes, and the competitive environment in which organisations operated. In its most basic form, ABC assigns costs to activities rather than products or services. This enables resource and overhead costs to be more accurately assigned to the products and the services that consume them.

Although there are numerous examples of companies that have successfully implemented ABC, the 1980s became a graveyard of abandoned projects, which had incurred more costs than they saved. Despite its chequered history, however, it remains a popular methodology as it is seen to provide three major benefits: more accurate costs, an improved understanding of the economics of production, and a picture of the economics of activities performed by organisations.

The Benefits of ABC

ABC attempts primarily to gain a clearer picture of product costs through a better identification of the costs of activities consumed by products. Second, but perhaps more importantly, it goes beyond this to provide clues as to whether such activities are necessary in the first place.[2] Traditionally, costs were regarded as generating value and measuring production activities rather than merely representing the utilisation of resources by an organisation's activities. In this way, using cost as a substitute for activity does not pose any difficulty, if the manufacturing process is relatively simple and produces homogeneous products. Production costs may be readily traced and allocated to product units. But in more sophisticated manufacturing and service environments, product quality, diversity and complexity are viewed as critical success factors for maintaining competitiveness. In these contexts, activity-based information can be more useful than traditional costing data as it attempts to more effectively capture factors that create costs. As such, activity-based information may comprise any relevant data about activities across the entire chain of value-adding organisational processes including design, engineering, sourcing, production, distribution, marketing and after-sales service. This type of information focuses the attention of managers on the underlying causes, or drivers, of cost and profit on the premise that people cannot manage costs – they can only manage activities that create costs.

The underlying foundation of all activity-based costing systems is the belief that the organisation is made up of activities. These activities transform resources into outputs demanded by the firm's other activities. From an activity perspective, activities consume resources and cost objects consume activities. In a departmental unit, the starting point is not with general ledger costs such as wages, equipment, etc., but on the costs of activities undertaken by it. Thus, conventional costs of a department would be assigned to the organisational activities contributed to by the department.

The manufacture of a product entails many processes that add *cost* to the product but not all such activities necessarily add *value* to it. One of the advantages of activity-based costing is that it can help to differentiate between value-added and non–value-added activities according to whether or not the elimination of an activity from the manufacturing process would result in a deterioration of product attributes such as performance, function, quality and perceived value, and thus reduce value to the customer. However, there is the widely held view that an activity approach to accounting should be grounded in the management of the organisation by managing through activities rather than the traditional organisational functional unit. Activity-based management (ABM) can therefore be defined as a discipline focusing on the management of activities as the route to continuously improve both the value received by customers and the profit earned by providing this value. This process includes cost-driver analysis and utilises activity-based costing as a major source of information.

Reflecting this wish for activity-based costing to extend its role in management, the practical emphasis has switched from product costing to activity-based cost management and activity-based budgeting, where the emphasis is on reducing costs by seeking to eliminate non-value-added activities, and on managing and planning the organisation using activity analysis. These processes shift activity-based approaches from being a contribution to accounting, to being more general management tools.

The Relevance of ABC in Today's Financial Environment

Today's business environment demands more relevant information on the organisation's activities, processes, products, services and customers. With this in mind, leading companies are using their enhanced cost systems to do the following:

- design products and services that both meet customers' expectations and can be produced and delivered at a profit;
- signal where continuous or discontinuous (re-engineering) improvements in quality, efficiency and speed are needed;
- assist front-line employees in their learning and continuous improvement activities;

- guide product mix and investment decisions;
- choose among alternative suppliers;
- negotiate on price, product features, quality, delivery and service with customers;
- structure efficient and effective distribution and service processes to targeted market and customer segments.

Kaplan and Cooper[3] claim that many companies are not gaining these competitive advantages from enhanced cost systems. Their managers rely on information from cost systems designed for a simpler technological age, when competition was local not global, and when speed, quality and performance were less critical for success. In their view, these managers do not have timely and relevant information to guide their operational improvement activities. Nor are they receiving accurate, valid information to shape their strategic decisions about processes, products, services and customers.

Deficiencies of Traditional Cost Systems

The evolution of ABC reflects the gradual shift in management accounting from mainly operational control and management control activities to supporting strategic planning and shareholder wealth creation.

According to Kaplan,[4] a traditional costing system which allocates overhead using a unit-based cost-driver, e.g. direct labour hours (DLH) is inappropriate where: (1) DLH has fallen to an insignificant percentage of the total cost; (2) the range of products has diversified; (3) product complexity, design and use of activities vary; (4) overhead is increased as a percentage of the total cost; or (5) automation has replaced DLH. Focusing on allocating overhead to products based on DLH has distracted management attention from the expansion of indirect costs. Poorly designed or outdated accounting and control systems can distort the realities of manufacturing performance.

Cooper[5] identified that traditional cost systems treat a large proportion of manufacturing overhead as fixed because management accounting teaching traditionally has concentrated on information for making short-run (one to three months) incremental decisions based on variable or relevant costs. These 'fixed' costs have been the most variable and rapidly increasing costs. Many overhead costs are driven by the complexity of production, not the volume of production, so non-volume-related bases are required to allocate these cost pools to product. Product costs are almost all variable; some vary directly with the volume produced while others arising from overhead support and marketing departments vary with the diversity and complexity of the product line. Traditional cost systems did not reflect this, using a two-stage cost allocation structure but with a single-unit-based second stage cost-driver usually based on direct labour hours or machine hours.

The Case for ABC

ABC is a methodology that can help companies to gain competitive advantage in an increasingly competitive environment. According to Gartner Group research director, Lee Geishecker, there are four ways of gaining competitive advantage with ABC:

- ABC and ABM can help organisations to obtain better information about their existing processes and activities, thus efficiency of operations can improve continuously.
- An organisation is able to rationalise and optimise its development of people, capital and other assets.
- The new activity-based organisation becomes more nimble and market-focused which results in an enhanced competitive position.
- More accurate product costs are delivered.

Since ABC first of all assigns the cost of resources to activities and, second, assigns the cost of activities to products, using unit, batch and product-sustaining cost-drivers to assign the cost of equivalent classes of activities, this results in more accurate product costs. Cooper states that it is essential that managers know what their products cost as the anticipated cost and profitability of the product will influence decisions such as product design, new product introductions, marketing effort and discontinuance. The cumulative effect of decisions on product design, new product introductions, discontinuance and pricing helps define a firm's strategy. If the firm's product costs information is distorted, the firm may follow an inappropriate and unprofitable strategy, for example, the strategy of being a low-cost producer, or of being a differential producer hoping for premium prices.

So, better product costs should result in the following:

- better pricing decisions;
- better product mix decisions;
- better product outsourcing decisions;
- better decisions regarding customer, channel and market segment profitability decisions.

All of these should result in improved financial performance.

How to Achieve Cost Reduction

Leading ABC exponents Cooper and Kaplan recommend that companies should 'firstly explore ways to reduce the resources required to perform various activities. Then to transform those reductions into profit, they must either reduce spending on these resources or increase the output those resources produce.' If this step is not completed, management will merely have created excess capacity, not increased profits. ABC helps managers reduce demands for resources by focusing the product line.

Low-volume, high complexity products can be hived off to a focused facility.

Activity-based budgeting

There is a growing belief that budgets prepared using ABC concepts can give superior results in terms of helping managers anticipate the effects of planned changes. ABC budgeting can be used to simulate the effect of planned changes in activities. ABC budgeting links projected revenue to activities and activities to resources required, thus producing a more realistic budget. Actual activity and resource drivers or budgeted activity and resource drivers may be used in the budgeting process. Budgeted activity and resource drivers will have planned efficiencies and planned reductions in surplus capacity built in. ABC budgeting greatly aids workload and resource requirement planning.

Customer profitability analysis

Few organisations carry out rigorous and frequent analysis of the profitability of their products and clients. Too often decisions are made on the volume discounts and levels of service to give clients or assign to product lines based on 'gut feel' and simple assumptions made around sales levels – leading to statements like 'they are our biggest client so they deserve more discount'. Unfortunately, the reality can be far from obvious, and may at first seem counter-intuitive.

In an analysis of the impact of individual customer profitability, Cooper and Kaplan[6] used ABC analysis to discover that Kanthal, a heating wire manufacturer, had established the following profile:

- 20 per cent of customers generated 225 per cent of profits;
- 70 per cent of customers generated 0 per cent of profits;
- 10 per cent of customers generated −125 per cent of profits.

In Kanthal's case, the customers generating the biggest losses were among those with the largest sales volume, a situation that is surprisingly common.

ABC and marketing

When analysing product profitability, too, Cooper and Kaplan found that organisations typically find that both the most profitable and the least profitable products are those with high sales volumes.

Although ABC is more normally associated with cutting and controlling traditional costs, the methodology is also particularly relevant for more 'peripheral' functions such as marketing. According to Lewis,[7] the cost of physical distribution and other marketing activities accounts for a significant proportion of total costs. The objective of market cost analysis is to provide relevant quantitative data that will assist marketing managers in making informed decisions regarding:

- product profitability;
- pricing;
- adding or dropping a product line or territory, or sales channel.

To achieve this objective, it is necessary to be able to trace costs directly to product lines or territories, and to establish a rational system of allocating non-traceable costs to the cost objective.

This is becoming increasingly relevant in respect of distribution channel profitability as products are now sold through a growing number of diverse channels, for example, distributors, mega-stores, direct mail and e-commerce. Needless to say, if the organisation serves a single channel, then channel profitability calculation is relatively straightforward. If, however, the organisation is aligned by production, region, or facility location, then calculation of profitability by channel becomes more difficult. By using ABC in this context, companies can cost products more accurately by recognising that costs are not only driven by production activity but by the customers served and the channels through which the product is offered. Examining the cost structure from this perspective allows management to understand cost differences related to one of these categories or related to interaction between the categories.

ABC also allows organisations to determine how a company's customers are consuming its marketing, distribution and customer service resources. According to Foster *et al.*,[8] customer profitability analysis is important because each dollar of revenue does not contribute equally to profit. Profitability depends not only on the unit cost of the product but also on back-end services (marketing, distribution and customer service).

Supplier relationships

It was Kaplan[9] who noted that ABC could play a major role in improving supplier relationships by working on the principle that the lowest cost supplier is not necessarily the cheapest in the long term. This is because the total cost of making a batch of components available to production includes costs of purchase, ordering, paying, receiving, moving, storing, scrap, rework, obsolescence, scheduling, expediting and downtime. The supplier that minimises the totality of these costs is the lowest cost supplier. The ABC model enables purchasing to estimate how much it is willing to pay a supplier so that the net gains can be shared between supplier and customer – the lean supplier paradigm. ABC enables an informed trade-off among price, quality and responsiveness and ultimately creates sustainable relationships with suppliers.

Product design

Research by Ford shows that an estimated 60 to 80 per cent of costs over a product's life cycle are locked in at the end of the product design phase, rising to 90 to 95 per cent by the time the design production process is complete. Therefore ABC offers tremendous cost reduction opportunities.

Implementing ABC

The following are the steps typically involved in implementing ABC in organisations:

1   *Planning.* This involves enlisting the services of qualified, knowledgeable consultants to advise and educate management on ABC. Factors such as the critical issues for the corporation, difficult decisions, the corporate culture and the prevailing approach to financial management must be identified. Based on the information provided through this process, the framework for ABC emerges.

2   *Resolving issues.* Issues such as the following need to be closely evaluated and resolved to enable the implementation of the ABC framework. These are:
    (a) loss of control;
    (b) re-evaluation of prior decisions;
    (c) learning the new process;
    (d) job accountability.

3   *Training.* Analysts need to be trained in the methodology of ABC. In the author's experience, those with an operations knowledge but no cost accounting background were better able to grasp the ABC techniques, while those with a cost accounting background needed time to readjust from traditional cost accounting.

4   *Procedural documentation.* This includes the preparation of a list of all activities in the various departments. These activity types are used to determine the cost distribution methodology within the ABC system.

5   *Expense analysis.* The process used to determine activity unit costs. Theoretically, expenses are redistributed from the

organisational and natural expense category into activity pools via first-stage drivers (see point 6). Then, activity volumes are divided into the pools to determine a unit activity cost. Activities are tracked to each product based on the second-stage driver and are aligned either directly or indirectly to products to determine the product cost.

6   *Collecting first-stage drivers.* This stage is used to align indirect expenses from the activity centre to activity pools. These drivers would include staff time measures, which need to be carefully tracked for each activity.

7   *Collecting second-stage drivers.* Second-stage drivers dictate how an activity is assigned to a product and they vary with activity type. Volumes of activities for the same timeframe are used to develop a per unit activity cost.

8   *Automating the process.* Our main area of concern is the complex process of building an automated system to support the ABC methodology. The system must be designed to be extremely flexible and dynamic. A software product capable of computing, storing and reporting the ABC cost data is required. In a large organisation, it is impractical to attempt to run a manual ABC system.

9   *Management training.* Management needs to be educated to the many uses of the ABC data and must be trained to play an interactive role in the ABC process. An essential prerequisite to success is corporate-wide acceptance of the new cost system, and a tailoring of the system to its own environment.

Activity-Based Management

Activity-based management (ABM) is a discipline that focuses on the management of activities as the route to improving the value received by the customer and the profit achieved by providing this value. This discipline includes cost–driver analysis, activity analysis and performance measurement. ABM therefore draws on activity-based costing as its major source of information (Figure 5.1).

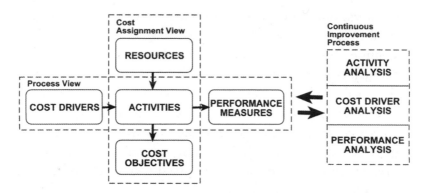

Figure 5.1. The activity-based management model. *Source:* (J. A. Miller (1996) *Implementing Activity-Based Management in Daily Operations*, p. 236).

Information determined by ABC helps guide ABM to direct resources to activities that yield the greatest profitability and helps improve the way work is carried out. This is achieved through activity analysis, cost-driver analysis and performance analysis:

- *Activity analysis*
  - Identify non-value-added activities and whether the activity is essential to the customer or essential to the functioning of the organisation. An example of a non-value-added activity is maintaining two independent sets of bills of materials, one for engineering and one for production. Non-value-added activities are candidates for elimination.
  - Identify significant activities. The organisation should focus on significant activities by applying the Pareto (80:20) rule.
  - Benchmark activities against best practice, thus identifying scope for improvement.
  - Examine the link between activities. Poorly performed activities earlier in the linked chain of activities can have knock-on effects on other activities later in the chain. For example, purchase orders generated by the purchasing department with incorrect prices result in extra non-essential work in the accounts payable department during

the activity of matching invoice price to the purchase order price prior to approving payment.

- *Cost-driver analysis.* This involves searching for those things that require you to perform non-essential activities or to perform activities below par. For example, moving a product internally between two processes is a non-value-added activity. This activity cannot be eliminated until the distance between the two processes is eliminated. The cost driver of the moving activity is the distance between the two processes. Corrective action is to reorganise the plant so that the two processes are side by side in sequence.

- *Performance analysis.* A performance measurement system (see Chapter 4) must foster improvement in the right areas. To do this, the organisation must determine its key objectives, communicate these objectives to the people in the organisation, and finally develop measures to access the performance of each activity. These measures should signify how each activity contributes to the overall mission.

Turney[10] noted that ABM has two goals: first, to improve the value received by customers and, second, to improve profits by providing this value. Customers want products and services that fit a specific need, provide good quality and service at an affordable price, they want to be delighted and they want it available on demand. In providing customer value, a firm must also provide an adequate return on stockholder investment. The firm's profitability should be important to the customer in the long run, since they generally want the supplier to continue to supply them in the long term.

Turney explains that a company does this in two ways:

- *Improving strategic position.* A successful business deploys resources to those activities that yield the highest strategic benefit. Taking a strategic choice determines the activities and resources needed. The firm must analyse the link between its

strategy and the activities and resources needed to put the
strategy into place.

- *Improving strategic capability.* Improve what matters to your
  customer. This has three steps:
  - Analyse activities to identify opportunities for improvement.
  - Dig for drivers – the factors that cause waste.
  - Measure the things an activity should be doing well if it
    contributes to an organisation's success and the profitable
    servicing of its customers.

All these goals are achieved through the management of
activities. Each activity makes a measurable contribution to
improving customer value through improved quality, timeliness,
reliable delivery or low cost. Managing activities is a process of
relentless and continuous improvement of all aspects of the
business.

Continuous Improvement Through ABM

Continuing improvements to processes and products leading to
increased customer satisfaction and higher profits is the key goal
of activity-based management. Continuous improvement of
products also means designing products that meet customer
requirements yet are easier and faster to manufacture, for
example, products designed with modular sub-assemblies and a
common chassis can be assembled on the same production line.
Continuous improvement of processes means the on-going
search for waste in operating activities and the elimination of this
waste; reducing set-up time on a machine reduces cost and
improves flexibility and quality.

Achieving cost reduction can be done in four ways.

- *Activity reduction* focuses on reducing the elapsed time and
  effort required to perform activities and translates into a
  reduction in resource requirements.

- *Activity elimination* where changes to the production process or products can eliminate the need to perform activities.
- *Activity selection.* A product or process can be designed in several ways with each activity having its own set of activities and associated cost. Design for cost reduction involves choosing a low cost alternative from several competing alternatives.
- *Activity sharing.* The designer of a product or process can choose design alternatives that permit products to share activities. Sharing activities provides economics of scale in using these activities.

All of the above cost reduction exercises can be achieved by either re-designing the product or re-designing the process. In each case, ABC is superior to conventional costing as it facilitates identification of activities to be targeted for cost reduction.

Case Study: Royal Mail

Royal Mail delivers around 82 million items of mail to 27 million addresses each day. It has more than 220,000 employees and an annual turnover of £8.3 billion (€12 billion, US$15.3 billion). In recent years the business has faced a multitude of challenges. A new regulatory and competitive environment, plus a weak economy, led management to seek out more reliable sources of information on performance and profitability. As part of a wider financial systems programme they created a dynamic costing system using an activity-based management application, linked into their ERP system and 60-plus data sources.

Following 25 years of profitability, 2001–02 saw annual losses hit £1.1 billion (€1.6 billion, US$1.9 billion). In the 1990s, the organisation had regularly delivered profits of several hundred million pounds. While business volumes grew, they failed to match predictions, and the high fixed-cost statutory commitment to provide a 'universal service' was a major drain on the company.

Royal Mail began a process of business renewal to return to profit with a positive cash flow. A new management team was put in place and the organisation was restructured. A major issue in trying to address the organisation's performance was the need to improve information support for managers in order to support better understanding of the drivers of value, cost and profit.

The Royal Mail is a complex organisation operating from thousands of locations and with multiple data sources. The Enterprise System Programme was tasked with improving Royal Mail's ability to collect, store, analyse and use data to support strategic decision making. The Revenue and Cost Model was at the heart of this approach.

Delivering Analytic Intelligence

The aim was to simplify the complex interconnection between the three financial activities that underpin the business; the planning and budgeting cycle; management accounting and reporting; and commercial analysis, such as which products and customers are profitable, together with its counterweight of regulatory analysis. Being in a regulated industry, the Royal Mail needed to demonstrate that their prices were sensibly related to their costs, and prove that there was no cross-subsidy between regulated services, such as letters, and non-regulated services, such as parcel deliveries.

To do this, Royal Mail needed to join up their processes and, most importantly, support all three financial activity areas with common data. Reconciling differences between them represented a major overhead, and one which did not add value. In 2001 Royal Mail deployed a general ledger and data mart solution. The ABM system was then implemented and linked to the data mart to create the intelligence layer.

The ABM system from SAS was flexible, had a good functional fit with current and likely future business requirements. Transparency was critical, not least because regulatory reporting meant having access to an easy audit trail. Its high modelling power was important, given the large computation volumes and the needs of regulatory reporting – the level of detail had to be high even on smaller product lines.

In a very complex network business like the Royal Mail it can be hard to identify individual costs to individual customers, so customers are treated as a 'bundle' of various products. While on the face of it they have relatively few products, all the variants and handling characteristics combine to provide 1100 products in the Royal Mail model, with 600 resource types assigned to 400 activities to cost those products. Indeed, in the performance management of the operation, the mail delivery process model assigns 20 000 resources to 200 activities. This adds up to some 20 million calculations required on a regular basis.

Integrating Systems

While the costing requirements were clearly complex, modelling the business was not the main technical challenge. A key issue was ensuring the costing system was integrated with the financial and planning software. This was vital in delivering a single view of the numbers.

The data mart is populated with financial and other data from the ERP system and numerous legacy sources. The vast majority of complex analyses – relating to customer and product profitability, regulatory requirements, and so on – are then generated by the ABM system. This gives the different facets of Royal Mail access to enhanced analytic capabilities. In operations it can look at issues such as the value chain and process management. Sales and marketing can focus on performance management and product/customer contribution. In planning, the business can, for example, undertake product- and customer-focused planning with a five-year horizon.

In the regulatory arena managers can review efficiency, explore price controls and provide regulatory accounts. Meanwhile executives have reports that cover areas such as business trends and product/customer performance.

The new ABM approach has created better integration between planning and performance management, allowing a proper understanding of cost drivers. Royal Mail now has purpose-built, fact-driven reports, faster processing, improved access to information in general, and a solid ABM platform to build on – all of which means improved organisational ability.

Royal Mail's fortunes are already improving – thanks, so far, to determined management direction to eliminate costs. The goal now is to recover normal profitability levels. For this, the improved costing capability and ABM infrastructure will help management to focus action even more effectively in the right places.

Reproduced by permission of Royal Mail Group plc.

ABC/M's Relationship to Other Accounting and Management Innovations

The past decade has been a time of many accounting and management innovations. In this section the link between ABC/M and innovations such as value chain analysis, life cycle costing, and target costing are discussed.

Value Chain Analysis (VCA)

According to Partrige and Perren,[11] activity-based systems help to create product-enhancing attributes, which prove useful in identifying separate value chain costs. Shank and Govindarajan[12] look at value chain analysis as evaluated by Michael Porter and argue that strategic cost management insights that emerge from value chains analysis are different from and better than the insights available from traditional management accounting approaches. Managing costs requires a broad focus on what Porter calls the value chain – the 'linked set of value creating activities'. The focus is external to the firm with each firm viewed in the context of the overall chain of value-creating activities of which the firm is only a part, from basic raw material to end-use consumers.

'Value added analysis', on the other hand, is internally focused to the organisation with each firm viewed in the context of its purchases, processes, functions, products and customers. The aim of value added is to maximise the difference (value added) between sales and purchases. The strategic insights yielded by value chain analysis are superior to those offered by value-added analysis. The 'value-added' concept starts too late and ends too early when compared to value chain analysis.

A business can develop a sustainable competitive advantage by following either a low cost strategy or a differentiation strategy. Whether or not a firm can develop and sustain cost leadership or differentiation depends on how it manages its value chain relative to those of its competitors. Competitive advantage ultimately derives from providing better customer value for equivalent cost or equivalent customer value for lower cost.

The value chain framework is a method for breaking down the chain into strategically relevant activities in order to understand the behaviour of costs and sources of differentiation. Gaining and sustaining a competitive advantage require the firm to understand the entire value delivery system, not just the portion of the value chain in which it participates. Suppliers and distributors have profit margins that are important to identify, in understanding a firm's cost or differentiation position as end-use customers pay for all the profit margins throughout the value chain.

Value chain analysis promotes interdependence along the value chain. It promotes mutually beneficial linkages backward to suppliers and forward to customers.

Insights offered by value chain analysis:

- Value chain analysis is a first step in understanding how a firm is positioned in its industry. Building sustainable competitive advantage requires knowledge of the full linked set of value added activities of which the firm and its competitors are a part.
- Once a value chain is articulated, strategic decisions such as – make vs. buy or forward vs. backward integration become clearer. Investments can be viewed from their impact on the overall chain and the firm's place in it.
- Value chain analysis helps quantify buyer and supplier power.
- Value chain analysis highlights how a firm's product fits into its customer's value chain. It is readily apparent what percentage the firm's costs are of the customer's total costs. It encourages joint cost reductions.

Life Cycle Costing

Life cycle costing adds a new perspective to ABC programmes by highlighting the interdependence of activities and their associated costs at all stages of product lifecycles. Life cycle costing looks at products over their life cycle rather than just for one year. A product's life cycle encompasses initial research and development, proceeds through the product launch, growth in the market and ends with maturity, decline and end of life. A life cycle perspective yields insights to product costs and profitability not available from viewing a single year. A product that is in a start-up phase may appear uncompetitive with its low volumes and high marketing costs while a mature product with its higher volumes will appear highly profitable.

Cooper[13] notes that the application of the timing rule where only the expenses that relate to current outputs should be assigned to 'today's outputs' allows ABC systems to automatically generate life cycle costing reports. Life cycle costing offers several benefits over the traditional single year view. In other words, it allows:[14]

- more intelligent strategic perspective, for example, the commitment of scarce engineering resources requires a lifecycle perspective;
- the activities and resources needed to take a product from development to end of life to be highlighted;
- more informed decisions on early abandonment, or to commit extra resources part way through the life cycle.

The key to the success of life cycle costing is the accuracy of product life estimates and costs. The basis for target costing is profitability over the lifetime of the product.

So Why the Controversy?
The Problems with Implementing ABC/M

ABM and ABC, as we have shown in this chapter so far, are powerful linked methodologies for managing and costing modern organisations. Techniques and tools have developed considerably, and in recent times we have seen the approach being considered and applied in industries far removed from the traditional manufacturing sector where it started.

There are undoubted strengths of this approach, and the theory is compelling. However, it is in the application and implementation of ABC/M that it has earned its controversial reputation for too often being 'a good idea, poorly executed'. Time and again we hear of organisations undergoing a large and complex ABC project at huge cost and effort, which brings up interesting results and then atrophies and decays until it ceases to deliver meaningful results and is discontinued.

As Peter Hill, of ABC experts Bellis-Jones Hill admits: 'A lot of organisations that implemented ABC came away unhappy with the results' (see interview). There are many reasons for this, and we will explore them here.

Implementation issues broadly fall into two categories:

1   Technical issues concerning the development of the ABC/M model such as choosing a set of usable activities, establishing a set of cost drivers, gathering cost data, frequency of model update, or integration with the main accounting system.
2   Organisational factors, which are common to all major projects. These are linkage to business strategy, getting the support of top management for the initiative, education and training, end user buy-in, transfer of ownership from the project team to the end users, moving from the analysis stage to the action stage, effective project management and organisational change management. These organisational factors have a bigger bearing on the likely outcome of the ABC/M initiative than technical concerns.

Interview: Peter Hill, Bellis-Jones Hill Group

Peter Hill, operations director of UK-based ABC consultancy Bellis-Jones Hill Group is only too aware of the source of ABC's unpopularity.

'A lot of organisations that implemented ABC came away unhappy with the results,' he admits. 'There are two reasons for this. Either the organisation failed to bring in the right people, or they extracted so much detail that there was no way they could sustain the level of information and so dismissed the exercise as a one-off.

'Back in the late 1980s and early '90s there simply weren't the IT systems to support that level of extraction as there are today. The volume of data simply became too difficult to manage.' Hill believes that a number of companies also failed to properly recognise 'cause and effect' and subsequently the real cost-drivers.

'As customers buy products, activities therefore increase. These activities require processes, so costs therefore increase. For example: processing sales orders, which is normally measured by counting the number of orders processed. But sometime sales orders are hard to deal with, as are some customers. You need rigour to identify real cost drivers. ABC is not just an accounting exercise.'

Another area of criticism often thrown at ABC is its alleged preoccupation with time and motion data. Hill is quick to dispel the myth. 'Yes, ABC looks at activities, but going into the detail required for time and motion analysis again brings us to the problem of having too much information. You simply do not need that level of data.'

Simple is Best

Bellis-Jones Hill Group is keen to promote a simple model for the methodology, in contrast to its complex reputation. According to Hill, an increasing number of organisations are reaping the benefits of both repeatable ABC and one-off exercises, which can be completed in six to 12 weeks.

But it is the advent of CPM software that now allows organisations to use ABC-derived data for planning and forecasting. 'Companies want to know how possible market changes will affect production in terms of volume and price,' explains Hill. 'ABC can supply the information they need on which to base a decision.'

ABC – Not Just Manufacturing

Although its origins are firmly in the manufacturing sector, ABC is suitable for any industry sector, as long as it has 'complexity and variability'. In other words, companies that have one product or service line need not apply! However, Hill is quick to add that even if the business is relatively simple, services, products and indeed customers can themselves be complex.

Despite its manufacturing parentage, ABC is fast becoming the methodology of choice for shared service centres. 'Shared service centres have turned back-office functions into factories,' says Hill. 'The same level of information is needed to accurately price services as is needed to price products.'

A Tool for Compliance

Hill is equally as keen to push ABC's compliance capabilities. 'Sarbanes–Oxley is definitely going to have an influence on the number of companies implementing ABC,' he says. 'Companies need to know they are compliant. ABC gives you the high level view across the organisation, that is essential for that level of assurance.'

Problems Experienced in Implementation

Player and Keys,[15] list nine major pitfalls of implementing ABC/ABM.

Lack of top management buy-in

Executives fail to go through the set-up process and the ownership phase is never reached. The company may not get past the awareness stage. Supportive top management includes management of the parent and plant management.

*Failure to understand financial,
operational and strategic cost*

These different views of costs entail different users, purposes and levels of aggregation, reporting frequency and types of measures. ABC/ABM can serve all three purposes but not simultaneously. It is essential to understand how cost information from the new cost system will be used. Costs calculated under Generally Accepted Accounting Principles (GAAP) will differ from costs generated for strategic purposes, e.g. selling and G&A costs included in strategic costs but not GAAP costs. Strategic costs may include future costs even though GAAP will not recognise these costs until they are incurred.

Lack of clear objectives

This is closely related to the lack of top management buy in. ABC/ABM projects should be set up only to solve a business problem.

Lack of employee involvement

Employees must be involved in creating, implementing and continuously improving the ABM system. The team involved in identifying the activities and cost drivers should be mainly made up of non–accountants, even if accountants or consultants facilitate this process. Where non–accountants are involved, they are more likely to use the information the system generates and to make suggestions for improving the system. ABM must be viewed as a continuous process, which is constantly improved. It must evolve to accurately model organisational changes over time.

Lack of funding

ABM projects are expensive so adequate funding is necessary to cover:

- software
- consultants
- a full-time project team
- management time
- training.

The company should estimate the value of better decisions resulting from an ABC/ABM implementation. This may be critical in getting adequate resources to move forward on a rapid and focused basis.

Lack of training

Many employees must be trained in ABM. A symptom of no training or too little training is that managers and users do not understand the operation of the system and what the system will do for them in their jobs. As a consequence, users resist the change. Initial training should be done by consultants, subsequent training should be done by company personnel who can apply their knowledge of the company to the ABM training. Both the ABM implementation team and users must be trained. Most training should be done early in the process but some must take place after implementation. A periodic follow-up should be made to see if training has proved effective.

'It wasn't our fault'

Consultants should facilitate management's taking ownership of the system. Consultants should not prescribe solutions, but should model what company personnel want rather than what the consultants did on their last project. It is vital that they transfer knowledge so that the team members are as knowledgeable as the consultants by the end of the project. The ABM model should fit the circumstances of the company rather than fit the consultants' ABM software model.

Lack of cost management expertise

By the end of the project at least one employee in the company should be an ABC/ABM expert and responsible for the functional and technical aspects of the ABM system. The company should regularly benchmark cost management practices within the company against global best practices and understand the differences.

No link between ABM and other management initiatives

ABM should not be implemented in isolation, but must be linked to other management initiatives. Implemented correctly, ABM can support the other management initiatives. Having improvement efforts work together rather than competing is better than trying to implement them in isolation. ABM can be used to develop performance measures for JIT (just-in-time) or TQM (total quality management), and can generate continuous improvement ideas for such initiatives. Include people from other activities on the ABM team.

Technologies that Support ABC/M

The specialist ABC/M software market has developed steadily over the past decade. Software packages fall into three groups: (1) software developed by major consulting firms; (2) those developed by specialist independent software houses or; (3) those that form part of ERP (enterprise resource planning) suites. The latter category of ABC/M software has the advantage of integrating with the manufacturing, logistics and finance modules contained in these packages, but obviously is only applicable to those who have implemented those end-to-end suites across their business.

Most of these software packages and their author companies have been around for some time – several decades in some cases –

and their fortunes have reflected the uptake of ABC/M generally; they have enjoyed limited success with a small number of large organisations adopting them but often failing to build on initial success with a longer-term adoption.

However, with the development in recent years of improved technology in the areas of data marts, data warehouses and business intelligence, along with the advent of CPM (Corporate Performance Management – see Chapter 4), ABC/M has started to show signs of moving into the mainstream. The ability to extract, transform and load large quantities of data from an organisation's transactional systems into a data mart or warehouse provides the platform for delivering high volumes of meaningful data required for successful ABC applications.

Notes

1 H. T. Johnson and R. S. Kaplan (1987) *Relevance Lost: The Rise and Fall of Management Accounting*, Boston: Harvard Business School Press.

2 T. Hope and J. Hope (1996) *Transforming The Bottom Line: Managing Performance with the Real Numbers*, Boston: Harvard Business School Press.

3 R. S. Kaplan and R. Cooper (1998) *Cost and Effect: Using Integrated Cost Systems to Drive Profitability and Performance*, Boston: Harvard Business School Press.

4 R. S. Kaplan (1995) 'New roles for management accountants', *Journal of Cost Management*, Fall, p. 13.

5 R. Cooper (1996) 'The changing practice of management accounting', *Management Accounting*, March, pp. 26–35.

6 R. Cooper and R. S. Kaplan (1991) *The Design of Cost Management Systems: Text, Cases and Reading*, Englewood Cliffs, NJ: Prentice Hall.

7 R. Lewis (1991) 'ABC for marketing', *Management Accounting USA*, November.

8 G. Foster, M. Gupta and L. Sjoblom (1996) 'Customer profitability analysis: challenges and new directions', *Journal of Cost Management*, Spring, pp. 5–13.

9 R. S. Kaplan and D. P. Norton (1992) 'The balanced scorecard: measures that drive performance', *Harvard Business Review*, Jan–Feb, pp. 71–9.

10 P. B. B. Turney and J. M. Reeve (1991) 'How ABC helps reduce cost', *Journal of Cost Management*, Winter, 29–35.

11 M. Partrige and L. Perren (1994) 'Cost analysis of the value chain: another role for strategic management accounting', *Managing Accounting*. Vol. 72, issue 7, pp. 22–4.

12 J. K. Shank and V. Govindarajan (1992) 'Strategic cost management and the value chain', *Journal of Cost Management*, Winter, pp. 5–21.

13 R. Cooper (1988) 'Rise of ABC Part 2 – When do I need an ABCS?' *Journal of Cost Management*, Fall, pp. 41–8.

14 P. B. B. Turney (1991) *Common Cents: the ABC Performance Breakthrough*, New York: Cost Technology.

15 S. Player and D. Keys (1995) 'Lessons from the ABM battlefield: getting off to the right start', *Journal of Cost Management*, Spring, pp. 26–38, 'Lessons from the ABM battlefield: developing the pilot', *Journal of Cost Management*, Summer, pp. 20–35.

CHAPTER 6

FORECASTING, PLANNING AND BUDGETING

We should not let our past, however glorious, get in the way of our future.

(Charles Handy)

As the volume of information from processes grows, so too does the complexity associated with managing an organisation's performance. At the same time new technologies and increased market competition mean the pressure for change is greater. All these factors drive ever more complexity into the planning and budgeting process. For leading-edge businesses, budgeting is quickly changing from a once-a-year event to a dynamic process that is in a constant state of flux.

All too often, finance professionals end up building ever more complex systems to support this evolving planning and budgeting process, inevitably making considerable use of spreadsheets, email and *ad hoc* analysis. This leaves the finance department unable to keep up with advances in the business strategy. As a result, finance professionals and business executives are now looking at alternative ways of carrying out their organisation's budgeting so that the rapid changes can be taken into account and time, cost and effort can be dramatically reduced.

But despite this financial revolution, budgeting is still generally accepted as a static process largely reliant on manual processes. The traditional annual budget can be viewed simply as a 'top-down' exercise, whereby budget packs go out from corporate offices (hard copy or electronically) to various divisions and business units, accompanied by forms or procedures to uphold and adhere to. Once the exercise is completed and returned from the 'bottom up', the process is further enhanced with amendments until agreement is achieved. The final product is completed months after the initial process began and often looks totally different from any original submissions made by line managers.

Although many companies are now beginning to vary their approach to both planning and budgeting, a study published in February 2004 by CFO Research Services[1] found that over 60 per cent of the 287 mid-size US companies surveyed believed their planning process took too long.

Figures from benchmarking group Hackett give an idea of the gulf between the planning performance of average organisations and world-class companies. In an article in *Darwin Magazine*, the following benchmarks were given:

- Tactical and financial planning: Average company takes 4.1 months; world-class company takes 1 month.
- Strategic planning: Average company takes 4.7 months; world-class company takes 1 month.
- Level of budget detail (line items): Average company has 372; world-class company has 21.
- Per cent of time spent on forecasting/action: Average company spends 23 per cent; world-class company spends 44 per cent.
- Forecasting basis: Average company uses current year; world-class company uses a rolling year.

But times are changing. In 2002 a joint survey by consultants Accenture and Cranfield Business School[2] concluded somewhat dramatically that the days of traditional budgeting and planning are numbered. The study reviewed the financial performance of 20 companies, and showed that the move away from traditional budgeting had helped them outperform their peers. It also highlighted the link between well-executed budgeting and planning and overall company performance. The authors concluded that it was a mistake to conduct budgeting as a separate process, and instead recommended that it be part of an integrated procedure that includes strategic planning, performance reporting and target setting.

Case Study: Murray, Inc.

Murray, Inc. has been a fixture of the US consumer goods sector for more than a century. From its beginnings as a maker of supply fenders, gas tanks and running boards, Murray has grown into a major $1bn industry leader. Its portfolio of products now includes lawn tractors, walk-behind mowers, snow blowers and recreation vehicles, including state-of-the-art GoKarts and SnoRacer sleds. The company operates a global network of retailers and dealers – with 8000 dealers across the USA alone – and it has over four million square feet of manufacturing space in three assembly plants throughout Tennessee.

In order to keep ahead of its industry and optimise sales for its diverse product set, the company decided that it had to simplify and accelerate its financial processes. In particular, Murray was keen to transform its financial planning and budgeting process from an administrative burden – weighed down by hundreds of standalone spreadsheets – to an efficient, collaborative process that would make a strategic contribution to the company's success. As its sales are greatly influenced by the changing seasons, the company also needed to instantly view the health of its business through up-to-the minute reports and forecasts. This, in turn, allows managers to measure, monitor and control short- and long-term performance and to drive profitability.

'We wanted to implement a planning and budgeting solution that would provide us with more control and predictability through real-time reporting, monitoring and reaction,' explains Murray's financial systems manager.

'The only way to achieve this was to replace our existing planning process, which was heavily dependent on spreadsheets and provided fragmented information – not the business analytics we demand.

'This was further compounded by the fact that we had little integration between our business operating systems. So, we had vast islands of information sitting in our finance, manufacturing and CRM systems, leaving key business data spread out across a number of different databases. To make this information meaningful, we had to bring it together and have the power to report on it and analyse it from any angle.'

The new solution is a real-time, web-based enterprise planning system that integrates with Murray's core financial and manufacturing systems to provide a full service tool for budgeting, planning and consolidation, through to analysis and forecasting and financial reporting. This ensures that the CFO, COO and managers across the organisation can access real-time sales and customer information across the supply chain.

The move away from stand-alone spreadsheets to collaborative budgeting has revolutionised the planning process – making it both proactive and real time, according to Murray: 'Planning, budgeting and consolidation had previously been arduous tasks, slowed down by manual processes. We had no conformity. Individuals across our 268 departments were doing their own thing, so the process inevitably involved rekeying data, usually into separate spreadsheets that then had to be reported on manually.

'With the new planning system, users can now directly input budgeting information and, because it is integrated with the finance engine and other business operating systems, all information is in real time and we have instant consolidation and reporting. As a result, we have reduced our period close from five days to just three and in 45 minutes we can now calculate a year of actuals and budgets.'

The solution has enabled Murray to eliminate the hundreds of stand-alone spreadsheets it used to rely on for budgeting and planning information, and this has provided rapid return on investment by enabling the company to increase efficiency and produce instant reports and sales analysis for key customers such as Wal-Mart, Home Depot and Sears.

The Problems with Traditional Budgeting

> The traditional budget can undermine the growth potential of a company by forcing managers' attention exclusively on the short-term financial numbers.
>
> (David Axson, Managing Director of AnswerThink)

Much of the blame for corporate governance failure could be attributed to flawed budgeting systems, as traditional bottom-up budgeting not only consumes a huge amount of executives' time, but forces them into endless rounds of dull meetings and tense negotiations. Many believe the traditional approach also encourages line managers to 'play the game' by setting targets low and inflating results. The main concern is that budgeting has become so embedded in corporate life that it is now accepted as 'business as usual' – no matter how destructive.

The traditional budget also fails to allow for change within the fiscal year. Budgets based on a 12-month year generally do not allow room for innovation as they are unable to take unforeseen events into account. According to Hope and Fraser,[3] founders of the Beyond Budgeting movement, budgets not only act as barriers to change but actually fail to provide the order and control managers believe them to do. Hope and Fraser go on to condemn budgets because:

- They encourage incremental thinking and tend to set ceilings on growth expectations and a floor for cost reductions, thus stifling real improvement break-through.
- They do not deliver on shareholder value, an increasingly important issue.
- They fail to provide the CEO with reliable numbers, both current and forecast. Budgets are typically extrapolations of existing trends with little attention being paid to the future.
- They act as barriers to exploiting synergies across the business units – they endorse the parochial behaviour of 'defend your own turf'.
- They are overly bureaucratic, time-consuming exercises.

Other identifiable disadvantages include the following:[4]

1   They become obsolete too quickly and add little value given the time required to prepare them.
2   Budgets concentrate on cost reduction and not on value creation.
3   They are a form of corporate/central control.
4   There is little active participation from line managers and lots of interference from centre to 'make the numbers'.
5   They are time-consuming and costly to compile; they typically consume between 20–30 per cent of management's time.

6 They constrain responsiveness and flexibility and are often cited as being barriers to change. The focus is often on beating the budget and not maximising the organisation's potential.

7 Budgets are rarely strategically focused – they tend to be internally driven and focus on current year results.

8 Budgets add little value – finance personnel spend most of their time putting the information together while only about a quarter of their time doing any analysis.

9 Budgets encourage political game playing – this is evident when the budget results are linked to remuneration.[5]

10 One of the most dangerous shortcomings is that the process often ignores, and consequently sabotages strategic planning.[6] Budgets do not reflect the emerging network structures that organisations are adopting.[7]

Alternatives to Traditional Budgeting

Now that organisations are aware of the shortcomings of the traditional budget technique, many have turned their attention towards re-inventing the budget so that it becomes a continuous planning process.

Rolling Forecasts

As the organisation's objectives and strategies change, unlike the static traditional budget, this continuous budget can change with it. This method of dynamic budgeting is known as rolling forecasts, where forecasts are updated every few months – in effect, reassessing the company's outlook several times a year. In this way the financial forecast not only reflects a business's most recent monthly results but also any material changes to its business outlook or the economy. Rolling forecasts have a bigger emphasis on the strategic objectives of the organisation and help to narrow the gap between the overall strategic plan and the operational budget, which the traditional approach failed to do effectively.

'The budgeting process is quickly changing from a once-a-year event to a dynamic process that's in a constant state of flux. Organisations are finding that they can compete far more effectively when they truly understand business conditions and can adjust their budgeting to reflect the opportunities and challenges,' explains Lee Geishecker, a research analyst with Gartner in Stamford, Connecticut, US.

Geishecker believes that a dynamic budgeting model can produce enormous dividends by providing key insights into trends, patterns and changing circumstances. This enables companies to budget strategically rather than simply reacting to data that is six months or a year old. Geishecker adds that the dynamic budgeting process meshes with the trend towards a more strategic finance department. Instead of number crunching, managing data and distributing spreadsheets, finance managers can use dynamic budgeting to transform the numbers into knowledge.

Says Geishecker: 'For the first time, companies have the tools to execute their business plan and mission with a good deal of precision.'

A rolling budget demands that employees and managers adopt an entirely different mind set. It requires finance not only to collect, sort and analyse data, but also to strengthen organisational links and help company managers understand the dynamics of the enterprise. Company managers must share information appropriately and use it to maximum advantage.

Boston-based consultancy the Aberdeen Group[8] suggest in their report *e-Planning: Fixing the Broken Planning Process*, that organisations that have already successfully adopted rolling forecasts also have an integrated software system that can do the following:

- Gather information at weekly or monthly intervals, rather than annually or semi-annually.
- Adapt to the information needs of professionals in different positions throughout the enterprise.
- Reconcile as opposed to merely equalising top-down planning and bottom-up budgeting nearly instantaneously.
- Encourage what-if modelling, dynamic goal setting, gap analysis and financial analysis.

Zero-Based Budgeting (ZBB)

Unlike rolling forecasts, ZBB requires managers to budget their activities as if the activities had no prior allocations or balances – in other words, the starting point is zero. It became popular in the 1970s and 1980s and proved to be a useful one-off exercise to review discretionary overheads. As these are a large and growing proportion of total costs in many firms, significant cost reductions and resource allocations can often be achieved through ZBB. When used effectively, it forces management to look at the upcoming operation and all the costs associated with those operations. Starting from zero effectively forces managers to forecast their anticipated resource requirements.[9]

However, it can be labour-intensive and relies on individual managers to be able to construct their budget in the detail required. Another problem is that ZBB is applied hierarchically by functional department whereas the real opportunities for improvement are more likely to be found by reviewing costs by business process.[10]

Activity-Based Budgeting (ABB)

ABB is a concept developed to consider costs from the perspective of their relationship with the activities and through-puts of the organisation. Whereas activity-based costing (see Chapter 5) attempts to improve the understanding management has of costs, ABB takes the next step in this process and uses the information for developing detailed targets and forecasts.

This approach offers a number of advantages including better identification of resource needs, the ability to set more realistic budgets, increased staff participation, and clearer linking of costs with staff responsibilities.[11]

Beyond Budgeting

The Beyond Budgeting movement began life as a research project carried out by the Consortium for Advanced Manufacturing International (CAM-I) – a professional organisation created to improve the strategic process. According to Beyond Budgeting advocates, the traditional performance management model is too rigid to reflect today's fast-moving economy. As such, they view the traditional budget as acting as a form of 'control by constraint'.

Their research concludes that not only do firms need more effective strategic management but also need to redesign their organisations to devolve authority more effectively to the front line. Beyond Budgeting companies therefore aim to create consistent value streams by giving managers control of their actions and using simple measures based on key value drivers geared to beating competition. Leading and lagging indicators help to monitor value creation and provide an early warning system against a financial downturn.[12]

At the core of the Beyond Budgeting philosophy lies a shift in emphasis from performance management based on agreed budget targets to one based on people, empowerment and adaptive management processes. This concept is further underpinned by the following Beyond Budgeting principles:[13]

- *Governance* – use clear values and boundaries as a basis for action, not mission statements and plans.
- *Performance responsibility* – make managers responsible for competitive results, not for meeting the budget.

- *Delegation* – give people the freedom and ability to act, do not control and constrain them.
- *Structure* – organise around the networks and processes not functions and departments.
- *Co-ordinate* – co-ordinate cross-company interactions through process design and fast information systems, not detailed action through budgets.
- *Leadership* – challenge and coach people, do not command and control them.
- *Goal setting* – beat competitors not budgets.
- *Strategy process* – make the strategy process a continuous and inclusive process, not a top-down annual event.
- *Anticipatory management* – use anticipatory systems for managing strategy, not to make short-term corrections.
- *Resource management* – make resources available to operations when required at a fair cost, do not allocate them from the centre.
- *Measurement and control* – use a few key indicators to control the business, not a mass of detailed reports.
- *Motivation and rewards* – base rewards on a company and unit-level competitive performance, not pre-determined targets.

To date, there have been a number of adopters of Beyond Budgeting including IKEA, Volvo Cars and Swedish bank Svenska Handelsbanken, which abandoned budgets in 1970. Since adopting this technique Handelsbanken has grown to 8000 employees, 530 branches, earning 80 per cent of the group's profit. It now has one of the lowest cost to income ratios of the 30 largest universal banks in Europe.[14]

However, according to a survey conducted by CIMA in 2000,[15] which asked 1000 of its members for their budgeting experiences between 1995 and 2000 and what they thought the future might hold, budgets were and will continue to be the most important tool for management accountants in fulfilling their organisational role.

Process Improvement Techniques and the Challenge for Budgeting

Leading companies are achieving more accurate, faster and lower costs by using explicit forecasting models. They are deliberately separate from their financial management systems. The models are based on clear assumptions, when the criteria change, the assumptions change and a new forecast is generated quickly with virtually no manual intervention.

Best Practices

- Forecasts should be 'Assumption not opinion based'.[16]
- 'Lean not mean'[17] – the cost of budgeting and planning. Many companies are reducing the costs of the financial planning and reporting by judicious investment in IT to create common, widely accessible, cost and revenue databases. They are designed to create a single view of the company, reducing duplication of effort in running separate systems. Leading companies are also light on their review process, focusing on a few key financial measures and not reviewing every line item.
- Strategy execution[18] – competition not budget focused. Leading companies are extremely externally focused; comparisons are made not with budget but with competition. Targets are not based on current performance but by reference to external benchmarks. Incentives are disconnected from budget achievement and focused on beating the competition – both financially and in terms of achieving externally benchmarked non-financial targets.
- Action not explanation oriented. Leading companies are less concerned with the explanation of past performance than managing future results. This is done by forecasting and explaining variances before the variance occurs; managing the forecast and not the actual results; focusing on taking the actions that really drive performance, most of which are non-financial.

- Strategically not financially managed. Those who lead in the approach understand that better financial performance comes from developing and executing good competitive strategies; it does not come solely from better financial management. They plan and manage investments separately from the day-to-day operation of the business. They focus more on achievements of non-financial targets than they do on the monthly financial results. Under traditional budgeting, control was exercised by business units and divisions reporting their actual performance and variances with HQ virtually left to use this information to predict what the year-end result would be. Now those who take the non-traditional approach trust their managers to tell them what they will achieve.

In conclusion, it is evident that the traditional budget is simply inadequate in today's fast-changing climate. Many improvements have been sought by all and the chosen approach will depend much on the individual organisation itself. To date, the most common approach seems to be the process of rolling budgets or re-forecasts which do attack the problem of inefficiencies involved with the annual budget. However, the literature does seem to show that although these rolling budgets are an improvement, they still do not solve the problem of the cost and effort involved in the budgeting process.

This highlights the argument for web-based applications. These applications are all aimed at streamlining the budgeting cycle and evidence shows that many organisations are advocating this. They take into account the process of rolling forecasts and with their web capability shorten the time and effort involved mainly through a central database and multiple user allowance. To some, these systems may be seen as being in their infancy and very costly to deploy, however, the question is whether they improve the budgeting process and the literature finds they do.

As the countless advertisements for consultancy and software firms remind us, the rules of the game are changing. In today's environment of global competition, situations can change rapidly and new competitors enter markets with ease. Organisations have long been involved in planning and evaluating their performance through measuring financial returns, setting performance standards and comparing budgetary outcomes with plans. For effective enterprise management, this involves the measurement of both overall and business unit performance in relation to the objectives identified in the planning process. In this way, corporate performance management systems are a key factor in ensuring the successful implementation of an organisation's strategy.

Even with excellent budgeting and forecasting systems in place, predicting customer behaviour and revenues is fraught with difficulty:

> It all comes down to demand. The limitations of any system are always going to be tied to the fact that you are waiting on inputs from somebody or something. If you are really going to forecast demand correctly, you have to know – with absolute certainty – that a customer is going to give you in three weeks the order you are forecasting today. Unfortunately, nobody has yet invented the virtual crystal ball or crystalball.com. If they have, I would love to see it.
>
> (Jonathan Chadwick, VP of Corporate Finance and Planning at Cisco, following the company's write-off of $2.2bn excess inventory in early April 2001.)[19]

Collaborative Planning – Reinventing World-Class Budgeting

One of the criticisms of the alternatives to planning and budgeting is that they attempt to replace the existing process rather than fix or remedy its shortcomings. Our research shows that while many of the criticisms levelled against budgets are well founded, in many cases finance professionals recognise that budgeting does play an important role with respect to cost control, resource allocation and other important areas.

So why has the traditional budget survived for so long? We believe that despite the bad reviews from academics and consultants that budgeting survives because:

- It is simple, if time-consuming, but not as resource hungry as some of the alternatives proposed.
- It is scalable and can be used by organisations ranging from a corner shop to a global corporation.
- It was the first tool devised to enable strategy to be turned into action.
- It encourages a consistent view across the organisation.

As previously discussed, the CIMA (2000) survey showed that budgets were, and will continue to be, the most important tool for management accountants in fulfilling their organisational role.

Although alternative methods may give the suggestion that overhauling the budget is the necessary requirement in today's volatile environment, the need for forecasting and planning is still required. Cash flow forecasts, rolling forecasts and cost forecasts are still a major part of Beyond Budgeting, which therefore still leaves the problem of time and quality of information.

What if instead of trying to replace or move beyond budgeting, we could fix budgeting and make it better? Richard Harborne, a management consultant with PwC, suggests that the budgeting process is missing two critical important characteristics: (1) it should be a fully integrated process; and (2) it should contain a complete set of process components (Figure 6.1). Since business planning cuts across internal functional and geographic boundaries so it demands that the components of the process and activities of the people involved are seamlessly integrated.

Producing a strategic plan that is disconnected from the operations or tracking performance measures that do not reflect corporate realities will probably cause decision-makers to make incorrect and costly decisions. In addition, a fully integrated set

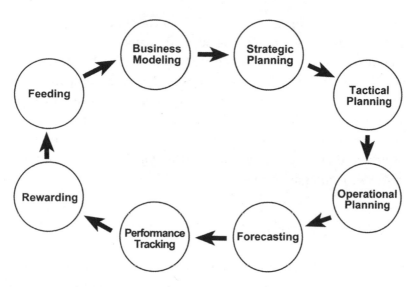

Figure 6.1. The integrated business planning process.
R. Harborne, 'Power Planning: the integrated business planning process', *Strategic Finance Magazine*, October 1999, pp. 47–53. Reproduced by permission of Institute of Management Accountants (IMA).

of components is required that fits your company's size, structure, industry and business model. It means taking the time to clarify the reasons why you plan and define the outputs of the process. Doing this requires a collaborative environment in which managers can work together to share insights, ideas and their mental model of the business across time and locations.

Moving from Advocacy to Collaboration

Under existing approaches managers spend large amounts of time and energy trying to convince the CFO of the merits of their resource requirements. Other disagreements arise because of the lack of a shared understanding of the organisation's business model and the likely future environment facing the firm. Under the collaborative planning approach, the focus shifts from arguing about outcomes to surfacing the assumptions that underpin the organisation's actions. The debate is therefore shifted from arguing about how much I need as a manager and is instead focused on me communicating my view of the future trading environment to the CFO and others. Leading companies are achieving more accurate, faster and lower costs forecast by collaboratively building explicit planning and budgeting models. The models are based on clear assumptions, which have been distilled through the organisations many stakeholders in an open, iterative but integrated process.

Collaboration is Key

Under the collaborative planning approach, the focus of the planning process shifts from the mechanical completion of templates and other activities to creating a rich environment in which tacit knowledge of markets, demand and other factors is made explicit through a combination of workflow and collaborative technologies.

One Size Does Not Fit All

The extent of the divergence from the traditional model should depend on the needs, objectives, size and complexity of the business. The time frames, level of complexity and degree of harmony required for each of strategic plan, annual budget and short-term forecast will vary considerably. Rolling forecasts are clearly being used successfully and widely and should be adopted if at all appropriate. Under the collaborative planning approach the tools support the process which is contingent on the organisation's needs. In some cases where the business model is well understood and widely communicated, the focus may be on driving cost efficiencies by supporting flawless execution of the plan. In other cases the focus may be on getting inputs from diverse specialists groups such as sales, marketing production and even supply chain partners on the likely future trading environment.

Many companies fail to recognise the value that exists in building a budgeting process that provides the opportunity to feed business intelligence back into the process. To be adaptable, an integrated planning process must have the ability to capture information that has been learned through meetings, interaction among personnel, intranet sites, and the transfer of knowledge in the course of business.

Collaborative Planning (CP) Technology

Collaborative planning (CP) technology makes use of the latest web developments to allow access for dispersed users, combined with the latest in collaboration technology to allow multiple users to share documents.

Our research shows that the most effective budgeting processes are those where the team share a common approach. Budgeting works best when the process is simple, the information delivered is concise and where bureaucracy is kept to a minimum. The team can design and agree a single global process based on the unique needs of the industry vertical. Traditional approaches to budgeting and planning rely on a budgeting 'tsar' who is seen as an enforcer of deadlines and budgeting pack requirements, is expected to produce poor process performance and often alienates the very business FDs that are needed to deliver the value added insights that the CFO is looking for. Under CP the team as a whole is accountable with team members jointly setting the quality threshold. As such, this implies mutual help, mutual trust and mutual dependency.

For the past three decades budgeting has been viewed as a data processing problem with the solution inevitably seen as more data processing capability. With the CP approach the emphasis is widened to address the real causes of delays and inefficiency: out-of-date processes, expensive and cumbersome manual hand-offs, serial workflow and lack of accountability and co-ordination. CP makes extensive use of intelligent documents that are self-directing within the workflow, can trigger task such as emails and information requests, push and pull content and activate emails, and raise alerts. Also key to CP systems is the ability to store narrative with any budget items and changes to plan, as well as a trail of changes and the associated explanations. This gives valuable context to a plan or budget, making the whole process more valuable and useful to an organisation.

Conclusion

As we have seen, the traditional budgeting process does not provide sufficient flexibility, responsiveness and alignment with the realities of how organisations and markets operate today. The common response of organisations has been to adopt a process of rolling budgets or re-forecasts, which address the timeliness issue but not the inefficiencies of the process. To make the process more efficient, organisations are starting to adopt sophisticated, web-based planning and budgeting technologies. These enable the move away from advocacy to a more collaborative planning approach, which is further supported by emerging collaboration technology and specialist applications.

Notes

1 A. Dragoon (2002) '8 ways to take control', *Darwin Magazine*, May (www.darwinmag.com).
2 A. Neely *et al.* (2001) 'Driving Value through Strategic Planning and Budgeting'.
3 J. Hope and R. Fraser (2001) 'Figures of hate', *Financial Management*, February, pp. 22–5.
4 A. Neely *et al.* 'Driving Value through Strategic Planning and Budgeting'.
5 R. McNally (2002) 'The annual budgeting process', *Accountancy*, vol. 34, no. 1, February, pp. 10–12.
6 Heyns and Sutcliff, 'How to beat the budget blues'.

 7 Neely *et al.*, 'Driving Value Through Strategic Planning and Budgeting'.

 8 Aberdeen Group, *e.Planning: Fixing the Broken Planning Process*.

 9 N. Rasmussen and C. Eichorn (2000) *Budgeting, Technology, Trends, Software Selection, Implementation*, Chichester: John Wiley & Sons, Ltd.

10 J. Hope and R. Fraser (2001) *Making Elephants Dance*, CAM-I Fraser and Hope.

11 J. Brimson and R. Fraser (1991) 'The key features of ABB management', *Accounting*, vol. 69, no. 1, pp. 42–3.

12 Hope and Fraser 'Figures of hate'.

13 Ibid.

14 Hope and Fraser *Making Elephants Dance*.

15 CIMA Members survey (2000). Available online at: www.cimaglobal.com.

16 M. Bourne, A. Neely and H. Heyns (2001) 'Strategic planning and budgeting', CAM-I Website.

17 Ibid.

18 Ibid.

19 R. Myers (2001) 'Budgets on a roll', *Journal of Accountancy*, vol. 192, no. 6, December, pp. 41–6.

PART II

Conformance

CHAPTER 7

BETTER ENTERPRISE GOVERNANCE THROUGH BETTER REPORTING

*I*n order to achieve significant improvements in Enterprise Governance, finance professionals must recognise the need to improve both the reporting processes and content and focus of reporting. In the past two years, our extensive research into corporate performance management and reporting challenges facing firms has highlighted a lack of time for thinking and analysis, among finance professionals. In the face of increasing corporate velocity many finance executives simply do not have any spare hours in the day to focus on the more strategic value-added priorities.

So what are finance departments doing to take up such valuable time? According to research from major consulting firms and benchmarking groups such as AnswerThink, much of the working day is being consumed by the month-end close. A survey by AnswerThink showed that the average company takes up to 15 working days to complete month-end close, while our own research suggests that while there are some differences across regions, many firms still struggle to close in under ten working days (Figure 7.1).

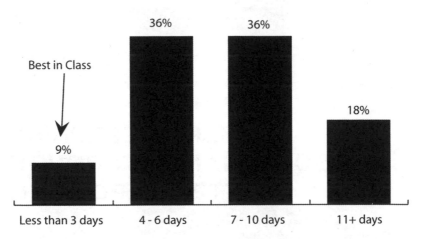

Figure 7.1. Month-end closing: length of the closing cycle. *Source:* (CODA Group, 'CPM Survey 2002'. © CODA Group).

But while it is difficult to draw firm conclusions about the causes of the long closing cycle, research suggests that delays are likely to arise from the large assortment of data extraction routines needed to deliver information to the closing process. The main source of issues surrounding data integration appears to coalesce around the large number of different operational systems in place combined with the failure of past systems projects designed to eliminate or cope with the 'hand offs' between systems. So bearing in mind that there are only 22 working days in the month, it is hardly surprising that the finance profession is so impoverished from a time point of view (Figure 7.2).

The Importance of a Timely Close

The month end typically forms the basis for all financial, management and statutory reporting. It is also the essential foundation for other activities across the organisation, such as performance management and compliance. As a consequence, every month, organisations around the world invest – or waste – vast resources in the month-end close. However, the real challenge is to drive down the amount of time spent on the

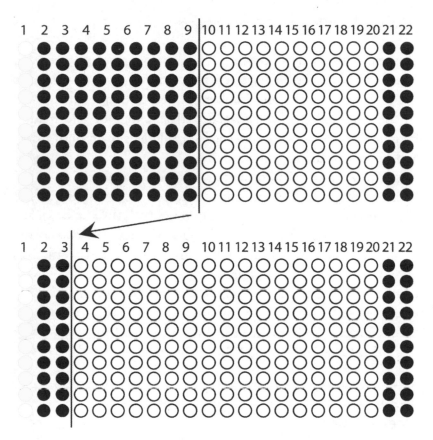

Figure 7.2. The staff time released for other analysis in moving from current close to a best-in-class three-day close. *Source:* (© CODA Group).

mechanics of month end reporting, thus freeing up value resources for value-added analysis. Many non-finance executives, particularly sales and marketing professionals, struggle to understand the importance and significance of the month-end close. As one marketing executive put it: 'There's value in closing a sale, but where's the value in closing out the books? It seems little more than an antiquated ritual left over from some out-moded vision of management control.'

So, what do we get from such a time-consuming and costly process and why do finance professionals consider it so important?

Shorter Windows of Opportunity

Shorter windows of opportunity and the emergence of speed as a competitive dimension have led to a situation where managers are expected to make and implement decisions faster than ever. At the same time, they are faced with a deluge of information ranging from emails to multi-page spreadsheets from both inside and outside of the organisation.

The real value of information ultimately depends on timeliness, accuracy, reliability, conciseness, completeness and, above all, relevance. The debate surrounding fast, flash and virtual month-end close, however, has tended to focus on *time* as the single dimension. As a result, many firms have found themselves investing considerable resources in improving reporting cycle times, with little or no improvement in decision-making effectiveness. There can be no doubt that *speed* is important, but ultimately only delivers value when accompanied by a commensurate improvement in information *quality*.

Month-end Close Lets Organisations Check their Progress

At a simple level, an effective closing process allows business unit managers, product managers and heads of functional areas to monitor business execution. It highlights shortcomings in expected performance and allows the executive committee to prosecute performance. At the same time, the close allows useful 'peer-to-peer' and 'like-for-like' comparisons across segments and units. As such, it allows senior executives to gain insights into business execution and determine progress towards the key strategic goals.

Closing Facilitates Good Corporate Governance

Corporate governance is now at the forefront of the executive committee agenda. With reporting regulations such as

Sarbanes–Oxley emerging thick and fast, along with the requirements of International Financial Reporting Standards (IFRS), executives are challenged to put in place systems that provide a realistic, timely and up-to-date assessment of the organisation's position and results. The month-end close remains a key part of the mechanisms put in place to ensure that management controls and reporting procedures are satisfactory, reliable and accurate.

The Monthly Executive Committee Briefings that Flow from the Close are the Basis of Many Business Decisions

Monthly reporting from the close will typically show the contributions of different business units, legal entities, products, markets, channels, and so forth. Therefore, it reflects the success of the firm's business model and positioning strategy and, when done effectively, puts control of the business model directly in the hands of the business managers. It ensures that business decisions are based on reliable, timely and accurate information and it provides 'across-the-board' consistency and accuracy.

The Shortcomings of Current Approaches to Month-End Close

Research indicates that almost all finance professionals struggle to put in place effective closing solutions. Typically, firms rely on a mixture of specialised and spreadsheet-based solutions to deliver month-end enterprise-wide information. Traditional solutions for month-end close focus only on the processing and consolidating of the data once the finance department receives it. However, much of the data required is spread around the organisation, locked away in the heads, systems and spreadsheets of other departments outside of Finance. The data cannot be processed until it is chased, collected and verified, and it is this that accounts for much of the elapsed time in the month-end close. The following quote from a finance director will sound all too familiar to many.

> Like most companies, we spend up to 50 full-time equivalent person days every month sorting and checking data to close the books – a process that adds little value in itself. For ten or 15 days a month, leave is forbidden and late nights and early mornings are standard. By the time we get it finished, we don't have time to analyse the figures, interpret anomalies or explore trends. We print out the management packs for the next day's board meeting and go home to reheat the dinner that we missed two hours ago.

The larger or more complicated the organisation, the more messy and time-consuming the whole process can be and, despite all the advances in technology, automation and communication, period-end consists of dozens of manual, tedious and repetitive processes. Technology solutions to help period close have traditionally focused on document processing and financial consolidation, as well as the reporting and analysis of the numbers. But they have failed to spot the vital and overriding element in the process. Period close is a complex process of collaboration between individual people, of chasing, collecting and confirming, of hassling and haggling, and of re-typing and re-formatting data that drags the process out to take too long and saps the resource and the strength out of our companies' finance departments.

If firms are to make progress towards more effective closing solutions they need to address the key organisational bottlenecks that plague the closing process. What are these bottlenecks?

- *Poor systems integration and an over-reliance on Excel to lick the data into shape.* The closing technologies in place in many organisations more often than not resemble spaghetti.

Important knowledge is locked in spreadsheets and people's heads, with many firms relying on the re-keying of fundamental data every month. More specifically, firms fail to automate the interface procedures between sub-ledgers and the general ledger and, in many cases, have not even automated the generation of month-end financial statements. In a world-class close, end-to-end automation is the starting point. In the absence of such systems, inefficiency creates work and time-consuming manually intensive work-arounds and re-checks become the norm.

- *Automating yesterday's processes.* Many of the consolidation and closing solutions currently on the market have been in existence for more than a decade. The key feature of these solutions is that they attempt to automate the closing process. The problem with that approach is that in many cases it has led to firms automating yesterday's processes. More specifically, as Figure 7.3 on page 139 illustrates, the existing approach involves placing a large processing engine at the corporate centre. This sucks data in through the stovepipes of the business units, geographies and other structures. As a result, bottlenecks or delays in any one of the stovepipes prevents data flowing to the consolidation engine. In this Kremlin-type model the finance function becomes a slave to the closing machine.

- *Lack of communication.* The closing process is a complex exercise in collaboration, involving submission and sign-offs from multiple stakeholders, often in different geographies. With multiple dependencies and the complexity of language, currency and culture, communication is key. Our research shows that many FDs or CFOs struggle to maintain regular and meaningful communication with operating site controllers. With time and distance, lines of communication become stretched and misunderstandings and delays are frequent.

- *'The only usable figure is an actual figure'.* While many finance professionals talk the rhetoric of business partnering, many are still obsessed with or bogged down in historical cost accounting. Under this 'standards' driven approach, only actual figures are allowed into the closing process. In our research we found many firms that delayed month-end close, while many minor figures were confirmed. By increasing the use of estimates for those items that can be estimated – interest, expenses and bank charges, for example – firms can significantly reduce the time taken to close. However, to reduce risk and preserve integrity the methods for estimating these should be carefully calculated, documented and controlled. The estimates can be revised and actual figures entered in the following month. By simply switching to the use of estimates of accruals for payables and receivables, firms can take days off the closing time.

- *Complexity in corporate legal structures.* A cursory glance at the annual report of any reasonably large company reveals a maze of subsidiaries and associated companies. Organic growth or sophisticated legal structures designed to optimise tax exposures can lead to a complex organisational matrix. As a result, a large amount of time at month end is spent on inter-company eliminations and adjustments. These adjustments and the need for local compliance reporting significantly increase the complexity and heterogeneity of the month-end processes.

- *The demands of the industry and its regulators.* While every vertical market sector has its challenges and demands, the month end will often be most affected. In the retail sector, for instance, the need for like-for-like comparisons to take into account changing public holiday periods or new stores puts additional strain on the reporting solution. In many cases, finance professionals end up relying on spreadsheet-based work-arounds to overcome the comparability problem, since many closing and consolidation tools fail to deliver the required functionality. In heavily regulated industries like financial services, petro-chemicals and energy, the closing process must also meet the additional burden of reporting to regulators. Central bank requirements, not to mention Basel II, all place an additional burden on the closing process.

- *Do we need all this information?* Organisations are consumers, managers and purveyors of information and, as a result,

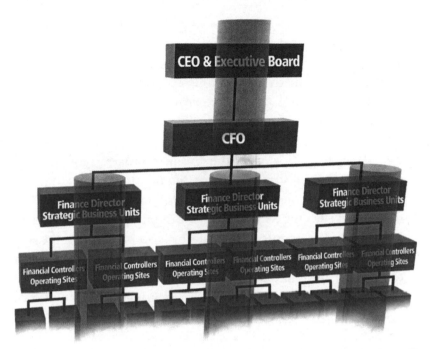

Figure 7.3. The Stovepipe Machine approach to month–end close. *Source:* (© CODA Group).

processes for gathering, storing, communicating and using information are essential elements of organisational operating procedures. Research on the use of information in organisations shows that organisations systematically gather more information than they use; that they continue to ask for more; and that the use of information is embedded in social norms that make it highly symbolic. In other words, getting reports makes us feel important. In many cases, the reporting burden of the closing process reflects the cumulative information demands of the organisation for the last ten years – new reports are added regularly but older reports are seldom, if ever, retired or pruned.

The Alternatives – Fast, Flash and Virtual Closing

In the past decade we have seen the emergence of three principal schools of thought with respect to the problem of closing.

- *Virtual closing* – most often associated with Cisco Systems who leveraged its expertise in networking to put in place real-time accounting systems that could be closed at any point in time. In the movement to a virtual close, managers establish their key metrics upfront, since under the virtual close model the information the company gathers is the critical information that managers need to make decisions.
- *Fast closing* – grew out of the business process redesign and TQM (total quality management) literature, which sought to identify and eliminate delays in the closing process by reducing the critical path time for delivery of the month-end financials.
- *Flash reporting* – adopts a satisfying or 'good enough' approach based on the belief that a first estimate of the likely outturn for the month has significant value to decision-makers and that the delay associated with full close brings little additional insight.

While many consultants and software vendors advocate fast, flash or virtual closing, our view is that these approaches do not provide the comprehensive, 'over-the-horizon' perspective that firms really need to execute effective strategies.

Virtual closing gives firms an accurate and fairly complete accounting perspective on what has happened in the past month, and while this is useful in supporting the narrow stewardship approach that used to characterise traditional corporate govern-ance, it lacks the predictability needed to support the more forward-looking, over-the-horizon capability which is required to deliver on the new vision for enterprise governance. As many companies find to their cost, virtual closing can tell you about the revenues you booked last month but it does not address the issue of the revenues you did not book nor the revenues you are likely to book in the future. Increasingly, firms need a more 'heads-up' approach to reporting, so that they can steer an appropriate course.

Both flash and fast closing assume that, given the timely availability of information, the firm will be able to react quickly to changing circumstances. Under these models, the month-end reports signal problem areas and then management take appropriate action. In what resembles a rather 'Kremlin-like' view, information is fed to the executive committee who are expected to steer the firm around the market hazards and emerging problems. This approach assumes that the organisation can react quickly to problems and change strategy or tactics. Take, for example, the issue of growing inventory, which may highlight the need to reduce output. However, in many industries, sub-supply contractors have six- and nine-month contracts for delivery, which cannot be amended without penalties. Similarly, unprofitable or under-performing market segments may signal a need to exit that segment but interdependences may prevent quick or erratic market moves. However much we might like firms to be agile and flexible, the reality is very different. Organisational change requires long lead times and cutting the reporting cycle by four working days does not have a discernible impact on the time to alter direction.

Virtual and fast closing processes may also institutionalise a flawed business model. As finance professionals resort to fast closing techniques in a bid to meet international best practice benchmarks, there are powerful behavioural reasons not to alter the scope and content of the month-end reporting. Changes to the process will often lead to poorer cycle times and finance staff become reluctant to make substantial changes to the consolidation or analysis models. As a result, over time a decision support gap emerges, driven by the diverging interest of the business managers and the performance demands of the closing process.

The recent debate on corporate governance has raised concerns about the appropriateness of flash reporting as a strategy for month-end closing and consolidations. From our experience, however, the real drawback of flash reporting is that the ambiguity that it allows creeps into what should otherwise be fact-based decision-making. As senior executives strive to prosecute performance, those responsible use the less-than-complete features of flash reporting to dismiss underperformance as little more than noise in the system that will disappear in the fully reconciled close.

New Approaches to Closing

The Collaborative Close

A research and development project in 2003 by CODA using new collaborative technology from Microsoft sought to respond to the challenge of period close by addressing the collaborative nature of the processes. The result was CODA Collaborative Close (CCC), a solution designed to bring openness and transparency to the closing process. This reflects its crucial role in corporate governance and the need to remove the blame, name and shame culture, which has often characterised established approaches to closing. With Collaborative Close the many and diverse activities that make up the closing process may be viewed by all the relevant stakeholders and can be monitored in real time.

With CCC, the unique portal technology allows a finance manager to keep track of data submissions from different regional offices or centres, thus allowing the performance picture to develop in real time rather than arriving at the last minute, when all the numbers are finally in. The objective is to eliminate the lack of ownership over data submissions, the bottlenecks and the expensive work rounds. As such, the focus is on integration of the team and the tasks, not of the technology.

Research shows that the most effective closing processes are those where the team shares a common approach. Closing works best when the process is simple, the information delivered is concise and where bureaucracy is kept to a minimum. With CCC, the team can design and agree a single global process based on the unique needs of the industry and the organisation.

For the past three decades closing has been viewed as a data processing problem with the solution inevitably seen as more

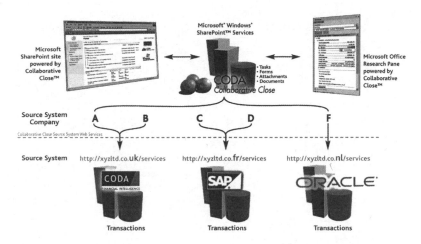

Figure 7.4. The Collaborative Close technology. *Source:* (© CODA Group).

data processing capability. With the Collaborative Close approach, the emphasis is widened to address the real causes of delays and inefficiency: out-of-date processes; expensive and cumbersome manual hand-offs; serial workflow; and a lack of accountability and co-ordination. Collaborative Close consists of a sophisticated task modelling engine that drives tasks, circulates documents and can automate data retrieval and process steps, where appropriate.

In essence, the Collaborative Close solution exploits portal, workflow and CPM technologies to allow firms to make their month-end closing process more controlled, repeatable, visible and auditable (Figure 7.4).

Case Study: CODA Group

As part of a global software firm, CODA has a presence across EMEA, Americas and Asia Pacific. In addition to its software licensing and maintenance revenues, the company also offers an extensive range of consulting, training and advisory services across a wide portfolio of products and technologies. In mid-2002, the CODA board took the decision to leverage its own technologies to generate operating efficiencies and deliver improved strategic management processes.

A key issue was the quality and timeliness of information available to inform decision-making on a monthly basis. With the development of CODA Collaborative Close (CCC), Jason Eames, the company's International Financial Controller, was asked to deploy the solution and prove that it could deliver real value to user organisations. As part of its commitment to realistic proof of concept, Eames pays the going rates for any CODA technology and consultancy used within his own team.

Current Status Assessment

The Collaborative Close project began with an extensive mapping of the existing month-end close process, which highlighted and detailed more than 200 distinct tasks, which have to be performed. Eames estimated that these tasks took anywhere up to ten working days to complete and a further day to produce the executive committee reporting pack. The CODA approach was highly interactive with continuous involvement by Eames and his team in the project to ensure transfer and development of the new process 'champions'.

Eames and his team began to incrementally develop a more explicit model of the closing processes and tasks. According to Eames, the project forced the team to rethink many of the activities it carried out and highlighted some obvious inefficiencies. Collaborative Close enabled them to identify which actions take the longest and where integration with the finance system could improve efficiency through automation of key processes.

Gaining this level of actionable insight into the closing process is clearly a major benefit for organisations and offers a swift return – not only on the investment of time and resources to implement Collaborative Close, but also the investment already made in the organisation's other systems.

In CODA's case, for example, consulting billing runs on a specialist time recording system and getting information from this system delays the closing process. Under the Collaborative Close approach, Eames can monitor the data feeds and submissions from the time recording systems and identify late data submission early in the closing process. If the close is late, Eames can identify which specific areas have held up the progress, such as timesheet submission, and make the case for a review from within that department.

A key feature of the Collaborative Close approach is that as a system it is self-monitoring and reports back performance metrics for the closing process. This self-reporting allows the company to adopt a *Kaizen* (or continuous improvement) approach to improving the close processes. More specifically, Collaborative Close supports time-lines analysis, to help identify process bottlenecks and shortcomings with respect to: capturing data; delays from errors; backlogs in data submission; inappropriate timing of work; cumbersome processing procedures, etc. In addition, Collaborative Close facilitates root-cause analysis to identify issues that could be corrected now, issues that required process changes, and issues that required new systems.

Improving Reporting Content

Timeliness Is Nothing Without Quality of Content

The second key theme that has emerged from our research is the so-called 'information gap' between the current decision support capabilities of firms and the information needs of senior

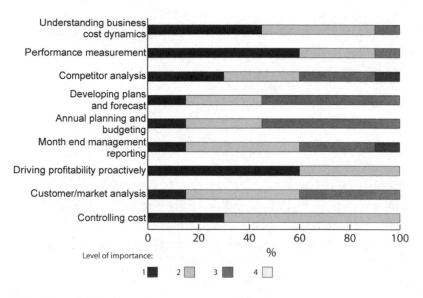

Figure 7.5. Challenges with respect to providing information and analysis (©CODA Group).

executives. As Figure 7.5 illustrates, finance professionals appear to be struggling to get a better understanding of the organisation's business model and to get real insights into the sources of value. The specific activities which finance professionals and other providers of CPM are most concerned with at present are:

- understanding business cost dynamics;
- driving profitability proactively;
- performance measurement;
- controlling costs.

Conversely, senior executives appear to have clear priorities with respect to the information and analysis they need. As Figure 7.6 illustrates, much of this additional information and analysis lies outside the traditional financial reporting which has characterised many finance departments to date.

Although organisations have long been involved in evaluating their performance through measuring financial returns, setting

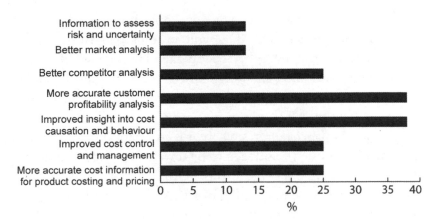

Figure 7.6. Additional CPM information/capability firms would like to have. (© CODA Group).

performance standards and comparing budgetary outcomes with plans, to achieve good enterprise governance, the measurement of both overall and business unit performance in relation to the objectives has to be identified in the planning process. Consequently, performance measurement systems are a key factor in ensuring the successful implementation of an organisation's enterprise governance strategy.

In addition, companies also need to understand how well they are making progress towards all of their strategic goals. Traditional reporting systems have been largely based on historical financial performance, but the performance of the business must be measured over all aspects critical to its success. It is also important that measurement be directed to influence and forecast future performance, rather than merely understand and record past results.

In many organisations, most of this information already exists; what they lack is the knowledge management skills and systems to capture, disseminate and leverage its true value. A company's store of market insights and foresights needs to be constantly updated and accessible to the teams who can leverage its value.

It is vital to have the right measurements since the very act of measurement affects behaviour.[1] If measurements are not carefully aligned with the strategic, operational and process objectives of the business, they will prompt behaviour which will run counter to these goals – people tend to focus on the areas that are being measured and assume their role is to improve them. The way employees are rewarded and recognised also affects the way they behave. Many companies are now seeing the need to develop performance cultures where it is contribution to corporate goals that is rewarded – and seen to be rewarded – and not political skill, level or age. To achieve this performance culture requires coherent direction setting and performance measurement aligned with reward and recognition support systems.

Research suggests that there is no single set of performance measures, no single basis for setting standards for those measures, and no universal reward mechanism that constitute some perfect performance measurement system applicable in all contexts. An analysis of service industries[2] published by CIMA (Chartered Institute of Management Accountants) found that the set of performance measures used is dependent on the competitive strategy being adopted and the type of service being delivered. Their research of a number of companies showed that they were all actively using their performance measurement systems to translate strategy into action. The systems and measures used were under constant review and had been changed, and will continue to change over time as the focus of strategy changes.

The Balanced Scorecard

In response, the range of current developments in performance measurement and management accounting and control systems continues to evolve. One significant development relates to the balanced scorecard concept, first put forward in 1992 by Kaplan and Norton,[3] and which encompasses both the combined use of non–financial and financial information and the use of the balanced scorecard as a key element of the strategic management process.

Their view is that managers need a balanced presentation of both financial and operational measures, which led to the development of the balanced scorecard. Kaplan and Norton liken it to the dials and indicators of an aeroplane cockpit; just as pilots need detailed information about many aspects of the flight, the complexity of managing an organisation today requires that managers be able to view performance in several areas simultaneously.

The balanced scorecard provides executives with a comprehensive framework that translates a company's vision and strategy into a coherent set of performance measures. It goes beyond the vision or the mission statement and translates mission and strategy into four different perspectives: financial, customer, internal business process, and learning and growth.[4]

From these perspectives, Kaplan and Norton describe the balanced scorecard as providing answers to four different questions:

- How do we look to shareholders? (financial perspective)
- How do customers see us? (customer perspective)
- What must we excel at? (internal perspective)
- Can we continue to improve and create value? (innovation and learning perspective)

Financial perspective

Financial measures are valuable in summarising the readily measurable economic consequences of actions already taken. They indicate whether an organisation's strategy, implementation and execution are contributing to bottom-line improvement. Financial measures typically relate to profitability, e.g. operating income, return on capital employed, or economic value-added. Alternative financial measures could be sales growth or cash-flow generation. The right financial measures for the balanced scorecard can depend on the stage the business is at in the economic lifecycle. Whether it is at the growth, sustain or harvest stage will require different emphasis in the chosen measures.

Customer perspective

In the customer perspective of the balanced scorecard, managers identify the customer and market segments in which the business will compete, and the measures of performance in these targeted segments. Core outcome measures include customer satisfaction, customer retention, new customer acquisition, customer profit- ability and market share in targeted segments. There should also be specific measures relating to the value propositions that the company will deliver to the target segments. These are factors that are critical in making customers switch to or remain loyal to the organisation. These could include short lead times, on-time delivery or innovation in products and services.

Internal perspective

In the internal business process perspective, managers identify the critical internal business processes in which the organisation must excel. These processes enable the business unit to deliver the value propositions that will attract and retain customers in targeted market segments, and satisfy shareholder expectations of excellent financial returns. They focus on internal processes that will have the greatest impact on customer satisfaction and achieving an organisation's financial objectives. These measures include aspects of both the short-wave operations cycle and the long-wave innovation cycle.

Innovation and learning perspective

The fourth perspective in the balanced scorecard identifies the infrastructure that the organisation must build to create long-term growth and improvement. Organisational learning and growth come from three principal sources: people, systems and organisational procedures. The financial, customer and internal business process objectives of the balanced scorecard typically will reveal large gaps between the existing capabilities of people, systems and procedures and what will be required to achieve breakthrough performance. To close those gaps, businesses will have to invest in giving new skills to employees, enhancing information technology and systems, and aligning organisational procedures and routines. These objectives are articulated in the learning and growth perspective of the balanced scorecard. Employee-based measures include employee satisfaction, retention, training and skills. Information systems can be measured by real-time availability of accurate, critical customer information to employees on the front-line of decision-making and actions. Organisational procedures can examine alignment of employee incentives with overall organisational success factors.

The four perspectives permit a balance between short-term and long-term objectives, between outcomes desired and the performance drivers of those outcomes, and between hard objective measures and softer more subjective measures. While the multiplicity of measures on a balanced scorecard may seem confusing, properly constructed scorecards contain a unity of purpose, since all the measures are directed towards achieving an integrated strategy.

Problems Associated with the Balanced Scorecard

Adoption rates of balanced scorecarding techniques has been low.[5] For example, a survey of companies in Ireland in 1998 found that only 4 per cent of responding companies use the technique regularly, and the literature reports an estimated 70 per cent failure rate in general for attempted balanced scorecard implementations.

Lack of awareness is unlikely to be an explanatory factor. Performance may be deemed satisfactory and there may be no incentive for changes. Furthermore, the cost and potentially disruptive effects of such changes may be deemed a high price to pay in return for uncertain, less measurable and distant benefits.

Lack of top management support is often cited, as is poor communication, inadequate training and failure to secure widespread participation and support. A further reason is failure to tailor and adapt innovative practices to suit local circumstances, arising from a failure by systems designers to adequately consult users.

Some managers may be reluctant to let their operations become more visible and may see accountants who stray beyond their traditional domain of pure financial matters as intruders. Some accountants may see the decentralisation of accounting information as the erosion of their power base. One answer seems to be to take a 'softly, softly' approach, integrating sophisticated systems through a naturally evolving process rather than a 'big bang' approach.

Used correctly the balanced scorecard empowers an organisation by operationalising the strategy discussion, and then by assigning the accountability for well-defined results.[6] In theory, it is a tool for decentralisation, giving control and responsibility to the line managers. First, it breaks down the organisation's financial targets, thus creating a dialogue as to the strategy to achieve them. Second, it makes the strategy transparent, thereby reducing the risks of delegation. Third, the non-financial indicators provide a sense check to see whether targets have been set legitimately, or through financial manipulation.

Unfortunately, it often ends up feeding management's tendency to fall back into the central planning trap. If the balanced scorecard is run from the centre, it tends to become formalised. To empower the organisation, the balanced scorecard must remain the language of ongoing strategic discussion. It should not lock managers into a solution, nor tie them into a centrally run 'straitjacket'.

According to specialists in this area,[7] it is logical to drive the scorecard down to the level where profit and loss occurs. At this level the scorecard has the greatest impact, and yet can do the least harm. The scorecard helps the profit centre manager understand the business drivers and, since he or she has the financial accountability, it acts to impose complete focus on the key drivers.

Unfortunately, the central planning tendency can be strongest in the staff functions of an organisation, and in some organisations it is the functions outside the core business which implement an internally focused scorecard. The scorecard must be owned by the line of business and not staff, and must reduce and not increase support activity.

At the profit centre level the balanced scorecard is a strategic tool. Since its goal is to operationalise the strategy, the key to setting up the scorecard is to understand the factors critical to the success of the strategy. Only these indicators are strategic and needed for monitoring at top level. Not every indicator has to be on the scorecard. Operational managers use operational measures for operational control. There is no need for these to be balanced scorecards.

Indicators have a habit of multiplying and there can be a tendency for confusion to arise if managers are measured against a battery of indicators. This can be avoided by making certain important indicators 'threshold indicators' – ones that are important to achieve, but not to optimise.

Once the scorecard becomes viewed as a central planning tool, it rapidly becomes part of the corporate politics. Managers use it to 'cover themselves' while claiming to follow strategy. For the scorecard to work, it must be a tool that sets managers goals without interfering in how they will be achieved.

Financial indicators can provide a distorted perspective and the need to enhance them is clear. Equally clear is the need to supplement them with lead indicators and long-term indicators. Sometimes less is more and the idea of balancing these indicators leads to new distortions. The scorecard is best compiled against the business strategy, and only once the strategy has been operationalised and articulated should it be checked against the four quadrants.

It is important to align the scorecard to incentives, though beware of incentivising the scorecard directly. Managers, incentivised on a weighted scorecard, will seek to achieve the balance at the expense of a goal (see box). The scorecard focuses managers on long-term, and this is the clue to the optimal incentive structure.

Examples of 'Un-Balanced Behaviour!'

The linking of balanced scorecard systems to incentives can create unexpected and dysfunctional behaviour from employees, leading to a wealth of anecdotes, including:[8]

- The telephone company which pledged to have at least 90 per cent of payphones working, then achieving this figure by simply removing all public payphones from those areas most often vandalised.
- The bus operator which, plagued by delays, decided to pay bonuses to drivers who arrived at the terminus on time. As a result most buses arrived on time, however, drivers no longer tended to stop for passengers along the way!

As always, widespread change in an organisation is difficult, and using a scorecard to implement strategy is such a change. Buy-in is achieved only with participation of the essential players. Unfortunately the balanced scorecard has a habit of becoming 'corporate strategy by laundry list' whenever large numbers of managers are involved in a brainstorm. Managers and staff must buy in to the process.

In conclusion, the balanced scorecard appears deceptively simple at first glance. However, if the do's and don'ts are ignored, it has the potential of being very appealing but doing more damage than good.

Information Systems to Support the Balanced Scorecard

Information systems play an invaluable part in assisting managers to analyse beyond the summary level balanced scorecard measures. When an unexpected signal appears on the balanced scorecard, managers need access to underlying data to investigate the cause of any problem or to analyse trends and correlation. If the information system is unresponsive, however, it can significantly impact the effectiveness of performance measurement.

Such an information system must, therefore, incorporate all of the following features:

- at-a-glance exception alert;
- rapid access to summarised data;
- drill-down to successive levels of detail;
- easy-to-follow dependency paths to identify the causes of performance other than drill-down;
- reporting of initiative, objective and process information including responsible owner, team members, and definitions as well as current status;
- reporting of impacts of underlying objectives upon scorecard measures;
- reporting of the impacts of objectives upon each other;
- graphical creation and modification of objectives, measures and relationships;
- integration with existing corporate data sources – with support for additional direct entry of values and annotations.

Figure 7.7 provides an example of the emerging functionality with respect to scorecard functionality.

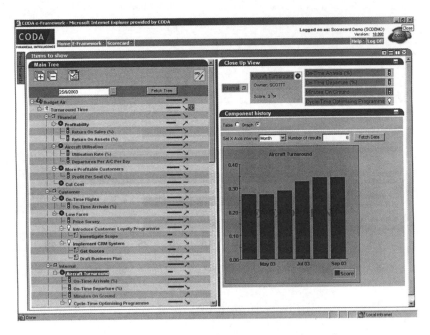

Figure 7.7. Example of a balanced scorecard screenshot for an airline.

Measuring and Reporting Customer Profitability

The modern focus on customers is also gaining increasing impact in performance measurement discussions. One of the criticisms is that most companies produce an annual plan that includes targets for market share and sales by market segment, channel, brand and product, but the plans often exclude any evaluation of which customers (both existing and targeted) are worthwhile. There is little concern with which customers to keep, which have untapped potential, which are strategic, which are unprofitable and which should be abandoned.[9]

One of the principal assets owned by most companies is their customer base, but few either measure the changing value of customer capital explicitly, or set specific targets for its improvement. Yet companies should be interested in measures that track profitability, size and share of business, growth and potential growth, stability, satisfaction, loyalty and repurchase levels, organisational learning capabilities, and the image-enhancing effects of dealing with market leaders.

Because accounting systems gather, record and report costs and profits by function and department, determining exactly which customers are profitable is difficult. The best that most accounting systems can do is provide some measure of gross profitability. Most often they apply variable costs only, giving a resultant contribution margin. But contribution analysis encourages and reinforces the mentality that there is always a valid reason to add or retain a customer, and seldom a good reason to abandon one. Similarly, there is always a valid reason to accept a price that generates a contribution to overheads.

Hope and Hope[10] note that once the full cost of supporting customers is taken into account, the majority of customers are not profitable at all. However, companies have no real idea as to which customers make up the profitable segment. Activity based costing (ABC) techniques can be employed to give an alternative view of customer profitability and cost behaviour. ABC attempts to charge costs to products, channels, and customers for the resources they consume.

The use of ABC has been discussed earlier in this book (see Chapter 5) and need not be reviewed again, but it is an important element in determining customer profitability, particularly in service organisations. The large component of apparently fixed costs in service organisations arises because, unlike manufacturing companies, they have little or no materials, the prime source of short-term variable costs. Service companies must supply virtually all their resources – people, facilities, etc. – in advance. These resources provide the capacity to perform work for customers during each period. Fluctuations in the demand by individual products and customers for the activities performed during the period by these resources do not influence short-term spending to supply the resources. In effect, marginal costs are almost zero, and are not a valid basis for measuring customer profitability. ABC systems can step in to provide the cost basis for measuring customer profitability.

Kaplan and Cooper,[11] similarly note that for service companies, there is an almost complete separation between decisions to incur costs and the decisions by customers that generate revenues. They argue that service companies are ideal for understanding why companies need different systems for operational control and for measuring the costs and profitability of products and customers. For short-term control, a traditional system that measures expenses by cost centre will suffice, but only the end-to-end process analysis from an ABC perspective reveals the cost of performing basic services for individual customers, leading on to customer profitability.

There is also an emphasis on the existing profitability of customers, which could give rise to short-term disengagement actions by management. But analysis of customer profitability needs to go beyond the short term, placing more emphasis on potential or lifetime profitability. This then drives management decisions around customer retention, loyalty and niche marketing. The use of customer profitability information has implications for behaviour in organisations and the long-term impact of these behaviours on business profitability and growth needs to be examined.

In summary, organisations must adopt a broader and more enlightened approach to assessing and managing company performance. If they do not, they will have increasing difficulty in coping with the challenges they face and achieving the goals they set themselves. If they do, they will be starting to focus on what is really important, be able to manage resources more effectively and measure and report progress towards their goals. This will help create the ability for a performance-enhancing and continuous-improvement culture to flourish.

Performance measurement issues and techniques continue to evolve, but what is important for organisations is the means to implement changes on a practical basis. Many of the techniques have been developed or extended with the development of new technologies and commercially available software packages. One of the dilemmas facing organisations is to be able to rationally evaluate the benefits of the new techniques away from the focus of the systems sales pitch.

Managing for Value and the Rise of Shareholder Value

As we have discussed, measurement systems have broadened in recent years. From a narrow focus on financial numbers, anything and everything is now being measured. Some critics argue that firms have too many measures,[12] yet financial measures have retained their primacy in the boardroom and in the investment community. However, such is their disenchantment with traditional financial numbers, that many investors and executives are now adapting these numbers to represent measures of value-adding performance. In the early 1990s commentators were arguing that it was time to move shareholder value from the arena of investor relations into an integrated operational framework for managing publicly held companies.[13] By making shareholder value the standard for measuring performance, management imposes on itself the long-term view so critical to gaining competitive advantage.

One such measure of shareholder value is market value-added (MVA). This is calculated by taking the total capital entrusted to management, aggregating the money raised through share issues, borrowings and retained earnings, and comparing it with the current market value of shares and debt. The difference between the two is market value-added, which at a very simple level measures how well managers have fared with the capital resources available to them.[14] A positive difference represents value creation for the shareholders. However, while useful over the long term, it can be distorted by significantly volatile share price movements.

Another measure is shareholder value-added (SVA), which has total return to the shareholder – the dividend received and the capital appreciation – as its central tenet.

Companies are also beginning to use a proxy measure known as economic value-added (EVA). Under economic value-added, the only bottom line that really matters is the one drawn after charging the full cost of capital. By deducting the full cost of capital from the accounting profit, shareholders can measure the real underlying increase in their wealth. It is therefore a measure which holds a company accountable for the cost of capital that it uses to expand and operate its business, and attempts to show whether the company is genuinely creating value for its shareholders.[15]

Economic value-added was developed by a New York Consulting firm, Stern Steward & Co. in 1982, in an attempt to give corporate management a clear and unequivocal focus on value-maximising behaviours. It has gained in popularity because it is regarded as a complete measure of performance. It enables an integration of capital budgeting with operations, in terms of both planning and control. It can be used to set clear targets for management, linked to appropriate incentives that generate behaviour in line with shareholder expectations.

Measures like economic value-added can be broken down into component parts and these can then be individually managed to improve the outcome. But economic value-added tends to be measured at too high a level in the organisation, and the link between management actions in the marketplace and the effect on organisation economic value-added may not be simple. Likewise, attempts at financial re-engineering can contribute to changes in economic value-added, in the same manner as return on investment can be manipulated.

Conclusion

We have tried to demonstrate in this chapter that Enterprise Governance can only be delivered if executives receive the right information in the right format, measured against the right criteria, and have time to analyse it. They need to ensure that the 'basics' of closing the books and compiling data is as efficient and automated as possible, freeing up the time of finance staff to provide better and more timely information. Companies need to set in place the right criteria for measurement of performance, and ensure that not only senior management but all staff are incentivised correctly to ensure their behaviour is in line with the expectations of the shareholders and wider stakeholders.

At present, shareholder value measures are more likely to be used at the top of the management hierarchy, and are portrayed as another measurement technique. The merits of shareholder value and other lessons from finance and investment need to be explored in the context of the whole of management accounting rather than just as a single item. In particular, care must be taken to ensure that measurement and incentives focused heavily on shareholders do not cause behaviour detrimental to the wider stakeholder community, since this will not deliver broad Enterprise Governance and so will eventually lead to issues that will impact overall performance. We will go on to consider some of these wider issues in the coming chapters.

Notes

1 A. Miskin (1995) 'Performance management', *Management Accounting*, November, p. 22.
2 L. Fitzgerald and P. Moon (1996) *Performance Measurement in Service Industries: Making it Work*, London: CIMA.
3 R. S. Kaplan and D. P. Norton (1992) 'The balanced scorecard: measures that drive performance', *Harvard Business Review*, Jan.–Feb., pp. 71–9.
4 R. S. Kaplan and D. P. Norton (1996a) 'Using the balanced scorecard as a strategic management system', *Harvard Business Review*, Jan.–Feb., pp. 75–85. R. S. Kaplan and D. P. Norton (1996b) *The Balanced Scorecard: Translating Strategy into Action*, Boston: Harvard Business School Press.

5 B. Pierce (2000) 'Low take-up of management accounting innovations', *The Sunday Business Post*, 30 April.

6 M. Gering and K. Rosmarin (2000) 'Central beating', *Management Accounting*, vol. 78, no. 6, pp. 32–3.

7 Ibid.

8 M. Binnersley (1996) 'Do you measure up?' *Management Accounting*, November, pp. 32–4.

9 J. Hope and T. Hope (1997) *Competing in the Third Wave: The Ten Key Management Issues of the Information Age*, Boston: Harvard Business School Press.

10 Ibid.

11 R. S. Kaplan and R. Cooper (1998) *Cost and Effect: Using Integrated Cost Systems to Drive Profitability and Performance*, Boston: Harvard Business School Press.

12 T. Hope and J. Hope (1996) *Transforming The Bottom Line: Managing Performance with the Real Numbers*, Boston: Harvard Business School Press.

13 A. Rappaport (1992) 'CFOs and strategists: forging a common framework', *Harvard Business Review* May/Jun., pp. 84–91.

14 Hope and Hope *Competing in the Third Wave*.

15 M. Binnersley (1996) 'Do you measure up?' *Management Accounting*, November, pp. 32–4.

CHAPTER 8

CORPORATE GOVERNANCE

Businesses that embrace a culture of transparency, honesty and social responsibility will enhance their business performance and maintain sustainable shareholder value.

Those that fail to embrace or accept corporate governance, corporate social responsibility and risk management practices will eventually fail.

What Is Corporate Governance?

Despite a proliferation of material, there is still much confusion surrounding this subject. Put in its simplest form, corporate governance is the systems and processes put in place to direct and control an organisation in order to increase performance and achieve sustainable shareholder value. As such, it concerns the effectiveness of management structures, including the role of directors, the sufficiency and reliability of corporate reporting, and the effectiveness of risk management systems.[1]

Where the confusion arises, however, is that corporate governance appears to embrace everything from budgeting to internal auditing, the role of non-executive directors to business ethics. It is very difficult therefore for finance professionals to define their changing responsibilities and ensure they are doing what is now expected of them.

In a joint in-depth survey of more than 300 CFOs and senior finance executives by CFO Research and Ernst & Young, nearly three-quarters of respondents said that better decision support was the main reason for improving their finance systems. Only half cited the need for better regulatory compliance.

In order to achieve good corporate governance a company must adopt a clear stance on each of the following:

- strategy
- stewardship
- corporate culture
- corporate reporting
- IT systems
- board operation.

There is plenty of evidence to show that if those pieces of the corporate governance jigsaw are not put together properly, the effectiveness of risk management systems across an organisation will prove inadequate.

The Good, the Bad and the Ugly – Examples of Corporate Governance

The Good: Unilever[2]

Unilever is one of the world's largest packaged consumer goods companies with more than 700 brands in its portfolio. Owned by Netherlands-based Unilever and

UK-based Unilever Plc, it operates as a single company, linked by equalisation agreements, which regulate the mutual rights of respective shareholders.

The company has grown to become a dominant force in the food, home and personal care markets, and is not only one of the largest ice-cream manufacturers, and the biggest producer of packet tea, but a world leader in deodorants, anti-perspirants and skin cleansers. It also operates a prestige fragrance business boasting designer brands to include Obsession, Eternity, CK One and CK Be.

It has made an impressive series of sales and acquisitions over the past ten years, to rationalise its operations and focus on core brands. Sales of these brands grew by more than 5 per cent in 2002. The company also took a number of its traditional brands into new markets.

As an organisation divided into two companies operating under two different sets of financial reporting regulations, there are obvious anomalies in corporate governance requirements. For example, the supervisory board as recognised in Holland is not known in the UK, neither are non-executive directors recognised in the Netherlands.

However, Unilever has created a governance structure often held up as an example of best practice. Advisory directors, as required under Dutch reporting regulations, act as non-executive directors, chosen for their broad experience for an initial period of three to four years. All appointments and re-appointments are based on the recommendations of a Nomination Committee.

Board committees are divided into an executive, audit, corporate risk, external affairs, corporate relations, nomination, remuneration and routine business committees.

Directors' service contracts, under Unilever's Articles of Association require all directors to retire from office at every AGM. Directors are expected to retire by their 62nd birthday.

The Good: General Electric[3]

In 2002, GE was ranked the world's second most admired company in the Fortune 500. Not only highly regarded for its financial services, GE is also involved in engineering, broadcast media, power generation and medical imaging.

Its good standard of governance has no doubt helped keep its stocks at such consistently high levels and contributed to its continued brand strength. When in 2002, the company faced intense investor scrutiny over earnings from its financial services operation, GE Capital, it resolved the situation by dividing GE Capital into commercial finance, consumer finance, equipment management and insurance. In the same year, GE also announced plans to further strengthen its governance standards to serve the long-term interests of its stakeholders.

The Bad: HIH

The problematic aspects of the corporate culture of HIH can be summarised succinctly. There was blind faith in a leadership that was ill equipped for the task. There was insufficient ability and independence of mind in and associated with the organisation to see what had to be done, and what had to be stopped or avoided. Risks were not properly identified and managed. Unpleasant information was hidden, filtered or sanitised. And there was a lack of sceptical questioning and analysis when and where it mattered.

(Royal Commission on the collapse of the Australian insurance company HIH)[4]

The Ugly: Boeing[5]

In December 2003, Boeing, one of the world's most famous aerospace companies, found itself caught up in a scandal that was to see its CFO sacked and its CEO resign – albeit not as a 'direct consequence' of the scandal.

The scandal followed investigations by a number of military and civilian departments into allegations that Boeing acted improperly in the $18bn sale of 100 Boeing 767 tankers to the United States Air Force (USAF).

The firm had already been rocked by a similar 'unethical practices' scandal involving the possession of documents belonging to rival Lockheed Martin during bidding for a military rocket launch contract in 1998. As a result of the allegation the Pentagon subsequently suspended Boeing from bidding on future rocket contracts pending a review of its practices. Lockheed Martin sued Boeing for alleged theft.

Alleged accounting irregularities surrounding the acquisition of McDonnell Douglas cost the company $92.5m after shareholders accused the then CEO Phil Condit of using accounting tricks to massage the company's financial health. In 2003, Boeing paid out more than $1bn in deal-related write-offs.

Alleged Unethical Practice

In February 2001, Boeing, already feeling the corporate pinch, bid to supply the USAF with re-engineered 767s for a price tag of $124.5m each. Although the proposition was initially well received, research later showed that the air force did not need any new tankers until 2010.

The terrorist attacks of September 11 brought about more financial misery for Boeing as airlines worldwide reduced the number of flights. Shortly after the world-stopping events, Boeing laid off around 30 per cent of its commercial aviation workforce. By 2002, it had also scrapped plans for a new faster, smaller long-range aircraft – the Sonic Cruiser.

A short-lived turnaround followed, with the announcement of a $9bn deal to supply Ryanair with 100 new aircraft, and a $9.7bn deal with the USAF for transport aircraft. However, the run of good luck was brought to a halt when strike action threatened to halt production.

But in 2003, the *Washington Post* broke an article alleging that Boeing executives had met with USAF official Darleen Druyun, who, it was alleged, had provided bid details to Boeing. It was also alleged that she suggested ways of finding the money to fund the deal through a leasing agreement.

Druyun then entered discussion to join Boeing in October 2002, but continued to work on the deal for the USAF until November. She then officially joined Boeing in early 2003. Following the story, Boeing publicly defended itself, publishing a number of articles in leading US newspaper titles. But the scandal still persisted.

According to a *Wall Street Journal* report, Boeing had committed $20m to Trieme Partners, a firm set up by Richard Perle, a key political ally of the Pentagon's right-wing leadership, who had long supported the Boeing/USAF deal. It was alleged that articles written by him supporting the deal were ghost written, as were a number of other articles by leading military figures, who later became Boeing consultants.

As the scandal deepened, CEO Condit fired his CFO Michael Sears. Druyun was the next to go. Condit's resignation was alleged not to be 'related to the scandal', but opinion to the contrary persists.

Former vice-chairman of the Boeing board, Harry Stonecipher, came out of retirement to replace Condit in

December 2003. He maintained that in spite of the controversy the tanker deal would remain on the table.

Market Position

In 2002, commercial aircraft accounted for 52 per cent of Boeing's sales. By 2003, its 70 per cent market share had dropped to 50 per cent with fewer than 300 planes delivered. Boeing spent more than 10 to 20 per cent more on building costs than its main rival Airbus.

Shortly before Thanksgiving 2003, aircraft manufacturer Boeing fired CFO Michael Sears and vice-president Darleen A. Druyun after an internal investigation alleged that Sears personally lobbied to hire Druyun in late 2002 while she worked for the Air Force – with whom Boeing was negotiating a $21 billion contract. A week later, Boeing CEO Phil Condit resigned as well, just as book reviewers received their copies of *Soaring Through Turbulence: A New Model for Managers Who Want to Succeed in a Changing Business World* – a primer on ethical business management by former Boeing CFO Michael Sears.[6]

The Historic View

Traditionally organisations held the view that capital markets were only interested in the share price. Corporate governance was therefore considered a necessary evil at the cost of developing business. As it concerns financial reporting, achieving compliance was deemed the responsibility of the finance function, which in turn adopted the view that governance could best be achieved through internal audits.

According to research by consultants McKinsey, good corporate governance practice is now strongly tied to investment decisions the world over. The group's 2002 Global Investor Opinion Survey showed that an overwhelming number of investors were prepared to pay a premium for companies with high governance standards. In North America and Western Europe purchase premiums averaged 12–14 per cent, in Asia and Latin America 20–25 per cent, and 30 per cent in Eastern Europe and Africa. Institutional investors have also begun to look closely at the corporate governance records of companies they invest in.

Case Study: What Good Corporate Governance Means to a Company like Shell

Upholding the Shell reputation is paramount. We are judged by how we act. Our reputation will be upheld if we act with honesty and integrity in all our dealings and we do what we think is right at all times within the legitimate role of our business.

(Extract from Shell's Statement
of General Business Principles, 1997)

NGOs (non-governmental organisations) and ethical share-holders have in the past taken a poor view over the business operations of oil companies like Shell. Since 1976, however, the petrochemical giant has gone to great lengths to achieve high levels of corporate governance, corporate social responsibility and socially responsible investment (SRI).

The company, which is spending considerable time and effort into developing its alternative fuel operations, now tops CG and CSR ethical investment indices, including the FTSE4Good Index. It works closely with the UN Development Programme and NGOs on proposed projects. Extensive environmental and social impact studies are always carried out prior to any project start.

Shell is also addressing the HIV/AIDS pandemic by working in partnership with other organisations to help reduce the spread of the disease. Throughout sub-Saharan Africa, the company runs AIDS prevention and care programmes for employees and their families. Free treatment is also offered to employees infected with the disease.

Its high level of corporate transparency and 'honesty' has been achieved through its Statement of General Business Principles (SGBP) – a guiding framework based on the core values of honesty, integrity, and respect for people, as well as openness, trust, professionalism and teamwork. Included in those principles is a clear and unequivocal stance on the non-acceptance of bribes or facilitation payments, or the support of political parties in any way.

The SGBP, which was the first statement of its kind made by a quoted organisation, has been revised five times since its first publication in 1976, with the most recent revision in 1997. In that year, further focus was placed on human rights issues and sustainable development, transparency and implementation. Successes and failures of KPIs (key performance indicators) set within those principles are printed in the annual Shell Report. The report, which Shell plans to include as part of its financial results, highlights environmental, social and economic performance. Readers are encouraged to make comments on the company's progress by using the 'Tell Shell' facility on the corporate website.

The company uses a combination of 'soft' and 'hard' implementation tools to create an integrated approach. Measurement of set Assurance Policies is achieved by a combination of internal audit, an assurance questionnaire (Assurance Collection Tool), and a free-format assurance letter, which is written by the chairman of each country operation each year. Responses are evaluated by Shell's Committee of Managing Directors and local KPIs are mutually set. The company has also introduced an employee Reputation Tracker survey, which judges the level of compliance within each individual operation. This not only maintains a high level of internal control, but also gives a good picture of the overall health of the company. Additionally, Shell uses the Global Reporting Initiative guidelines to measure the success of CSR policies and materiality.

The company also strongly believes in training, both for senior and middle management positions. A web-based self-teaching program is used for training on issues ranging from human rights to health and safety. Managers take an exam once they have completed the program and are then expected to impart their knowledge to their fellow employees. Access to information and clear communication are of key importance to Shell. For example, the company is planning to create a website detailing successful risk management solutions implemented by the company over its corporate history to help managers deal with 'unplanned' events. Shell is also looking at making a number of its internal learning resources available to an external audience.

'These are the "heart and mind" systems of corporate governance,' says Albert Wong, Shell global policy advisor. 'Upholding our reputation and protecting our brand is of great importance to Shell. We have a duty to our shareholders, many of whom have pensions linked to their investment, to our employees, customers, business partners and to society as a whole.

'We know that wherever we operate we will have an impact. From day one we want to balance any issues in order to minimise negativity and maximise positive impact. This is all part of the decision-making process.'

Mr Wong adds that good corporate governance also acts as reassurance to the governments of developing nations. This in turn allows Shell to pursue opportunities with the co-operation of all parties involved.

'You can have the best business plan in the world, but if you do not have co-operation on the ground level, it will be useless,' says Mr Wong. 'We are increasingly being pushed to help develop developing nations, which often have weak levels of corporate governance. Our experience and track record has led a number of governments to approach us for advice on this subject.'

He adds that Shell's existing corporate governance measures mean that it is already Sarbanes–Oxley compliant. In fact, the company welcomes the Act, which it claims will help level the energy industry playing field.

'Bidding for a contract is a very stressful time. In the past we could not be sure of the "honesty" of a rival bid. With Sarbox, the assurances are in place.'

Note: Issues that emerged in 2004 surrounding the over-reporting of oil reserves by Shell caused considerable damage to the company's reputation, led to the dismissal of senior executives and the company was forced to pay substantial fines. This serves to highlight that despite the best intentions, processes and systems in the world, corporate governance must be adhered to at every level in order to maintain and not destroy stakeholder value.

So What is the Case for Corporate Governance?

Generating consistently superior shareholder returns is the most challenging task a company can set itself.

It is a tough discipline to accept and people will wriggle like mad to escape the discipline. It requires extraordinary commitment and belief to stick to it over the long haul.

(Sir Brian Pitman, senior adviser to Morgan Stanley and former chairman of Lloyds TSB addressing a CIMA conference)

If You Do Not Have Good Corporate Governance You May Go to Prison

Until the collapse of US energy giant Enron in 2001, corporate governance was not in the public arena. The calls for transparent financial regulatory compliance, balanced board structure and performance-based remuneration for senior executives were loosely regarded as back office idealism. Shareholders rested secure in the knowledge that financial regulatory bodies competently investigated any 'accounting irregularities', and quoted companies diligently ticked the necessary boxes to meet with market rules. The Securities and Exchange Commission (SEC) in the USA, for example, has investigated 1,200 companies for accounting irregularities since the late 1990s. As such, traditional risks normally associated with stock market investment, such as market fluctuations, were automatically taken into account.

But in truth Enron's accounting cloak and dagger collapse was not the first of its kind. During the 1980s and 1990s, a significant number of quoted companies failed just as dramatically and misreported just as frequently. Among the named and the shamed are Robert Maxwell, BCCI, Polly Peck and Barings in the UK, Credit Lyonnais in France, Metalgesellschaft & Schreider in Germany, AWA and Spedley Securities in Australia, Lernout & Hauspie in Belgium, Yamaicki in Japan, and the Canadian Commercial Bank. Although there had been much discussion on the state of the world's reporting standards, including strong words of warning from the United Nations Conference on Trade and Development, Enron's failure still served as a rude and costly awakening for global stock exchanges, shareholders and governments alike. As market analysts, forensic accountants, lawyers and politicians raked over the company's ashes, the call to better regulate listed corporations grew ever louder. Those calls were not confined to the behaviour of stock listed companies.

The Global Scale of Corporate Failure

Since Enron, most major markets outside the USA have also experienced spectacular corporate collapses or accounting investigations, including:
- Australia – HIH Insurance
- Germany – Comroad, Babock-Borsig, Kirch, Philipp Holzmann, EM.TV
- Italy – Parmalat
- Korea – SK Group
- The Netherlands – Royal Ahold
- UK – Equitable Life, Independent Insurance

The subsequent collapse of global accounting firm Arthur Andersen amid allegations of collusion also brought the role of the external auditor under closer scrutiny. Corporate executives, who only months before had enjoyed public adoration normally reserved for film stars and pop idols, were publicly criticised for their greed and corporate irreverence by shareholders, furious at the loss of investments and life savings. The love affair that had survived stock market crashes and recession was finally over. Corporations would now not only have to earn investors' trust, but prove their accountability.

Ironically, closer scrutiny has brought about yet more business failures. Just as the financial markets thought they had convinced stakeholders that Enron's failure was just an unfortunate, if colossal, one-off, telecommunications giant WorldCom drastically devalued its stock after it admitted misreporting to the tune of millions. The scandal only strengthened investor scepticism over existing regulation. The US Government, having been heavily criticised over its lack of direct action following Enron, finally ordered a comprehensive review of America's financial regulatory environment in an attempt to reassure investors. But the floodgates by now were wide open. Major US conglomerates

Xerox, Computer Associates, Global Crossing, Tyco and Qwest Communications all joined the former energy giant in the hall of corporate shame. Despondent investors the world over united in the hope that the combined legislative amendments made by the US Government would put an end to what former SEC chairman Arthur Levitt described as accounting 'hocus-pocus'.

Shareholder Scrutiny

Although the long-term effects of the introduction of new legislation remain to be seen, the expectations of shareholders look set to remain high. In the USA, institutional investors the Teachers Insurance and Annuity Association-College Retirement Equities Fund (TIAA-CREF), and the California Public Employees' Retirement System (CALPERS), have publicly stated that corporate governance records will be scrutinised prior to investment. The influence of such groups cannot be ignored; according to recent figures, institutional investors own around 50 per cent of all US listed shares, and 60 per cent of outstanding shares in the country's largest 1,000 corporations.[7]

Shareholder bodies across the world's financial markets have also openly criticised 'excessive' CEO remuneration and severance packages, which they claim are disproportionate to company performance. They have a point. According to compensation consultant Graef Crystal,[8] the average American-based CEO now makes about 450 times more than an average worker. According to research by *The Guardian* newspaper in the UK, the average pay for a FTSE 100 CEO in 2002 was £1.7m. Managers of the UK's biggest companies also benefited from a 23 per cent increase in pay in the same year.[9] So-called 'golden parachutes' or severance packages that award failure as well as success have generated even greater hostility. Dennis Kozlowski, former chairman of Tyco International, for example negotiated a severance package worth around $100m,

Bernard Ebbers, former CEO of WorldCom Inc, received $1.5m annually for life on his dismissal, and former Andersen consulting chief George Shaheen, who served as head of Webvan for 18 months, secured $375,000 a year for life. The company no longer exists.[10]

As a result, US-based bodies such as the Pension Rights Center and the Institutional Shareholder Services have actively encouraged shareholders to vote against 'unjustifiable' executive remuneration packages. In the UK investors have watched the downfall of companies such as Marconi, Railtrack and ITV Digital to the tune of millions, with senior executives seemingly rewarded for their failure. Even Tory MP Archie Norman, the former chairman of supermarket Asda, put together a Private Members Bill to impose a limit on so-called 'golden parachute' deals; it was later abandoned on the grounds that it would violate contract law. The UK's Department for Trade and Industry (DTI) did go some way to address the situation in its Rewards For Failure report, which offered suggested guidelines on executive contracts. But professional business bodies, that had pledged support to the remuneration revolutionaries, claimed this was not enough. The Confederation of British Industry (CBI), which stressed that salaries needed to be sufficiently high to attract the best candidates for the job, suggested that senior executives should only be given one-year contracts instead of multi-year deals.

Such public and damaging criticism by shareholders and professional groups alike has resulted in a number of significant shareholder 'victories'. In 2003, the CEOs of Barclays Bank, Shell, GlaxoSmithKline, Tesco and HSBC all had their pay deals rejected, and Pierre Bilger, former chairman of troubled French engineering group Alstom, was humbled into paying back his £2.7m 'golden-parachute' cheque. Other troubled executives, however, have not been extended the luxury of choice. Jean-Marie Messier, the former CEO of Vivendi Universal, had his £14.5m pay-off frozen while the company was investigated for accounting irregularities.

It is the Law: The Sarbanes–Oxley Act 2002

Following months of comprehensive research into America's existing legislation, the Sarbanes–Oxley Act 2002 (SOX) eventually arrived dressed as a big legislative stick. Although the USA already has 4,000 pages of legislation governing accounting and auditing, the new rulings, which are overseen by the Securities and Exchange Commission (SEC), include a significant number of amendments. The Act is essentially divided into six regulation criteria: reporting, roles, conduct, enforcement, penalties and relationships (Figure 8.1). The key points are as follows, though this is by no means a full and detailed account of the SOX legislation:

Reporting

- Companies must review quarterly and annual reports.
- Financial statements must be fairly presented and reports have no untrue statements or omission of fact.
- Companies must enhance disclosures related to off-balance sheet transactions and pro-forma/non-GAAP financial information.
- Companies must ensure rapid and current disclosure of material changes, financial conditions and operations.
- Companies must ensure that annual reports include management assessment of the effectiveness of the internal control over financial reports.

Roles

- Companies must ensure increased communication between auditors and the audit committee on critical accounting policies and practices, alternative accounting treatments and other material written communications with management.

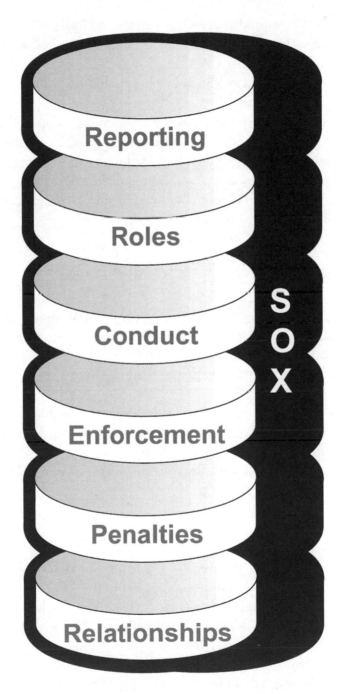

Figure 8.1. The elements of the Sarbanes–Oxley Act. *Source:* (© CODA Group).

- Companies should make clear that the auditing committee is directly responsible for the appointment, compensation and oversight of auditors.
- The audit committee's membership should be limited to non-executive directors.
- There should be procedures for whistleblowers and others.
- Personal loans to officers and directors must be prohibited.
- Audit committee should be provided with funding for auditors and other advisors as the committee deems necessary.
- Companies must disclose whether a financial expert sits on the audit committee.

Conduct

- It is unlawful for any director/officer or other acting at their direction to fraudulently influence, coerce, manipulate or mislead any independent auditor.
- Insider trading during pension fund black-out periods is prohibited.
- Accelerated reporting of trades by insiders is required.
- Companies are required to disclose whether they have a code of ethics as well as any changes or waivers.
- It is unlawful for companies to retaliate against whistleblowers.

Enforcement

- The Public Company Accounting Oversight Board (PCAOB) is to oversee the auditing of public companies. It has the authority to establish standards for auditing, quality control, ethics and independence of auditors of public companies who must register with the PCAOB.
- The PCAOB shall conduct a programme of inspections to assess the degree of compliance with registered accounting firms.

- The SEC may recognise 'generally accepted' accounting principles as established by an appropriate standard setting body.
- The SEC must conduct a study of principles-based accounting standards.
- Expand SEC review of 10 Ks and 10 Qs to at least once every three years.

Penalties

- Requires CEOs and CFOs to forfeit certain benefits received and profits realised on the sale of securities following a financial report that is later re-stated as a result of misconduct.
- Criminal penalties for officers providing certification knowing it to be untrue.
- Criminal penalties for corruptly altering documents or destroying documents or impeding official investigation.
- Increased penalties for accountants who fail to testify, produce documents or co-operate with investigation.

Relationships

- Prohibits auditor from providing certain non-audit services to company audited.
- Requires lead and concurring auditor partner rotation every five years.
- Requires a 'cooling off' period for one year before the audit firm employee who worked on the account can be hired in certain key financial oversight positions.

According to the international accounting and advisory organisation, Ernst & Young, US businesses are working hard to meet the new regulatory amendments. Dialogue with external auditors is being improved, disclosure committees are being formed, and boards are implementing risk management strategies beyond financial reporting. However, fundamental issues are emerging with SOX and the way it is causing organisations to behave. An extreme focus on the recording of processes and transactions means that enterprises face soaring audit fees and growing costs of internal audit. All the while, business professionals are questioning what benefit SOX compliance will ultimately bring to companies, their shareholders and wider stakeholders. It is causing companies to focus huge resources on areas that fail to create value, but arguably would be unlikely to prevent creative fraudsters from wreaking havoc.

Neither has SOX proved to be the legislative 'godsend' for auditors in need of regaining their professional credentials. In fact it has created a climate of fear and uncertainty that has left audit firms as afraid of failure as their clients, and creativity and growth stifled.

Finance professionals therefore must seize the initiative and take forward a new mantra – *automate, automate, automate*! Only by automating business processes will the finance function stand a chance of breaking out from the misery of transactional drudgery to start supporting their fellow business managers and adding value to their companies. Fortunately, groundbreaking new collaborative technologies are now available that not only automate processes, but make them controlled, visible, repeatable and crucially – auditable.

For more information on the Sarbanes–Oxley Act, visit www.law.uc.edu/CCL/Soact.pdf

Other Regulatory Changes

NASDAQ and the New York Stock Exchange (NYSE) have also dutifully rewritten their respective rulebooks. In conjunction with SEC actions, the NYSE appointed a Corporate Accountability and Listing Standards Committee in 2002 to review its current listing requirements in an effort to improve accountability and transparency of the Exchange's companies. The resulting listing standards, known as Section 303A, apply to all listed companies, limited partnerships, and business trusts.[11]

The standards require listed companies to do the following:

- Have a majority of independent directors and conduct executive sessions of non-management directors.
- Tighten the definition of 'independent director'.
- Establish nomination and compensation committees with the requisite charters.
- Increase authority and responsibility of the audit committee, adopt the required audit committee charter and establish internal audit function.
- Adopt corporate governance guidelines and a code of business conduct and ethics.
- Provide foreign private issuer description of significant differences from NYSE standards.
- Get CEO certification of compliance with listing standards.

The new regulations governing financial reporting also apply to the US-based subsidiaries of non-domestic stock-listed companies. As a consequence, investigations into the accounts of the world's third largest retailer Royal Ahold revealed a $856m accounting hole at its US foodservice unit plus 73 million euros in accounting irregularities, French engineering company Alstom disclosed that it would have to take a 51 million euro charge after understating losses on a railcar contract at its US transport arm, and British construction equipment rental firm Ashtead Group revealed that past profits had been inflated by £11.5m at its US Sunbelt Rentals business.

International Financial Reporting Standards

Another outcome of regulatory reforms has been the pressure to move to common financial reporting standards across the globe, to provide greater transparency and accountability for investors and other stakeholders. By 2005, listed companies based in the EU will have to comply with IFRS (International Financial Reporting Standards) accounting practices, and not domestic GAAP.

The history of IFRS, formally known as International Accounting Standards, goes back to 1973 when a group of academics and accountants realised the need for a globally standardised set of accounting practices. However, it was not until 1989 that the International Organisation of Securities Commissions (IOSCO) endorsed IAS. A few years later and a number of countries, including Cyprus and Switzerland, had adopted the new practice.

Since then, the International Accounting Standards Board together with domestic and international accounting bodies have been working on the completion of a final set of codes designed to be universally accepted by all. As of late 2004, one of the only remaining countries left sitting on the fence was the USA, although it is widely anticipated that they will adopt the standards.

In the meantime, the EU, perhaps spurred into action by Enron, decided that all member states would adopt IFRS, especially as accounting practices within the Union are disparate. The introduction of IFRS is expected to have a huge impact on the way companies report, their corporate strategy, and the culture of compliance.

According to the European Federation of Accountants (EFA), only Britain, France and Italy of the current 15 member states have effective financial scrutiny. In May 2001, France took the moral high ground to become the first country in the world to pass company law that obliges publicly listed companies to publish triple bottom-line reports (Financial, Environmental, and Social Performance). France's non-voluntary lead on stakeholder empowerment means that the public will be given insight into how companies manage their performance. This will give them the power to influence performance direction, risk assessment, and priority.

The UK has long been held in wide regard for its 'true and fair' accounting practices. In fact, IFRS is similar in philosophy to the UK's existing code, which is based on English common law. Countries like Germany, France and

Japan are expected to struggle a little more with IFRS as it is radically different from Roman codified law.

However, for UK registered companies, and US businesses, if accepted, there will be a number of significant changes. IFRS is due to come into force in many countries in 2005. However it is not the intention of this book to go into details of IFRS, which are complex and still changing at the time of writing. For details on the latest position, visit www.iasb.org

Higgs, Smith, Tyson and the Revised Combined Code

In an effort to heal investor confidence in the UK, the Government commissioned Derek Higgs, a former chairman of Prudential's fund management business, experienced FTSE 100 non-executive director and chairman of both Partnerships UK and the British Land Company, to review corporate transparency and shareholder accountability within stock listed companies. Sir Robert Smith, chairman of The Weir Group and former managing director of Charterhouse Development Capital, was asked to examine existing UK accounting and auditing practices. Finally, and making slightly less controversial reading was a report by Laura Tyson, dean of the London Business School, on broadening pools of talent to enhance board effectiveness.

But it was the eagerly awaited publication of the Higgs review that stirred up corporate emotions, especially over his recommendations on the future role of the non-executive director and executive remuneration. Despite intense criticism, the public company rulebook has now been re-written using the majority of recommendations made by Higgs and Smith, with a few conciliatory amendments. In July 2003 the Financial Reporting Council (FRC) finally agreed the final text of a revised Combined Code. The code, which is not yet mandatory, replaces the 1998 Code, which was previously annexed to the Financial Services Authority (FSA) Listing Rules. It includes 14 corporate governance 'principles', which act as a guide in how to achieve the more concrete provisions, 21 'supporting principles' and 48 detailed provisions. The 1998 code had just 14 principles and 45 provisions.

The key principles include:

- New definitions for the role of the board, chairman, and non-executive directors (NEDs).
- More open and rigorous procedures when appointing directors, and consideration of external candidates.
- Formal and rigorous annual evaluation of the board's own performance, as well as the performance of the main board committees and individual directors, with explanation of how the evaluations have been carried out.
- At least half the board, apart from companies outside the FTSE 350, and excluding the chairman should comprise independent non-executive directors.
- Audit and remuneration committees should consist exclusively of independent NEDs – while the majority of nomination committee members should also be independent.
- A chief executive should not be appointed chairman of the same company.
- Executive directors should not commit to more than one non-executive directorship or chairmanship in a FTSE 100 company.
- The audit committee's role in monitoring the integrity of the company's financial reporting should be strengthened, reinforcing independence of the external auditor and reviewing the management of financial and other risks.

The full code can be viewed at www.frc.org.uk/combined.cfm

There have been a number of detailed examinations of corporate governance and reform throughout the European Union member states. These include the Winter Report in the Netherlands, the Bouton Review in France, the Cromme Review in Germany and the Aldama Report in Spain. The EU itself conducted an extensive review of corporate governance procedures and in 2002 recommended a 'comply or explain' approach.

A New Focus on Materiality – the Operating and Financial Review (OFR)

Until now, UK organisations have been in control of which non-financial issues they report on and to what extent. But in 2005, companies listed on the London Stock Exchange will be required by law to produce an extended non-financial narrative – the Operating and Financial Review (OFR).

Originally conceived as a 'persuasive framework' following a statement by the Accounting Standards Board (ASB) in 1993, the OFR was intended to reflect best practice when discussing the main factors behind a company's financial performance and market position.

In 2003, the ASB Statement recommended that the OFR should include a description of the business, including a consideration of its objectives and strategies. This reflected a new disclosure that the 'OFR should not assume that users have a detailed prior knowledge of the business, nor of the significant features of its operating environment'.[12]

However, the Government later announced that to improve company disclosure, quoted firms would be required by law to produce an OFR. This announcement followed the Company Law Review and the 2002 Modernising Company Law white paper.

So what is the Operating and Financial Review?

As well as a balanced and comprehensive analysis of issues traditionally considered as key to financial performance, firms will have to report on a series of new issues, where these could affect future performance, including workforce, environmental, social and community impact. The new style of report will be subject to Accounting Standards Board reporting standards. Although boards will be left to decide what is finally reported, any omissions will fall under a 'comply or explain' rule.

But it is not only quoted companies that will be affected by the push for greater corporate accountability. Companies with a turnover greater than £22.8m and 250 employees will be required to produce a 'balanced and comprehensive analysis of the development and perfromance of the company's business, to include financial, and where appropriate non-financial key performance indicators under the Accounts Modernisation Directive'.

So what needs to be reported, and in how much detail?

The OFR, however controversial, reflects a wider recognition that non-financial factors are inextricably linked to corporate governance and ultimately quality of management. That aside, companies are now left with the monumental task of deciding what is a material risk to their business and then putting in place the processes and systems needed to extract, measure and report that information.

According to OFR guidance from the Department of Trade and Industry (DTI), processes relating to the review should be planned in the same way as any other major board-led projects. Emphasis should be placed on transparency, appropriate consultation, relevant information and internal processes. Comparison should also be made with other companies operating within the same industry sector.

Directors will therefore have to strike a balance between historical analysis of past performance and likely trends affecting future performance. However, companies will be able to determine their own appropriate time period.

Summary[13] according to guidelines published by the Department of Trade and Industry

An OFR shall be a balanced and comprehensive analysis of:

- The development and performance of the business of the company and its subsidiaries during the financial year
  - the position of the company and its subsidiaries at the end of the year
  - the main trends and factors underlying the development, performance and position of the business of the company and its subsidiaries during the financial year
  - the main trends and factors which are likely to affect their future development, performance and position.
- The review should include a description of:
  - the business objectives and strategies of the company and its subsidiaries
  - resources available to the company and its subsidiaries
  - principal risks and uncertainties
  - capital structure, treasury policies, objectives and liquidity.
- The review shall include information about:
  - employees
  - environmental matters
  - social and community issues
  - professional relationships, which are essential to the company's business
  - receipts from, and return to, company members in relation to shares held.
- The review shall:
  - include analysis using financial and non-financial KPIs, plus information relating to environmental and employee matters
  - refer, where appropriate, to amounts included in annual accounts.

Any omissions should be fully explained within the review. Companies with numerous business units – perhaps following a series of mergers and acquisitions – where standardised information may not exist, are encouraged to comment on the 'quality' of information included and their consequent judgements.

Although widely accepted as 'a good idea', the legislation has not been without controversy. In November 2004, the DTI agreed to drop the term 'due and careful enquiry' following warnings that it would create legal problems for auditors, and have a significant effect on future director liability insurance. However, the requirement that 'auditors should consider whether the OFR is consistent with the company's accounts, and whether it contains any inconsistencies based on any matter that have come to their attention while conducting the company audit' will remain.

Risk and Internal Control

Failure to adopt good corporate governance suggests that the company has inadequate risk management strategies and weak internal control. Although risk is an integral part of business, it is important to have transparent strategies in place to cover every possible scenario, whether it is an industrial accident, environmental catastrophe or a product recall.

Corporate governance enables an organisation to accurately assess those risks and track any developments with the use of real-time data systems. The ultimate goal in reducing risk exposure is to increase shareholder confidence. Investors need the reassurance that if the unlikely, unpredictable or unfortunate does happen, visible systems are in place to act on those situations as quickly as possible.

The Importance of Enterprise Governance and How to Achieve It

Effective corporate governance requires that organisations not only have the ability to monitor and measure historic performance on a monthly basis but that they are also able to meet the more forward-looking direction setting needs of the firm. While many organisations can monitor corporate performance on a monthly basis, our research shows that they often have a less than full insight into costs and performance drivers.

Firms that excel in the Enterprise Governance 'space', however, are characterised by a willingness to move beyond mere stewardship and accountability to open and transparent engagement with stakeholders. These firms have typically implemented a complex configuration of systems, processes and controls. In addition to these specific board level capabilities, these organisations also have systems for the effective measurement, reporting and evaluation of performance. Leading-edge exponents of value-based corporate governance such as Tesco and HSBC have put in place state-of-the-art information systems to enable managers at all levels to evaluate and monitor performance. In the case of Tesco, these systems incorporate store-wide point-of-sale systems, enterprise-wide financial systems, supply chain management systems and corporate-wide corporate performance management systems.

A study by Paul Gompers, Joy Ishii and Andrew Metrick[14] showed a 'striking relationship between corporate governance and stock returns'. The performance of around 1,500 companies throughout the 1990s was measured using a specially created governance index. The study showed that companies with the best governance scores outperformed those with the worst by 8.5 per cent. The research also showed that weaker shareholder rights were associated with lower profits, lower sales growth, higher capital expenditures, and a higher amount of corporate acquisitions.

Ensure Effective Board Operations

A recent Booze Allen Hamilton study[15] found that turnover of CEOs at the world's 2,500 largest publicly traded companies increased by 53 per cent between 1995 and 2001. Companies appear to be setting higher standards of performance for their CEOs. Despite the high-profile management flameouts in the US, CEO turnover is accelerating faster in Asia and Europe than in North America. Effective board operations require firms to assemble a cohesive, qualified and effective board which can drive performance and protect shareholder value. Successful companies tend to focus on a number of key areas. They encourage a strong, well balanced board with independent-minded directors who will balance the CEO's power. On-going training programmes are implemented for new and existing directors, with considerable emphasis placed on communication. A culture of continual improvement and evaluation is also fostered.

Balance the Role of the CFO as Controller and Strategist

As traditional custodians of the firm's performance measurement and control systems, finance professionals have a key role to play in ensuring that the necessary systems are in place to support corporate governance.

According to professional services firm Deloitte, the CFO's dual role as financial steward and corporate strategist 'confers important synergies'. Although the consultancy strongly advises against separating them, as it would create a competitive disadvantage, it does recommend achieving a better balance. For Deloitte, the CEO and board members need to know 'what factors are driving the numbers and what strategies can be put in place to improve performance'. Because the CFO as financial steward has a 'hands-on' understanding of the company's financial performance and the relationship between risk and return, he or she is invaluable in devising strategy. This is vital if a company wants to set strategies that are closely linked to financial realities.

So what should firms be doing to achieve better coverage in their governance efforts? Firms can begin by setting up a project group to review the current approach to governance. This team should undertake a 'root and branch' review of the systems in place in order to do the following:

- Assess the level of strategic alignment between governance priorities/capability and the needs of the firm.
- Identify the key governance processes of the organisation, and the owner of these.
- Measure relative performance across the key systems that support governance.

- Identify opportunities for improvement.
- Deploy problem-solving teams to begin addressing short-comings.

Recognise the Importance of Talent

> In looking for people to hire, you look for three qualities: integrity, intelligence and energy. And if they don't have the first, the other two will kill you.
>
> (Warren Buffet, CEO, Berkshire Hathaway)

There is increasing evidence to show that good corporate ethics will not only help a company to retain talent, but attract it. After all, who wants to work for a company that regularly attracts negative press over its alleged 'opaque' deal making? It makes sense that companies such as Asda, Microsoft, Barcardi-Martini and Harley Davidson, which have clearly defined corporate governance and corporate responsibility principles, regularly top the 'best company to work for' surveys. In 2003, Danone, Sun Microsystems and Bristol-Myers Squibb all scored highly in the Financial Times Best Company index.

Meeting the Challenge of Enterprise Governance

In 2004 the authors undertook a major research programme 'Corporate Response to Governance Pressures: A Global Survey'.[16] Commissioned by the CODA Group, and carried out by National University of Ireland and PMP Research, the survey focused on the realities of Enterprise Governance and the challenges organisations face in meeting the emerging demands being placed on them in the governance 'space'. The survey consisted of in-depth interviews with senior finance professionals from 147 international businesses across Europe, and the USA. One-third of those interviewed were based in the UK, with a further one-third based in the United States of America. The remainder of the survey participants were drawn from France,

Germany and the Netherlands. Of those organisations that participated in the study, 36 per cent had a US parent and 28 per cent had a UK-based parent. The interviews were drawn from a wide range of industry sectors with the largest group being manufacturing, at 27 per cent, followed by banking and finance at 14 per cent.

Here are the top ten findings from the survey.

1   *Enterprise Governance is not a fad and is here to stay.* It is clear from our research that Enterprise Governance will remain at the top of the management agenda for the foreseeable future. Market volatility, political instability, shareholder pressures, and general economic uncertainty have left many organisations facing a difficult Governance environment. They find themselves facing major challenges with respect to risk management, corporate responsibility, reputational risk and brand protection.

2   *Chief Executives and CFOs are taking a leading role in executing the Governance agenda.* In the post-Parmalat world of Enterprise Governance, CFOs and CEOs are taking responsibility for Governance issues (Figure 8.2). For over half of the survey participants, Governance is generally the responsibility of either the CEO (28 per cent) or the CFO (28 per cent). In the UK, dedicated risk management directors (38 per cent) are playing a significant role in driving Enterprise Governance while, in the US, CFOs (81 per cent) are taking the lead (Figure 8.3).

3   *Governance issues are driving changes in systems and processes.* Businesses have responded to the Governance challenge by putting in place mechanisms to protect the interests of the shareholders and ensure that executive management fulfils its primary responsibility to direct strategy and monitor performance. Nearly two-thirds (63 per cent) of respondents said that they had the mechanisms in place to ensure that executive management fulfil their primary responsibility to direct the strategy and monitor the performance of the business.

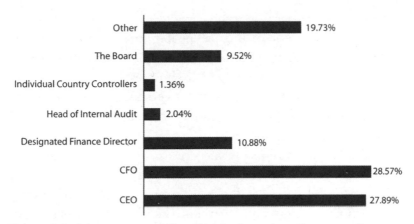

Figure 8.2. Primary responsibility for implementing Corporate Governance initiatives. *Source:* (© CODA Group).

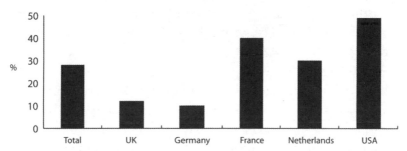

Figure 8.3. The role of the CFO in implementing governance initiatives, by geography. *Source:* (© CODA Group).

4 *Many organisations still see Governance in narrow ethical and corporate responsibility terms and have failed to make the shareholder value connection.* Over 80 per cent of the survey respondents viewed Governance in terms of professional ethics and corporate responsibility. Few of the businesses in the study had moved beyond the narrow Corporate Governance perspective where risk is seen as a hazard, to the wider Enterprise Governance view, where performance, conformance and responsibility are addressed in balance. In this respect, risk management procedures are the key focus of Governance efforts with Sarbanes–Oxley and Basel II compliance following closely. Risk as a hazard is the mental model for most businesses.

5   *Finding the time for Governance projects is a key source of difficulty.*
Some 40 per cent of finance professionals reported having
difficulties finding resources and time for Corporate Governance projects. 64 per cent of UK businesses are struggling to
achieve consistent standards of Governance across the group
because training and education of staff in the area of
Governance is insufficient.

6   *CFOs lead the way in risk management but risk directors have a
significant foothold in the UK.* There was a striking difference
between the USA and the UK with regard to primary
responsibility for risk management. The overall findings for the
study show that 43 per cent of businesses have given
responsibility to the CFO but this figure rises to 81 per cent
for the US businesses. Only 19 per cent of the participants have
a dedicated risk director with the UK leading the way with 38
per cent of businesses appointing a specific risk director.
Respondents believed that this is directly related to the
historical strength and influence of the UK's insurance industry.

7   *Companies have opted for standardised, integrated organisation-wide
approaches to risk.* Companies have pursued highly integrated
approaches to risk management that use common procedures
and periodic assessments for the entire organisation. As such,
businesses have made considerable progress in putting in
place systems to assess and identify risks. Risks beyond the
organisation's control are a cause for concern for a significant
number of survey respondents. One area of weakness appears
to be the identification and assessment of political, economic,
social and financial risks over which companies have very
little control.

8   *Reputation and brands are key elements of reporting going forward.*
While the rhetoric of reporting intangibles – such as brand
and risk – is well established, it is clear from our study that
businesses are now beginning to incorporate these areas into
their reporting. The survey found that in the near future
companies will explicitly include information on risk,
reputation and brand in their reporting.

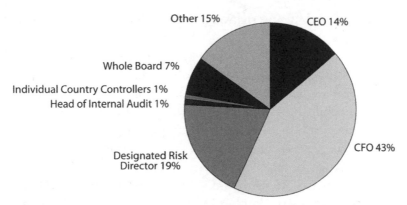

Figure 8.4. Primary responsibility for implementing risk management. *Source:* (© CODA Group).

9 *Businesses lack effective planning and forecasting processes to help them identify over-the-horizon risk and Governance issues.* In our study, we found that only a small number of businesses (just over 8 per cent) view planning and budgeting as a key to effective Governance procedures. For many businesses, the role of planning and budgeting is to operationalise strategy, and while this is understandable, in the future businesses will need to incorporate planning and budgeting into the Enterprise Governance framework.

10 *Enterprise Governance is about balancing compliance and performance.* The key challenge is one of balancing the requirement to comply with the duty to perform. Those companies that treat Governance as another layer of bureaucracy have missed the point. Whereas early Corporate Governance codes have been too focused on compliance with certain specified procedures and on having certain structures in place, the emerging focus now is on how a company performs against specified principles and strategic direction.

Notes

1 R. Sharman and T. Copnell of KPMG (2002) 'Performance from conformance', in *Management Risk to Enhance Stakeholder*

Value, London: International Federation of Accountants and CIMA.

2 V. Agarwal (2004) *Corporate Governance at Unilever*, Hyderabad, India: ICFAI Knowledge Centre.

3 V. Agarwal (2003) *Corporate Governance at General Electric*, Hyderabad, India: ICFAI Knowledge Centre.

4 Available online at: www.treasury.gov.au

5 A. Khan (2004) *Boeing Corporate Governance Crisis*, Hyderabad, India: ICFAI Knowledge Centre.

6 A. Horowitz, M. Athitakis, M. Lasswell and O. Thomas (2004) 'The 101 dumbest moments in business', January/February issue, published by business 2.0 www.business2.com

7 Available online at: www.CorpGov.net

8 Graef Crystal, quoted in *The Washington Post*, 8 June 2002.

9 Guardian Unlimited website. Available online at: www.guardian.co.uk

10 BSR News Monitor summary of article in *The Washington Post*, 5 June 2002.

11 Business for Social Responsibility paper. Available online at: www.bsr.org

12 Page 6, 'From carrots to sticks: a survey of narrative reporting in annual reports' by Deloitte, published 2004. See www.deloitte.co.uk

13 'The Operating Financial Review: a practical guidance for directors' by the Department of Trade and Industry, published May 2004. See www.dti.gov.uk

14 A. Gompers, J. Ishii and A. Metrick (2003) 'Corporate governance and equity prices', *The Quarterly Journal of Economics*, Feb, vol. 118, no. 1, pp. 107–55.

15 Booz Allen Hamilton 'CEO Survey 2003'. This survey studied the 253 CEOs of the world's 2,500 publicly-traded corporations who left office in 2002 and evaluated the performance of their companies and the events surrounding their departure. To provide historical context, Booz Allen evaluated and then compared this data to information on CEO departures for 1995, 1998, 2000 and 2001.

16 CODA Group 2004 'Corporate Response to Governance Pressures – A Global Survey', Ref. GRGP001.

SUPPORTING ENTERPRISE GOVERNANCE: THE EMERGING FINANCE ARCHITECTURE

S ince the mid-1990s there has been widespread recognition of the need for finance to move from the role of traditional scorekeeper to a business partner. At the same time, firms are striving to increase the efficiency of their finance and administrative processes and reduce costs as a percentage of revenues.

As a result of these pressures, many organisations have changed their finance function and begun shifting the emphasis away from operational finance/transaction processing and focusing instead on strategic decision support and more value added analysis in support of the key business decision-makers.

The rapid development of information systems has removed many of the tasks that traditionally occupied the finance department. Manual transaction processing in areas such as purchase to pay and order to cash are being replaced by e-procurement and e-fulfilment applications with strategic finance activities such as corporate performance management moving to centre stage.

In addition, the growing importance of the disciplines within Enterprise Governance – conformance, performance, risk management and corporate responsibility – has forced many

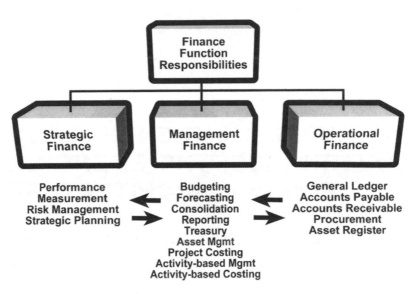

Figure 9.1. The finance function's area of responsibility. Emphasis and resources are moving from the operational to the strategic. *Source:* (© CODA Group).

CFOs to look for mechanisms to free up time and resources in the more routine areas of operational and management finance, and to ensure that processes are clearly visible, standardised, controlled and auditable across the enterprise, however complex. Two clear approaches that allow finance to focus on more strategic issues and to standardise processes have emerged; shared services centres and business process outsourcing (Figure 9.1).

Case Study: Whirlpool – An Early Player in SSC

Whirlpool Corporation is one of the world's leading manufacturers and marketers of major home appliances. Its headquarters are in Benton Harbor, Michigan, in the USA. Though now a global leader, the company began as a family-owned machine shop located in a small town on the eastern shore of lake Michigan. The company manufactures in 12 countries, has over 30,000 employees and markets products under 10 major brand names in more than 140 countries. Annual sales now surpass $8 billion and continue to grow as the company expands its current lines of business and seeks opportunities in new ventures around the world.

In 1994, Whirlpool examined its finance strategy and realised that:

1 The dynamics of the major domestic appliance business in Europe had changed dramatically.
2 The winners would only be those who are able to operate at a pan-European level.
3 Those who are able to provide business support at the lowest cost per unit.

Whirlpool's response to this changing market was to announce that the new organisation would focus primarily on processes and not on local geography. Finance and Administration's response to support this new organisation was to do the following:

• create a finance and administration organisation that would support and add value to all areas of the business;
• keep business planning and analysis close to the business;
• outsource non-core activities such as payroll, travel and fleet management;
• centralise at a single European location all transaction processing activities.

The main aim was to create competitive advantage both in services and cost for the finance function. To meet these goals it needed to separate the basic cost adding transaction processing from business planning and analysis which is the key value adding role for finance going forward. It also needed to enhance the analytical skills of the business planners to more effectively support the business and at the same time dramatically reduce the cost of the overall service. Finance had to become better aligned to supporting the information needs of the business. Issues to be resolved included:

- volume of reports: too much data and too many reports;
- clarity of information: data not information, recipients had to interpret reports, inconsistent data definitions;
- variance analysis: confusing morass of profit measures, full Profit & Loss reports drowned the key variances;
- exception reporting: multiple potentially contradictory benchmarks, which performance benchmark, plan, forecast, prior year;
- context of information: insufficient data to identify trends in performance;
- future vision: concentrated on historical information with little future vision;
- focus of information: did not pinpoint problems;
- level of detail: too much unnecessary information with insufficient focus on areas for concern and investigation.

Senior Whirlpool management agreed that there was a need to give the business what it wanted – headline news with fewer pages, clear signposts to problems, distinguish good news from bad, trend analysis, predictive data and timely information. The future vision was that Business Planning Analysis and Control would be the key value adding role in the support of the business. Whirlpool Europe benchmarked itself against its counterpart in the USA, NAAG (North American Appliance Group), the centralised NAAG finance and administration function required 33 per cent fewer staff than the decentralised European structure. Based on the above, it was agreed that major savings could be derived in Europe by consolidating and centralising transaction accounting. It was also agreed that the best companies were predominantly US multinationals operating in Europe. Companies at the leading edge in finance are those with strategies towards shared services and in the area of shared services in Europe there was little to emulate.

One of the main benefits which Whirlpool derived from changing to a shared services strategy was to re-align its finance strategy. The centralised North American Appliance Group (Whirlpool's US operation) required around 20 per cent less finance and administration staff than the decentralised Whirlpool Europe structure. All additional staff in Whirlpool Europe were involved in the area of transaction accounting. The business planning and analysis functions in the US represented around 40 per cent of the total finance and administration staff but only around 20 per cent in Europe. Whirlpool realised that as a US multi-national in Europe it encountered wide-ranging threats and opportunities.

Whirlpool believed the additional benefits of moving to a single centre were greater than from a series of regional centres, however, these benefits had also to be weighed against the increased complexity and difficulties of implementation, as well as the political considerations associated with the reduction in staff numbers and power in each of the countries where those functions and activities were currently located.

After a period of meticulous planning Whirlpool opened a shared service centre in Dublin, in September 1995 which took over work from 14 different finance operations in Western Europe. What made Whirlpool's case particularly fascinating is that it chose a big bang approach to reform transferring existing accounting and finance practices to a single location in a relatively short space of time. This challenged conventional wisdom which said that it is better to reform existing finance practices at country level first before transferring them to a single centre, otherwise organisations may end up centralising bad habits as well as good ones.

The next step was to decide where to locate, should it be in a place where the firm already had an existing site or should it be a greenfield operation. In the end the team opted for a greenfield site and it appointed Ernst & Young, a consultancy firm, to assist in finding a location offering a pool of skilled labour, excellent telecommunications infrastructure and suitably priced property. At the end of March 1995 the project team pulled together all of the company's financial controllers and human resource representatives from across Europe for a workshop to explain what the shared services project was all about. The following month the team carried out a series of road shows across Europe to explain to country heads the likely impact on their organisations and to enlist their support for change. This exercise had two crucial goals:

1 To enlist local support – the co-operation of the national human resource staff was needed in order to identify which local staff would have a job in the future and which staff needed to be persuaded to stay at least for the transition period.

2 To manage expectations – rather than selling the project as something that would revolutionise the finance function overnight, the team simply promised that after migration of the relevant activities to the shared services centre that the service provided would at least match that which the local country organisation was used to and there would be no disruption to the business. The main task now was to identify a site for the centre and enlist a recruitment team to anticipate staffing requirements. They also drew up a timetable for migrating the national finance operations to the shared service centre, planning and analysis and factory administration would remain local. For convenience this schedule was identical to the IT department's timetable for switching each national Whirlpool organisation to a new European wide area network.

In June 1995, Ernst & Young proposed Dublin as a suitable location and this choice was quickly endorsed by Whirlpool Europe's senior management. Some 30 staff were hired to fill the most important positions. A lease was also signed on a building and, in order to link the shared service centre to the rest of the organisation, a local area network was set up. After the initial induction course in Dublin which lasted four weeks, the centre's new recruits, about half were Irish, were sent out to workshadow people whose jobs they were assuming.

In countries such as France and Germany, where the company had major operations, they stayed up to five months to ensure that the company did not lose essential local expertise. People said there was a risk of centralising bad as well as good practices, however, this was limited due to the fact the centre was structured on a functional and not a country basis, one group handles Accounts Payable and this is further divided into processing and disbursements. One handles the statutory and fiscal accounting, another the general ledger management and the fourth fixed assets, intercompany and inventory. This allows for staff covering different countries to compare and identify best practices and implement these countrywide in the centre. As the company's finance centre is under one roof, it is easier to train and utilise the most up-to-date technology.

The main services which are covered in the Whirlpool SSC are:

- General Ledger accounting
- Disbursements
- Fixed Assets/Inventory accounting
- Reporting Consolidation
- VAT and Intrastat
- Statutory/Fiscal Accounting
- Accounts Payable Processing.

Shared Services – The Case for Centralisation[1]

Shared services centres (SSCs) first appeared in America in the 1980s as purpose-built business units specifically created to process high volume, low value transactions for the finance department. Since then the SSC model has evolved, with regional and global centres offering multifunctional services increasingly becoming the norm.

They are referred to as shared services as their activities are shared by units across entire organisations, rather than being duplicated by similar services within each individual unit. Typical services include finance, treasury, human resources, information systems, legal, marketing, purchasing and R&D. In recent years a significant number of organisations worldwide have established regional or global SSCs (Table 9.1).

There are a number of approaches to shared services being adopted around the world. They range from the most basic form of consolidation of transactional activities all the way to creating an independent business set up to provide shared services internally and to sell shared services externally to multiple clients.

Table 9.1. Examples of organisations that have established shared service centres

Microsoft	Whirlpool	Coca-Cola
Hewlett-Packard	Philips	Pepsi
Oracle	General Motors	Diageo
Xerox	3M	Mars–Masterfoods
Siemens	Lockheed Martin	Philip Morris
3Com	Goodyear/Dunlop	Procter & Gamble
Monsanto	Trw Automotive	Company
Mastercard International	National Australia Bank	McDonald's Corporation
Baxter Healthcare	Allstate Insurance	Disney Worldwide
Corporation	Company	Pfizer Bba Aviation
AstraZeneca	GE	Royal Mail
Symbol Technologies	Gillette	BP
RMC	Royal Bank of Scotland	Quintiles
GlaxoSmithKline	Group	Bristol-Myers Squibb

At the heart of the SSC approach is the simplification and rationalisation of process, systems, structures and locations:

- Processes are standardised, continually improved and automated where possible.
- Systems are rationalised to single versions on a single database.
- Organisational structures are simplified and streamlined where possible.
- Operations are consolidated into a single location.

The most obvious commercial opportunity comes from eliminating non-value-added activities such as multiple authorisation processes and reconciliations. Organisations can gain economies of scale and improved productivity by consolidating and centralising repetitive or transaction-based activities.

Research suggests that the main aims of moving into a shared services environment are to do the following:

- enhance corporate value;
- focus on partner service and support;
- liberate business and operating units to permit focus on the strategic aspects of their operations;
- lower costs and raise service levels;
- make the best use of investments in technology;
- focus on continuous improvement;
- harmonise and standardise common business processes to reduce duplication;
- standardise and control compliance processes;
- facilitate integration post-merger or acquisition.

But it is not only the prospect of achieving operational savings that makes SSCs such an attractive option. The potential tax savings can also be considerable. Governments in countries such as Holland and Belgium have already introduced specific tax regimes to encourage shared services activities. As a consequence, many firms are now using a 'Commissionaire' structure to achieve these savings. Under this concept, sales are made by a

Table 9.2. Top 10 services in initial shared services scope

Service	Proportion (%)
Accounts Payable	83
General Accounting	65
Fixed Assets	57
Accounts Receivable	56
Payroll	55
Travel & Expense	50
Reporting – Financial	48
Human Resources	44
Credit & Collections	43
Help Desk	39

Source: Results of the Annual Shared Services Survey conducted by the Shared Services and Business Process Outsourcing Association (SBPOA) in conjunction with Accenture, and A. Kris. Available online at: www.SBPOA.com

central unit, which then pays the local sales organisations a commission. With this structure it is possible to net off the group's profits and losses, and to move more of the profits to a low tax regime.

Recent research by the Shared Services and Business Process Outsourcing Association (SBPOA) suggests that an increasing number of firms are now transferring additional value-added services such as statutory reporting to an SSC model (Table 9.2).

Case Study: Shared Services at Carrefour[2]

With more than 9,000 outlets in 27 countries, Carrefour is the world's second largest retailer. It operates a variety of store formats including hypermarkets, supermarkets and convenience stores. When Carrefour adopted a new global vision: 'to embrace the challenge of building a worldwide company, not only geographically international, but truly global in vision, leveraging each country's experience as we optimize our resources and technology,' they called for systems that were consistent across the entire organisation.

Accenture was chosen as the partner to deliver upon Carrefour's first global system deployment initiative. The Carrefour and Accenture team designed, built, deployed and installed a fully integrated financial system to support effective accounting and financial activities. Local teams were involved at each step of the design and implementation process. This ensured that the solution addressed local needs and was being used in a similar manner across boundaries. The project team implemented General Ledger, Purchasing, Accounts Payable and Asset Management modules with additional modules to be added later.

Benefits achieved have been substantially in excess of predictions. The infrastructure can support rapid expansion and can add new stores with the flick of a switch. From a systems point of view, Carrefour now has a 'factory' in place to deliver high-efficiency systems, tools, processes, and training.

'From the onset, we established a vision to embrace the challenge of building a worldwide company, not only geographically international, but truly global in vision, leveraging each country's experience as we optimize our resources and our technology,' says Sergio F. Dias, Group Controller.

Source: www.accenture.com

The Importance of Information Technology in SSCs – Moving to Single Instance

If a shared services centre is to successfully deliver all its promised benefits, then the right IT strategy is imperative. The move to a shared services culture will often involve either an adjustment or extension of an organisation's IT arrangements, or even further implementation. The aim is to combine the various and frequently incompatible systems operated by different business

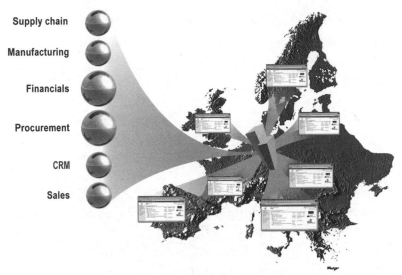

Supply chain

Manufacturing

Financials

Procurement

CRM

Sales

Figure 9.2. Single instance implementation. *Source:* (© CODA Group).

units into a common system platform. It may not be possible to switch from multiple systems to a single system overnight, but an initial target of a reduction to no more than five systems should be achievable. Therefore any move to a shared services environment must incorporate a clear understanding of an organisation's IT strategy. The shared services unit must not only be able to interact with other business units' IT systems, but be in a position to take advantage of new IT solutions while carrying out its services, which can lead to cost reductions and improved performance (Figure 9.2).

Mark Adams, CFO of STA Travel, on the benefits of single instance implementation

'STA is a complex company. We operate in 18 countries, have 450 branches and employ more than 3,000 staff. We are a very high volume business with an average turnover of $1.2bn a year. However, the profit margins are very tight. If we can make a 3 per cent return we are doing very well.

We are also in a highly crowded and competitive market. It's therefore key to manage the business in real-time terms. For example, a product could normally have a margin of 14 per cent, but if for any number of reasons that drops to 12 per cent, you need to know straight away. In order to react to that cut you need to have the right information at your fingertips. You need these types of systems, however complicated they may seem.

'Initially we did look at ERP, but felt it did not provide the information we wanted without a lot of work. Buying financial accounting software is a big decision, there is no doubt about that, and there are no guarantees. STA's IT spend on systems will be $25m over the next five years. Our total IT spend will cost around $50m. But it is a means to an end when striving for long-term sustainability.'

Workflow and e-Procurement[3]

In recent years a so-called second-wave of shared services centres began to emerge. These technology-enabled centres attempt to leverage web/Internet technologies in order to dramatically improve SSC performance. Under the web-enabled SSC, high volumes of detailed data are captured and processed automatically but exceptions may still occur. As a result, the role of the SSC changes from processing transactions and applying internal controls, to one in which the centre deals with processing exceptions while internal controls are embedded in the web applications.

These include not just traditional e-commerce applications in the form of Business-to-Business (B2B) procurement, but also services to employees and suppliers. For example, employees can fill in expenses claims with screen prompts highlighting invalid or excessive claims. Organisations such as Cisco have shown the effectiveness of web-based HR processes and this functionality is now becoming standard from many ERP vendors. Controls are becoming embedded in the processes, for example, accounts payable and fixed asset management are embedded in the supply chain process or revenue management as part of the customer care process. In addition, intranets allow suppliers to access internal organisational information to improve the co-ordination of the supply chain.

Within best-in-class shared service centres, technology is used as a vehicle to implement fundamental changes to business processes. Implementations typically cut across a large area of the business enterprise. For example, workflow management tools typically contain details on the routing of tasks throughout a business. Every single SSC business transaction from verifying an invoice or creating a new vendor in the master data records, to requesting a credit note from a vendor can become a task list. In this way, the SSC end user can process a task in an automated fashion by using a business model, the task list and appropriate data. By combining workflow technology with electronic document imaging, and Internet/intranet/extranet technology, SSCs can achieve important efficiencies (Table 9.3).

Significant increases in e-procurement spending are expected by organisations that have invested in these technologies for their shared service centres. E-procurement solutions offer significant cost reduction benefits to buying organisations through the following means:

- reducing administrative costs by between 60 per cent to as much as 95 per cent;
- curbing maverick purchasing;
- transforming the purchasing organisation to become more strategically focused;[4]
- reducing considerably error and dispute resolutions costs; up to 30 per cent of manual purchase orders require some sort of error-correcting rework;
- bringing a high return on investment and satisfaction, providing the highest ROI of any enterprise-wide application,

Table 9.3. Workflow and e-procurement technology types and benefits

Type	Benefits
E-workflow management	Reduced manual intervention
	Cost reduction
	Higher speed of processing
	Activity independent of location
E-procurement	Reduced purchase costs
	Improved spend control
	Strategic purchasing
XML and B2B technologies	Standardised 'language' for exchanging documents
	More open and cheaper than EDI
	Brings B2B application integration to new levels

paying for itself within a year and with up to 85 per cent of heavy system users being highly satisfied with the results.[5]

According to Forrester Research, the success of this hands–off procurement tool depends on three tightly linked assumptions:

1 Procurement applications will help the firm to keep down the number of suppliers and to draw up more favourable contracts.
2 All employees will use the installed e-procurement system, eliminating rogue spending.
3 When all buyers and suppliers are online, the firm's total spending on goods and services will fall to a natural low.

Global Payments and Cash Management Systems

In the early 1980s companies recognised that there were economics of scale and improvements in control to be had in the regional consolidation of treasury and banking functions into a separate, formal legal entity. The essence of the shared service centre concept is a greater integration of the treasury function with other key financial functions. Technological advancement has been a key factor in this integration process. Treasury centres previously were characterised by a focus on tax efficiency and worked in a stand-alone environment with little interface to other parts of the company's financial organisation

One example of advances in banking technology is the Bank of America automated accounts payable system. Clients send a single file directly from their accounts payable system containing payment instructions. On the date specified in the file, the bank initiates payment in the format requested: cheque, wire or automated clearing house. It has recently introduced a new payment enhancement that enables client's accounts payable system to automatically generate wire payment orders to Bank of America.

The bank provides the client with the electronic data interchange (EDI) file format so that the accounts payable system can build the file of payment orders, including remittance information such as invoice date. In order to protect the data, a security package is used, the system then dials up the bank or uses the Internet to send the file. The bank validates the file and sends the wire payment and remittance information to the appropriate clearing system. A few minutes after receiving the wire request, the bank sends an EDI advice to the company's accounts payable system acknowledging the order.

Business Process Outsourcing

With the growing trend toward focusing on core business capabilities, many companies are outsourcing selected business functions to expert partners who can perform them more efficiently and cost-effectively. A step beyond traditional IT outsourcing, business process outsourcing includes such functions as cash collection, claims processing, invoicing, payroll and customer support. As recent research by Accenture shows, a significant number of firms now consider BPO a realistic option for reducing overhead costs (Table 9.4).

The decision to outsource administrative and support activities is being taken by forward-thinking managers who question how work has traditionally been carried out and whether there is a

Table 9.4. Current and planned outsourced functions

	Already outsourced successfully (%)	Plan to outsource (%)
Employee payroll	27	26
Tax compliance and planning	21	27
Financial systems application support	16	27
General and financial accounting	13	24
Travel and expense processing	12	31
Accounts receivables and collections	12	20
Accounts payables and vendor management	9	21
Financial reporting	7	19
Other finance functions	7	32
Management report preparation and analysis	6	17
Treasury and cash management	4	11
Financial risk management	3	18
Budgeting and forecasting	1	11

Source: Accenture and Economist Intelligence Unit company survey, Jan.–Feb. 2003.
Reproduced by permission of Shared Services and Business Process Outsourcing Association (SBPOA).

better way of doing it. The availability of a new breed of third-party suppliers and complementary information technology (IT) makes outsourcing an increasingly attractive option for some. Many companies now outsource non-core and/or non-strategic activities – such as finance, human resources, legal and administrative processes – to third parties. These operate their businesses along shared services lines to provide services economically to several client organisations through sharing people and resources and by implementing common processes and systems (Table 9.5).

Table 9.5. Recent European BPO deals (2004)

Customer	Provider/Vendor	Description
CSC	Swiss Re	IT plus other activities
BAe Systems	Xchanging	HR outsourcing
Abbey	EDS	Finance BPO
Eastern Energy	Vertex	Customer Care
Procter & Gamble	HP	Finance
Thames Water	Xansa	Various
BBC	MEDAS	Various
ASC	GM	Finance
Rhodia	Accenture	Finance
Dairy Farm	Cap Gemini	Finance

Case Study: Dairy Farm and Cap Gemini Ernst & Young[6]

Dairy Farm International Holdings is a leading retailer of fast-moving consumer goods in Asia Pacific, with more than $6 billion in annual revenues and 60,000 employees in ten territories. In the late 1990s as competition increased dramatically in the Hong Kong market, Dairy Farm embarked on a restructuring effort, which focused on strengthening core competencies, reducing operating costs while growing revenue, and avoiding capital outlays in non-core areas.

Dairy Farm teamed with Cap Gemini Ernst & Young (CGE&Y) Asia Pacific to build OneResource Group (ORG). ORG provides accounting, finance, and procurement services to companies globally. During the first two years of operation, ORG radically reshaped the finance function for Dairy Farm. Now, Dairy Farm Hong Kong only employs one finance person outside of ORG.

In the first two years of its joint venture with CGE&Y, Dairy Farm accomplished the following:

- consolidated to a single financial system across business units;
- reduced the finance and accounting staff by nearly 50 per cent overall reduction;
- achieved a 30 per cent decrease in costs;
- negotiated more than $3 million in savings in the procurement of operating supplies;
- implemented online tools for budgeting, management reporting, procure-to-pay, and T&E processing;
- established a low-cost processing operation in mainland China.

The goal of Dairy Farm's BPO project: build world-class capabilities in finance and procurement while avoiding the associated capital outlays.

> The bottom-line: CFOs and their direct reports from across all types of organisations and industries are now examining finance and accounting outsourcing. They are looking for ways to improve various transaction-intensive areas of their operation such as auditing, reporting, accounting, receivables and payables.
>
> *Source:* www.ebstrategy.com

Reproduced by permission of Cap Gemini Ernst & Young.

Accenture, in association with the Economist Intelligence Unit, conducted a wide-ranging survey of global corporate leaders in early 2003. Based on this research, they identified a number of key patterns with respect to finance outsourcing.[7]

Around 71 per cent of survey respondents, expect finance outsourcing to become more prevalent over the next three years; 30 per cent are currently outsourcing finance and accounting functions, and a majority of these think the arrangement has been very successful (8 per cent) or successful (57 per cent).

Companies with metrics in place to measure their gains report significant savings from outsourcing finance and accounting functions. Some 66 per cent of survey respondents saw 'lower costs' as the primary benefit of outsourcing. Rhodia, the French speciality chemicals company, reduced spending by 30 per cent in two years.

Reduced costs are not the only – or always the most significant – benefit. Outsourcing enables companies to focus on their core competencies. It relieves finance managers of responsibility for repetitive or generic business tasks, allowing them to concentrate on high-level management and other value-added activities. And by enabling companies to review and reshape entire business processes with an outsider's discipline, it can help companies execute ambitious transformation plans.

Outsourcing is often perceived as a risky undertaking. Many executives worry that it means surrendering control over vital business functions, and survey respondents cited numerous potential pitfalls, including valuable data falling into competitors' hands (52 per cent), the costs of outsourcing exceeding expectations (48 per cent) and the erosion of in-house knowledge (45 per cent).

Executives are keener to outsource repetitive, generic finance processes than operations requiring higher level analytical thinking. Payroll is a common starting point; this was the activity to have been outsourced by the greatest share (27 per cent) of survey respondents. Niche and specialist areas, such as tax planning and compliance, are natural outsourcing targets, as are turnkey solutions that help companies enter unfamiliar or difficult markets. Budgeting and forecasting were activities respondents deemed least suited to outsourcing.

Nearly 75 per cent of survey respondents thought that finance outsourcing could improve the quality of a company's disclosure. Outsourcing can create a healthy separation between managers trying to achieve performance and accountants charged with measuring it, reducing the temptation to massage the figures.

There are a number of specific reasons why firms may choose to outsource some or all of their shared services activities. These include:

- cost reduction;
- poor performance;
- capabilities not core to strategy;
- better, cheaper, effective alternatives exist;
- insufficient expertise available to upgrade;
- potential loss of control not an issue;
- service no longer relevant;
- previous experience with successful outsourcing;
- too disruptive to make the changes internally.

The conclusion many managers reach when they realise they need to trim overheads and eliminate inefficient internal service units, is to outsource it. They see moving the problem out of the organisation as the most prudent and easiest course of action to end inter-departmental disputes, poor service and 'unreasonable' costs. Even after more than a decade of restructuring, corporations are still pursuing the goals of efficiency and 'right-sizing'. The decision to outsource can seem enticingly easy: just let someone else do it. Implementation can be complex and always impacts people and strategy. But in many cases, it may be the wisest alternative.

Case Study: Rhodia and Accenture[0]

Rhodia, a $7 billion maker of specialty chemicals headquartered in France, conducted a benchmark study and found that its support processes were falling into 'worse than average' category. To improve their support processes, Rhodia turned to finance & accounting (F&A) BPO to achieve improved performance and cost reductions.

In 2001, the company entered into a six-year contract with Accenture to transfer the bulk of its financial and accounting functions to a shared service centre in Prague. Why Prague? Rhodia decided that moving to a Central European location where salaries and operational expenses are about three-quarters less than in Western Europe was a sound business decision. Rhodia laid off about 200 local employees and replaced them with Accenture's staff in Prague.

Transitioning to the Prague shared services centre required a phased approach, starting with all the UK units and following with several waves (30–50 people at a time) from the French locations. By the December 2002 target date, almost 90 per cent of the transition was completed. The lower cost of living and salaries in Prague is estimated to have yielded several millions in annual savings.

Source: www.ebstrategy.com

In the context of existing shared services, outsourcing can be viewed as the 'third' phase. Having decided to create internal shared services (phase 1) and followed through by implementing best practices (phase 2), some shared services operators realise that they will never be able to reach the standards of world class operations in certain of their activities. Outsourcing parts of shared services operations becomes a viable alternative (phase 3).

Conclusion

Despite the increasingly delicate political and social issues emerging around shared services, BPO and off-shoring, these approaches will inevitably continue to gain popularity. The challenges of achieving a good standard of Enterprise Governance and the growing pressure on operating margins lead almost inevitably to the conclusion that centralising, standardising and even outsourcing non-core operations are the only viable options for organisations in the future.

Notes

1 M. Fahy and A. Kris (2003) *Shared Service Centres: Delivering Value from Effective Finance and Business Processes*, London: FT Prentice-Hall.
2 Available online at: www.accenture.com
3 Results of the Annual Shared Services Survey conducted by the Shared Services and Business Process Outsourcing Association (SBPOA) in conjunction with Accenture and A. Kris. Available online at: www.SBPOA.com
4 C. Waltner (1999) 'Procurement pays off', *Information Week*, 26 July, pp. 65–8.
5 S. Bonisteel (1999) 'Electronic purchasing brings business savings'. *Newsbytes News Network*, 11 October.

6 Cap Gemini Ernst & Young case study. Available online at: www.ebstrategy.com

7 Accenture and Economist Intelligence Unit company survey, Jan.–Feb. 2003.

8 Rhodia and Accenture case study. Available online at: www. ebstrategy.com

PART III
....

Corporate Responsibility

CHAPTER 10

CORPORATE RESPONSIBILITY

Corporate responsibility is the continuing commitment by business to behave ethically and contribute to
economic development whilst improving the quality
of life of the workforce and their families as well as of
the local community and society at large.

(The World Business Council for

Sustainable Development)

The Birth of the Collective Conscience

Before 2001, Corporate Social Responsibility and Socially
Responsible Investment were seen as philanthropic business
practices preached by 'militant' non-governmental organisations
(NGOs) and action groups. Ethical investment indices were still
few and far between, and 'green consumerism' had been written
off by market analysts as yet another middle-class 'flash in the
pan'.

Although regulation on environmental practices and corporate
stewardship already existed, particularly in the USA, Corporate
Social Responsibility (now more commonly referred to as
Corporate Responsibility) was widely regarded as a costly waste

of resources. As a result, many organisations chose to interpret CR solely as little more than a series of selective 'charitable donations' made through staff fund-raising initiatives.

But even before the Y2K frenzy and paranoia had begun, investors were already voicing unhappiness at the ethical behaviour of corporations who focused on increasing share value regardless of the human or environmental cost. Anti-globalisation sentiments increased dramatically as consumers began to question the policies and practices of organisations operating in, buying from or outsourcing to Third World countries. There had also been a sharp swing in lifestyle priorities; employees wanted to devote more time to themselves and their families, and not be a slave to the corporation. The phrase 'quality of life' had replaced the 1980s' mantra of 'greed is good'.

Key Influences behind the CR Movement[1]

- *Technology* – investors and consumers can now access vast amounts of information 24/7.
- *Transparency* – stakeholders can now choose who they buy from, invest in, and work for using measurable benchmarks such as environmental and community impact.
- *Sustainability* – organisations are facing increasing pressure to adopt sustainable development strategies.
- *Globalisation* – as global corporate expansion increases, particularly in developing nations, so too have the calls for the export of human rights and environmental policies.
- *Borderless governance* – reflected by the creation of global governance approaches such as the Global Reporting Initiative, the UN Global Compact, the Sullivan Principles, and the Kyoto Protocols.
- *Stakeholder pressure* – poor governance, including accounting irregularities and excessive remuneration, has led to a demand for greater corporate transparency.

- *Mega-risk* – organisations now face increasingly complex and potentially dramatic risks such as product tampering, terrorist action, human rights violation, genetic modification, climate change, pollution, and nutritional care surrounding rising obesity levels.

Despite these influential trends, it took the collapse of a US-based energy giant to really focus the world's attention on how organisations behave. In other words, the CR agenda moved from being consumer-driven to investor-driven. Enron's failure succeeded in focusing the attentions of the regulators, the financial sector and the stakeholders not only on corporate governance standards, but also on internal controls and risk management policies. As a result, public limited companies across the world's capital markets are now having their CR policies, or lack of them, thoroughly scrutinised. CR has therefore become the latest 'value-added platform' for many an executive board.

But good CR is not just about joining up environmental and social policies. Although the moral reasons for practising CR lend themselves to easily identifiable 'ethical' benchmarks such as the environment, employee opportunities and human rights, the financial benefits are asymmetric; in other words, a company will not just benefit from CR practice, but will improve its performance by being better at it.

Yet, to fully reap the benefits of this essential business discipline, organisations must be prepared to fully embrace it as corporate culture. Companies must ensure that this essential business discipline is present in all parts of the business, including board operation. Although CR should not be considered a performance guarantee in its own right, having the right checks and balances in place can help facilitate a soft landing rather than a crash when scandal or failed strategy strikes.

By early 2004 Coca-Cola, for decades one of the world's most respected companies, faced numerous accusations of corporate 'irresponsibility' despite a previously consistent CR record. Its troubles began in 1999, when amid fines and warnings from legislators over its business conduct, the organisation was forced into recalling and destroying 17 million cases of Coke after 200 people complained of illness. Although it took appropriate action, Coca-Cola's handling of the crisis was considered as 'unsympathetic and tardy' by many media sources and consumers. By September, market capitalisation had fallen US$34bn.

But even after troubled CEO Douglas Ivester was pressured into resigning by Coca-Cola's heavyweight institutional investors, the situation worsened. In 2003, the company's Asian bottling operations in Kerala, Varanasi, Tamil Nadu and Thane were alleged to have created local water shortages, polluted water supplies and supplied local farmers with waste effluent, thought to be a good fertiliser. The effluent was later shown to contain a high level of lethal chemicals, and the practice was immediately halted. A year later Coca-Cola launched its branded water, Dasani, into the UK market; its image was first dented by the revelation that it was simply 'purified' tap water, then fatally damaged only weeks later when it was revealed to contain potentially dangerous levels of the carcinogen bromate. Millions of cases were immediately withdrawn.

However, its enviable CR reputation has helped it weather shareholder devaluation. The company has a number of sustainable growth strategies, including an Entrepreneurs Development Programme in South Africa designed to encourage micro-business retailers of Coca-Cola. Nearly 13,000 jobs have been created. Of 5,000 new outlets, 3,500 were part of the programme.[2]

Coca-Cola is not alone. Fast food giant McDonald's, for many years regarded as stakeholder superstar, has also found itself under the media spotlight in recent years. Already criticised for its lack of social responsibility over rising obesity, the organisation was forced into a worldwide advertising campaign in 2004 promoting food preparation standards after a series of hygiene scandals in the USA. The campaign needed to be aggressive. At the Chicago Field Museum outlet, health inspectors discovered that the food preparation area was backed up with raw sewage and that employees had changed the expiration dates on 200 cartons of milk. It was forced into immediate closure. In the same year, the chain announced the launch of a range of 'healthy options' meals and the withdrawal of super-sized drink and fries options.[3]

The cost of 'getting it wrong' is high. Not only does a company face damage to its financial position, image and reputation, legislation is upping the ethical stakes. Under Sarbanes–Oxley, for example, shareholders can now prosecute directors for neglecting their interests. The increased significance of intangible assets including brand, combined with the implications of globalisation and government requirements for disclosure is having enormous effects on directors' duties and accountability and the trend is not going to quietly fade away; if anything, it is more likely to grow in prominence. Companies must now show that they are acting responsibly towards the environment, the community they operate in, and society at large in order to appease their stakeholders.

Case Study: Merck

US-based pharmaceutical company Merck takes CR very seriously. As well as hefty contributions to a number of disaster funds, either in the form of medicine or money, it created the Merck Company Foundation, a public to private partnership (PPP) designed to help Botswana's anti-retroviral therapy programme. Created in 2000, the foundation will contribute $50m along with anti-retroviral medicine to the African Comprehensive HIV/AIDS Partnerships (ACHAP) initiative. But the company's longest-standing PPP is the Merck Mectizan Donation

Programme. The programme, which was founded in 1987 with the backing of the World Health Organization, UNICEF, and the World Bank, has provided more than 850 million tablets free of charge to people at risk of onchocerciasis, a debilitating condition more commonly known as river blindness.

In 1998, Merck expanded the programme to the prevention of lymphatic filariasis, or elephantiasis. The disease, which causes extreme swelling to both lower and upper limbs, is common to large areas of Africa. Some 40 million people already have the disease, with around a further 300 million Africans at risk. However, by 2002 more than 15 million people in eight African countries were receiving treatment for the condition. Merck claims that its goal is to eliminate both diseases as 'public health problems'.

Source: www.merck.com

Note: On 30 September 2004 Merck & Co., Inc withdrew VIOXX® (rofecoxib), its arthritis and acute pain medication, from sale after a study showed people who took the prescription drug for more than 18 months were twice as likely to suffer a heart attack, stroke or blood clots as those taking a placebo. They were quick to set up a VIOXX® (rofecoxib) Information Center on their website, featuring it prominently on the homepage. This gave information on the withdrawal from a wide range of sources, as well as information for people currently taking the drug and for healthcare professionals. Such a response is a reflection of the company's strong commitment to acting, and being seen to act, responsibly.

At time of writing, Merck looks likely to face a number of law suits which allege that Merck knew for years that Vioxx had harmful side effects. Merck says it will 'vigorously defend' its actions. About 84 million Vioxx prescriptions have been filled since the drug's introduction.

So What are the Benefits of Corporate Responsibility?

The benefits of adopting CR or sustainable development as a corporate culture, although not immediately obvious, are substantial.

Improved Risk Management

CR enables an organisation to improve its risk management and risk assessment. Even in today's enlightened times, many senior executives still associate the word 'risk' with business failure, fraud, and ultimately the destruction of shareholder value. Yet there is substantial evidence to suggest that if CEOs understand their organisation's risk profile, and put in place strategies and mechanisms to deal with them accordingly, such as CR, they will generate superior shareholder returns year on year. In order to gain the necessary operational control to avoid confrontation with stakeholders, directors need an integrated, automated platform that delivers a single point of control, as well as enforcing business rules and compliance with policies, across the organisation. Combined corporate performance management (CPM) and risk management corporate control (RMCC) systems should ensure that important data travels more quickly to the right people, and that it is what they *need* to hear instead of just what they *want* to hear.

Ensuring Compliance

The global corporate governance environment is currently undergoing a dramatic evolution. Compliance is now a measurement of responsibility to the stakeholder, the environment and the community. Business leaders must be prepared to demonstrate and explain their societal contribution on training, employment, income generation, wealth creation, innovation, and supply chain development. Failure to do so incurs a high price. As such, CR is intrinsically linked to corporate governance – and financial reporting. In 2005, financial statements in the UK for FTSE listed companies and top private firms will include a new style of report known as the Operational and Financial Review (OFR), which will replace the traditional directors' report. By law, influential performance factors including employees, customers, supplies, and impact on the environment and the wider community will have to be detailed and explained. Although only public companies with a turnover of £50m or more and 500 employees, and private companies with a turnover of £500m or more and 5,000 employees will initially be affected, it is almost certain that the law will eventually extend to smaller public and private organisations.

The UK Government, which appointed the world's first CR minister in 2000, has publicly committed itself to improving CR levels within UK registered companies. As well as ordering more than 60 Government CR initiatives, it created the all-party Parliamentary Group on Corporate Social Responsibility and the Parliamentary Group on Socially Responsible Investment. A CSR Academy has also been created to further promote the benefits of corporate responsibility.

The European Union is also encouraging companies within its member states to adopt CR policies, with the vague suggestion of making it a mandatory reporting requirement. In 2002, the first official EU strategy paper on CR was published, closely followed with the launch of the European Commission's European Multi Stakeholder Forum, which aims to create dialogue between businesses, trade unions, NGOs and the EU. In the USA, the Sarbanes–Oxley Act has further increased social responsibility commitments, despite the existence of relatively tough regulation governing business ethics including the SEC and Environmental Protection Agency (EPA) regulations on corporate disclosure on environmental liabilities, and the Foreign Corrupt Practices Act, which legislates ethical company behaviour. A number of initiatives to encourage adoption, and ensure compliance, have been launched. Among these is the

United States–Asia Environmental Partnership (US-AEP), which aims to improve Asia's many social, environmental, and industrial problems, and help US-based private and public companies to implement CR policies through overseas contracts.

The UK, the USA and the EC are not alone in forcing organisations to measure and report their societal contribution. The Corporate Law Economic Reform Act in Australia, the Bouton Report in France, the Peters Report in Holland, and in particular the King Report II in South Africa, recognise environmental, social and ethical issues within a broader 'comply or explain' framework. Industry regulation is also having a significant impact on CR awareness. Admittedly many companies view the steady stream of directives pouring out of government departments as choking red tape, but if approached positively, they can successfully provide measuring and benchmarking opportunities.

Case Study: Yorkshire Water

Yorkshire Water, a UK-based water utility company that is part of FTSE quoted group Kelda, has achieved some of the highest water standards in Europe by undertaking projects and programmes that go beyond mere legislative box ticking. The company has also launched a number of community recycling initiatives, and actively encourages its staff to get involved in community-related projects. Its financial reports are only available electronically, thereby reducing the company's paper usage.

'We do not have CSR policies just to please our shareholders, but because it is the right thing to do for our customers,' explains environment manager, Tony Harrington. 'And it's not just about compliance. We take a fair and balanced view across the interests of all our stakeholders.

'We have worked hard and invested millions to meet and exceed legislation, working closely with NGOs and government bodies such as the Environment Agency.'

Improved Financial Performance

Although the wider ethical business case for CR is fairly self-evident, the financial motives have always been a little more difficult to measure. However, a number of reports linking improved financial performance with CR have been published, as have comparative reports between ethical indices and mainstream money markets:

- According to the London Business School, out of 100 studies carried out over the past 30 years, 68 per cent demonstrated positive correlation between CR and shareholder value.[4]
- An Institute of Business Ethics report in 2003 showed companies that had adopted CR into their strategy performed better on three out of four financial measures. The companies studied also had 18 per cent higher profits on average. Another study focusing on FTSE 250 companies showed that organisations with an ethical code in place for more than five years outperformed the average on economic and market value-added.[5]
- A review of the Dow-Jones Sustainability Index suggested that between 2002 and 2003, the index outperformed the mainstream market. At the same time the DJSI World increased by 23.1 per cent, while the Dow-Jones World Index went up by 22.7 per cent.[6]
- A study of 'stakeholder superstars' including Procter and Gamble, Johnson & Johnson showed that companies who consistently try to take into account stakeholder opinions outperformed the S&P 500 by more than twice the average over the past 15 years. Total shareholder return was 43 per

cent over the past 15 years, while the total shareholder return from the S&P 500 was 19 per cent.[7]

- In 2000, Harvard University produced a report showing that stakeholder-balanced companies showed four times the growth rate and eight times the employment growth when compared to companies that were shareholder-only focused.[8]

In addition, organisations, such as the UK-based financial institution the Co-operative Bank, which has long embraced CR, has released figures highlighting the direct business benefits. In 2002, the high street bank announced that its ethical positioning had contributed to 20 per cent of its overall profitability.[9] In 2004, a study by Echo Research of global CR-related press coverage showed that the bank, now part of Co-operative Financial Services, was ranked first in the UK and third worldwide in terms of positive coverage.[10]

UK telecommunications firm British Telecom has also linked its ethical policies to the maintenance of its brand, claiming that CR now accounts for more than 25 per cent of the impact of image and reputation on customer satisfaction.[11] Healthcare group BUPA is another company qualified to boast a boost in business turnover because of successful CR initiatives. Other global brands to have successfully integrated CR policies as part of their overall business strategy include Rio Tinto, Unilever, Canon and GE.

Institutional Investment

A decade ago, ethical investment simply meant avoiding arms manufacturers, tobacco companies, pharmaceuticals, petrochemicals and nuclear power generators. Today, it has a whole new meaning, and the commitment of a once cynical financial services community. Following Enron *et al.*, 'ethical' can now be measured in terms of corporate governance and CR practice, as well as industry sector. As such, ethical investment funds have grown considerably. In the UK, more than £120bn has been invested in institutional and retail funds with active Socially Responsible Investment (SRI) policies, with more than £100bn by insurance companies seeking investments with lower social and environmental risks.[12] According to US-based group the Social Investment Forum, CR screening measures have been used on more than $2 trillion in managed assets. A similar report by Russell Reynolds Associates showed that 50 per cent of European investors and 61 per cent of US investors had decided to reduce their portfolio or not to invest in a company because of poor governance.

> In 2003 Kraft Foods announced a partnership with action group the Rainforest Alliance to support sustainable coffee production in Mexico, Brazil, Colombia and Central America.
>
> The deal includes funding for technical training and the improvement of living standards on plantations and farms. It will also mean that increased quantities of certified sustainable coffee will reach European mainstream brands. The Rainforest Alliance together with the Sustainable Agriculture Network will grant certification.[13]

Despite this steady growth, the bulk of the investments are still almost entirely in retail mutual funds.[14] The capital markets have tried to redress this balance as part of their efforts to restore investor confidence. In 2001, the FTSE4GOOD index was launched, (which admittedly still excludes weapons manufacturers, nuclear energy producers and tobacco companies) but includes FTSE companies that have adopted CR policies. Since then, other initiatives designed to promote the benefits of good corporate governance and CR have appeared, including the Business in the Community Corporate Responsibility Index, which allows firms to compare their adoption of CR into core business operations against other companies in the same sector. Even pension fund trustees can now receive training on Socially Responsible Investment through the UK Sustainable Investment Forum.[15] Furthermore, all pension funds now have to annually disclose their level of achievement following SRI policy statements under the UK's Pensions Amendment Act 2003. UK insurers have also made similar adjustments to respective policies with the launch of investment disclosure guidelines as made by the Association of British Insurers (ABI).[16] Additional ethical indices have also been created including the Kempen Capital Management and SNS Asset Management Index.[17] The Socially Responsible Investment (SRI) index, which is the first of its kind, tracks the performance of smaller companies operating in Europe. Maintained by HSBC Bank, the index is made up of more than 70 companies from 14 countries. Europe now has around 300 SRI funds[18] attracting investment from international pension funds.

America's capital market has also responded to the growing number of ethical investors. The Dow-Jones Sustainability Group Index benchmarks the performance of investments in companies that have adopted SRI policies. Around 200 companies representing the top 10 per cent of firms that have already committed to CR are included in the index. Qualification includes an industry-related sustainability assessment, which looks at the integration of economic, environmental and social factors into strategy. Corporate governance and transparency are also given high priority. Regulation governing business ethics already exists, including the SEC and EPA regulations on corporate disclosure on environmental liabilities, and the Foreign Corrupt Practices Act, which legislates ethical company behaviour. Since Enron's collapse in 2001, however, the focus on CR has increased dramatically, as reflected in the number of new CR initiatives. These include the United States–Asia Environmental Partnership (US-AEP), which aims to improve Asia's many social, environmental, and industrial problems and encourage US companies to adopt CR policies as part of international operations. In 2001, Clean-Flo, a Minnesota-based water technology company, won contracts worth more than $1m to introduce their water body restoration systems to a number of Indian states through US-AEP. It has since submitted proposals to clean up the heavily polluted Yamuna River.[19] Influential business groups the Investors' Circle, Business for Social Responsibility and the Global Academy, work hard to keep CR on the American corporate agenda.

Although the UK, the USA and Europe can be seen as SRI fund trailblazers, other countries are quickly following suit. In 2004, Australia announced that it was creating its own CR index in an effort to persuade companies of the financial and performance benefits. The index's creation followed a report by the New South Wales Chamber of Commerce, which showed that one of the foremost disincentives for Australian businesses in engaging in CR was the complexity surrounding the measurement of returns from investment. The new index will cover key areas such as corporate strategy, integration, management (comprising community, environment, marketplace and workplace) as well as performance and impact.

Europe, the UK and the USA are not alone in trying to realign their respective capital markets. Thailand, India and Korea are all in active debate on how to best improve transparency in their home capital markets, amid drastic changes to their respective economies. The South African government has introduced tougher financial reporting regulations with heavy emphasis on HIV/AIDS-related CR and corporate governance compliance as the country's HIV/AIDS pandemic continues to accelerate. However, in 2003 Japan emerged as the leading market to adopt the international CR framework as devised by the Global Reporting Initiative. According to research by the Fujitsu Research Institute, more than half of the companies listed on the Tokyo Stock Exchange publicly disclosed information on their environmental performance.

The Equator Principles

In 2004, ten leading banks from seven countries adopted a voluntary set of guidelines developed by the banks for managing social and environmental issues related to the financing of development projects.

The Equator Principles, as they are known, are based on policies and guidelines set by the World Bank and the International Finance Corporation, and will be applied globally to project financings in all industry sectors, including mining, oil and gas, and forestry.

Loans will only be provided to projects whose sponsors can demonstrate their ability to comply with processes aimed at ensuring development will be socially and environmentally responsible.

The principles will use a screening process for projects based on IFC's environmental and social screening process. Projects will be categorised as A, B or C (high, medium or low environmental or social risk) by the banks, using common terminology. For A and B projects (high and medium risk), the borrower will complete an Environmental Assessment addressing the environmental and social issues identified in the categorisation process.

After appropriate consultation with affected local stakeholders, category A projects, and category B projects where appropriate, will prepare Environmental Management Plans which address mitigation and monitoring of environmental and social risks.

The banks to have adopted the principles so far are ABN AMRO Bank NV, Barclays PLC, Citigroup, Inc., Credit Lyonnais, Credit Suisse First Boston, HVB Group, Rabobank, Royal Bank of Scotland, WestLB AG, and Westpac Banking Corporation.

Case Study: ExxonMobil

In 1989, the oil tanker *Exxon Valdez* ran aground the treacherous Bligh Reef as it navigated the Prince William Sound en route to California. As a result, more than one million barrels of oil spilt into the sea. According to reports, the third mate, who was not qualified to take the tanker into the sound, was at the helm at the time of the disaster. A later investigation showed that the ship's captain, along with high numbers of the crew, had been drinking to excess.

But as thick black oil spilled into the sea, Exxon refused to communicate. It did eventually release details of what procedures it followed in the event of such disaster, but as film footage showed, these were a failure. Within two days, despite relatively calm seas, the spillage had spread into a 12-square mile slick. The arrival of bad weather made containment impossible. Yet Lawrence Rawl, Exxon's chairman, still refused to comment. Instead Frank Larossi, director of Exxon Shipping, was sent to the site to deal with the hostile press, environmentalists and townspeople.

It was not enough, and Rawl finally agreed to be interviewed. However, the interview did not go well. When asked what were Exxon's latest clean-up plans, Rawl said he did not know. When questioned why, he added that it was not part of his responsibilities as chairman.

The spill cost Exxon $7bn, of which $5bn was in fines for poor corporate responsibility. Exxon went from being the largest oil company in the world to the third largest. The company not only demonstrated ineffective risk management, but poor leadership and an indifferent attitude to the environmental destruction. Since then, the oil giant has made a considerable effort to improve its reputation. However, its views on climate change remain controversial. In 2002 environmental action group Greenpeace launched its aggressive shame campaign 'Exxon's weapons of mass deception'. The group accused Exxon of waging a 'cynical self-interested war' by derailing climate talks. In 2004 Exxon was issued official requests to improve its environmental policies from several leading New York pension funds.

Accountability

> More corporate democracy and better corporate behaviour will go a long way to improve the current business culture in the eyes of the public, but unless these changes are accompanied by a new version of the purpose of business, they will be seen as mere palliatives.
>
> (Charles Handy, *Harvard Business Review*, December 2002)

In today's highly competitive market, brand is undoubtedly king, therefore protecting the reputation of intangible assets is paramount. Recent research by advertising group Interbrand showed that 96 per cent of Coca-Cola's value is now in intangibles; in the case of Kellog's, 97 per cent; for American Express, 84 per cent.[20] Reputation management experts have long agreed that it is easier to build a reputation from scratch than to improve one damaged by scandal. One such example is mineral water giant Perrier, which never fully recovered its loyal customer base following the benzene contamination disaster in 1990. Despite accounting for 60 per cent of all mineral water sold in the UK, the scandal saw Perrier's market share plummet to 9 per cent.[21] Much of this can be attributed to the emotional way in which the public responds to corporate failure. A study by the Reputation Institute and Harris Interactive Inc in 1999, which took into account the views of more than 10,000 respondents, showed that consumers relate to basic primordial issues such as bargains, safety, trust and honesty.[22]

Although the media plays a significant role in highlighting corporate foul-ups, the Internet has become an even bigger threat to corporate and brand reputation. From self-starter rogue websites, to shareholder action groups, the Internet can have a significant effect on an organisation's reputation and accountability. In 2004, Greenpeace won a legal battle allowing it to continue parodying Esso's corporate logo through its campaign website www.stopesso.com. Esso's attempt to 'silence' the NGO provoked thousands of complaints to the company's board, and even led to an online design contest to create more parody logos.

Only by enhancing relationships with its stakeholders can a company truly create value. According to Jane Nelson, business leadership and strategy director at the International Business Forum,[23] CR innovators have quickly recognised the need to 'integrate' CR principles and values into core business structures and strategies. Accountability is then clearly traced to the executive management team and board, with some companies even integrating performance targets to SRI into management appraisals. Nelson adds that companies such as Shell, Procter & Gamble, Nokia and 3M have already introduced internal venture capital funds, competitions and other incentives to encourage a 'culture of innovation'. These companies are also working with government and voluntary agencies and NGOs to generate debate and accepted institutional frameworks. Such voluntary initiatives include the UN Global Compact, the Ethical Trading Initiative and the Global Alliance for Workers and Communities.

An Ernst & Young report in 2002 revealed that 94 per cent of CEOs interviewed believed CSR strategy could deliver real business benefits. A study by Hill & Knowlton's Reputation Watch found that one out of three executives thought that CSR would increase sales.

Employee Attraction and Retention

According to a study by US human capital consultants Aon, workers are now more concerned over control of their working time, intellectual challenge and working for an organisation with a clear vision and values than pay.[24] This, coupled with an ever-evolving employment landscape that has seen decline in manufacturing and growth in the services sector, has led to a greater awareness of corporate impact than perhaps experienced by the previous generation. Many organisations have acknowledged this fundamental shift in priorities; viewing their workforce not as a cost, but as an asset that needs serious investment. Attracting talent has therefore become like a male peacock's display – boastful and beautiful. Societal, environmental and workplace achievements and programmes have become a familiar element of job adverts, reflecting the high priority given to the triple-bottom line by potential applicants, and the recognition by corporations that successful CR is a commitment to all stakeholders.

As a result, benchmarking workplace indices, similar to those created by *Sunday Times* and *Fortune Magazine*, are increasingly hotbeds of competition, with companies desperate to publicly demonstrate full, equal and diverse commitment to their workforce. Companies such as Xerox, still recovering from its own painful accounting irregularities scandal, are now proud to be recognised for their support of ethnic and gender diversity. The document company was featured in no less than 12 workplace rankings in 2003, including being named as one of the most powerful and gay-friendly public companies. It was even awarded the accolade of being one of the best lesbian places to work by *Girlfriend Magazine*.

But the motives go beyond philanthropic idealism. According to a report by professional services firm PricewaterhouseCoopers (PwC) of more than 1,000 organisations in 47 countries, companies that had good human resources strategies boasted higher revenues of up to 35 per cent. The study also highlighted that successful people management resulted in increased employee productivity, employee satisfaction, as well as reduced absenteeism, a problem that currently costs the UK an estimated £13bn a year. Other studies have shown that good CR also helps to reduce high staff turnover as traditionally associated with the catering industry, increases organisational effectiveness through departmental co-operation, and enhances brand awareness and protection. In fact, many experts believe that a talented, motivated workforce is now essential in creating a competitive advantage, especially within the service sector where employees have direct contact with customers. According to an Institute of Employment Studies report on a leading British retailer, a one-point increase in an employee commitment score represented a 9 per cent increase in monthly sales. Health care group BUPA claims that since launching their 'Taking care of lives in our hands' initiative, it has boosted employee satisfaction by 20 per cent, and turnover by 39 per cent over three years.

CR in the workplace, however, is by definition a complex discipline. Benchmarks range from ethnic/gender equality and diversity, health and safety practice, training (research shows that companies with UK employment standard Investors in People outstrip the national average in business performance), to human rights policies – all of which have to be maintained across the enterprise. Multinationals such as Shell, which publishes an annual CR report, work hard to ensure that such standards are kept across all operations, using key performance indicators to measure success – and failure. Such intense data mining, while helping to achieve long-term shareholder value, not only safeguards reputation and improves risk management policies, but also demonstrates social accountability; an important factor when governments of developing countries are considering foreign investment that they know will create substantial social and environmental impact.

We believe that our employees are one of our strongest assets and by giving them the opportunity to do what they do best everyday, our employees feel engaged and fulfilled in their roles. Our vision is to create an environment where great people can do their best work and realise their potential.

(Stephen Harvey, director of people and culture at Microsoft, winner of the 2003 *Sunday Times* 'Great Place to Work' study)

Innovation

While it is true that many business leaders view legislation as merely suppressive, embracing regulation within the corporate responsibility agenda can in fact stimulate creativity. According to the Business in the Community Fast Forward report, 80 per cent of European CEOs believe that responsible business practice allows companies to be creative. As CR affords an enterprise-wide view, organisations are able to put better risk management policies in place, not only equipping them with the appropriate strategies to cope with the unexpected, but allowing them to take advantage of market opportunities (see Chapter 11 on Enterprise Risk for a more detailed explanation).

Instead of seeing a problem, innovators see a business or market opportunity or a means of improving efficiency or maintaining competitiveness. Organisations should also be willing to pursue 'parasitic' partnerships or joint ventures in which all parties benefit. Nike, for example, has programmes in place with six of its material suppliers to collect 100 per cent of their scrap and recycle it into the next round of products, thereby reducing production costs and waste.[25]

Another example is Hewlett-Packard, which after discovering a demand for wedding and identity photos in India developed technology to enable low-cost picture taking and development, the HP Photoshop Store, where basic image development was licensed locally and a high quality solar-powered camera was used. The initiative sparked a cottage industry made possible through micro-lending. HP benefited as most of its margins are made through selling paper and providing replacement cartridges.[26]

Measuring and Reporting CR

Despite a growing willingness by the corporate community to adopt CR or sustainable development, its measurement and how to report it remain a highly contentious issue. At the time of writing this book, materiality was still without a universal definition, making it difficult for organisations to decide on what constitutes as an actual or potential CR 'risk' in today's increasingly complex and diverse marketplace. Furthermore, the growth of CR has led to an explosion of ethical league tables and benchmarks, all offering a different perspective of the discipline. This growth, in line with the information demanded by institutional investors from Socially Responsible Investment rating agencies, has led to an increased number of questionnaires being sent out to participating organisations, and confusion over the purpose. The SRI community has also been accused of failing to deliver realistic 'insights into quality of management'.[27] and not limiting enquiries to issues that have a 'significant effect' on value.

The confusion surrounding SRI reporting is worsened by the lack of a single standardised reporting framework, which has led to the creation of numerous initiatives, codes, and guidelines. All the while, stakeholder pressure to produce these reports is increasing. This too has led to some serious concerns over consistent clarity, and in 2004 it was claimed by a handful of analysts that a number of PLCs were starting to 'spin' their CR reports in the fear that failure could lead to substantial loss in

Table 10.1. The SRI community

Category	Examples
SRI fund managers	Insight, Jupiter and ISIS
Indices	SAM
	The Dow-Jones Sustainability Group Index FTSE4Good
	Business in the Community's environment and CR indices
SRI research and screening agencies	Storebrand
	EIRIS
Pressure groups	Consumers' Association
	Naturewatch

Source: Arthur D. Little (2003) 'Speaking the Same Language; Improving Communications between Companies and Investors on Corporate Responsibility'. Available online at: www.adl.com

investment terms. Bad news, including environmental fines or health and safety figures, was being hidden deep within reports as throwaway facts bearing no relation to the glowing successes accompanied by glossy photography of happy smiling faces.

There are other dilemmas. Defining stakeholder priorities, matching expectations set by early innovators, and ultimately financial cost. Because the discipline is a relatively new dimension in corporate undertaking, CR is in constant development. Until now, organisations have been in control of what and how they report. However, it is likely that the same legislative influence exerted by stakeholders on financial reporting will further influence CR reporting before long. The largest obstacle organisations face is that no formal framework yet exists to enable them to carry out a comprehensive cost–benefit analysis.

Despite all these problems, and the obvious need for better dialogue between the investment community, rating agencies, and the organisations themselves, CR reporting can substantially add value (Table 10.1). Organisations that readily embrace Enterprise Governance will find that they not only have much of the information already available, but the internal management and information systems needed to provide relevant and reliable CR reports.

Materiality Explained

Defining materiality has so far proved problematic, both for legislators and professional organisations. Technically, material issues are those which have a non–financial risk at an operational level, or an impact on business performance; and which are relevant to stakeholder interests. However, organisations not only face common risks, such as those shared by the business community or industry sector as a whole, but unique risks or opportunities. As a consequence, legislative bodies have been reluctant to define materiality through law, even though there are a number of legal cases in the USA for alleged misrepresentation of non–financial performance by US companies. Organisations therefore need not only to identify material issues, but also to demonstrate transparent governance to avoid legal action and secure professional indemnity assurance; if premiums have not risen beyond reach that is.

AccountAbility, an international non–profit membership-based institute created to promote accountability for sustainable development, has worked extensively with governments and legislators on redefining materiality. The group has developed a 'materiality approach', which involves a five-stage test in determining what should be publicly disclosed.[28]

1   The traditional *direct short-term financial impacts* of sustainability performance, i.e. where they appear as significant items on profit and loss or balance sheets.
2   Aspects of *policy-based performance* where agreed policy positions of a strategic nature exist, irrespective of short-term financial consequences.

3 *Peer-based norms*, which can be determined where a company's peers are deeming and disclosing issues and aspects of performance to be material.

4 *Stakeholder behaviour and concerns*, which are relevant to organisations where this is reasonable evidence that their stakeholders' perspectives on the company are likely to impact decisions and behaviour. Stakeholder views are not sufficient to be deemed as material alone – behavioural change makes it material.

5 The consideration of *societal norms*. Beyond regulation, the test would include aspects of performance that are likely to become regulated in the future.

Reporting

> We define sustainable development reports as public reports by companies to provide internal and external stakeholders with a picture of corporate position and activities on economic, environmental and social dimensions. In short, such reports attempt to describe the company's contribution towards sustainable development.
>
> (The World Business Council for
> Sustainable Development)

Most reporting frameworks or guidelines are based on the triple-bottom line (Table 10.2), with some integrating financial

Table 10.2. The triple bottom line

Category	Sub-categories
Economic	Profitability, wages and benefits, resource use, job creation, outsourcing
Environmental	Processes, products and services on the environment
Social	Health and safety, employee relations, ethics, human rights, working conditions

performance. Essentially, CR and sustainable development reports ask businesses to acknowledge responsibility for their impact on both the community and environment.

Companies need to define what the overall purpose of the report is, who their audience is, what the relevant issues are, in what format it will be published (very few organisations publish electronically despite the obvious environmental advantages), and whether feedback from stakeholders, such as NGOs, will be included.[29] Organisations also need to define who is responsible for the report, as well as ensuring that the appropriate systems are in place to collect and measure the data needed. The report will then need to be audited both internally and externally.

Due to the complexity and confusion surrounding CR and sustainable development reporting, the World Business Council for Sustainable Development launched a 'reporting portal'[30] – an online service bringing together examples of how other WBCSD members are reporting. The site divides the core reporting approaches into four categories:

- *Company context* – information on top management commitment, company profile, impacts and market position.
- *Governance* – information on strategies, policies, management systems, stakeholder engagement, risk management and business opportunities.
- *Performance* – information on KPIs specific to CR.
- *Assurance* – the advantages of third party observations in promoting credibility and reliability.

The organisation, a coalition of 160 international companies from more than 30 countries and 20 industrial sectors, has dedicated itself to promoting sustainable development through eco-efficiency, innovation, and corporate responsibility. Members include 3M, Nokia, Petro-Canada, Toyota and ChevronTexaco.

Frameworks – the Global Reporting Initiative

In response to rising criticism over the number of 'loose' and inadequate frameworks being created, the Global Reporting Initiative (GRI) was created. The initiative, which is supported by business, NGOs, trade unions, investor institutions and accounting bodies, aims to disseminate and develop global sustainable reporting guidelines for individual industry sectors. More than 300 companies in 44 countries have adopted the guidelines, which include both reporting principles and content indicators. Among the UK firms to use GRI are AstraZeneca, British American Tobacco, Sainsbury's, mmO2 and Diageo. US firms include Abbott Laboratories, Anheuser–Busch Companies, Dupont and Hewlett-Packard. Those in mainland Europe include Carrefour, Saint-Gobain, Siemens and Volkswagen.

The GRI has also developed guidelines for companies wanting to report performance, policies and practice with respect to HIV/AIDS. The framework, which was initially funded by the Bill and Melinda Gates Foundation, enables companies to increase CR credibility and allows stakeholders to measure and compare with sector competitors.

How does GRI work? Through a series of 'tools' the GRI guidelines[31] enable users to do the following:

- measure and benchmark performance against their own targets and their competitors;
- increase comparability and reduce transaction costs of sustainability when GRI is used as the generally accepted reporting framework;
- ensure brand and reputation are not damaged by the action of others along the supply chain.

The benefits of GRI framework reporting include:

- helping increase the financial bottom line by identifying areas of waste and new business opportunity;

- providing a common language and set of indicators that can be used to discuss performance among stakeholders and reduce 'survey fatigue';
- providing valuable information on changing stakeholder interests and demands for legislation;
- offering one of the few forums where key stakeholder groups convene as equals to discuss and advance sustainability.

The GRI claims that the guidelines can also help companies reduce the volume and variety of information processed, while increasing focus and value. According to research by the initiative, GRI indicators cover around 80 per cent of indicators commonly sought in SRI ratings and surveys. The group also recommends its indicators to stakeholders looking to measure the quality of a company's corporate governance practices. Because the development costs of both the guidelines and other GRI documents are shared among its multiple users, the overall costs are lower than developing one's own company or own sector framework. The guidelines are also in constant development. Technical protocols for each individual indicator are being created to provide 'detailed definitions, formulae and references to ensure consistency across reports'. Moreover, the guidelines offer a commonly shared 'language' for investors, stakeholders, companies and regulators alike.

Other Voluntary Standards and Frameworks

In March 2003, UK-based non-profit business institute Account-Ability launched its AA1000AS international standard for sustainability assurance in an effort to improve the quality of assurance statements by independent auditors. The European Federation of Accountants (FEE), which is urging companies to carry out sustainability reports, believes that the standards will offer robust independent verification under one accepted methodology.

The AA1000AS recommends that assurors assess reports against the following principles:

- *Materiality*: does the report cover all the areas of performance that stakeholders need to judge the organisation's sustainability performance?
- *Completeness*: is the information complete and accurate enough to assess and understand the organisation's performance in all these areas?
- *Responsiveness*: has the organisation responded coherently and consistently to the stakeholders' concerns and interests?

SA800 – the Global Workplace Standard

Created by human rights organisation Social Accountability International,[32] the SA800 is based on international workplace norms in the ILO conventions and the UN's Universal Declaration of Human Rights and the Convention on Rights of the Child. Issues measured and reported on include:

1 *Child labour* – no workers under the age of 15; minimum age lowered to 14 for countries operating under the ILO Convention 138 developing-country exception; remediation of any child found to be working.
2 *Forced labour* – no forced labour, including prison or debt bondage labour; no lodging of deposits or identity papers by employers or outside recruiters.
3 *Health and safety* – provide a safe and healthy work environment; take steps to prevent injuries; regular health and safety worker training; system to detect threats to health and safety; access to bathrooms and potable water.
4 *Freedom of association and right to collective bargaining* – respect the right to form and join trade unions and bargain collectively; where the law prohibits these freedoms, facilitate parallel means of association and bargaining.

5 *Discrimination* – no discrimination based on race, caste, origin, religion, disability, gender, sexual orientation, union or political affiliation, or age; no sexual harassment.

6 *Discipline* – no corporal punishment, mental or physical coercion or verbal abuse.

7 *Working hours* – comply with the applicable law but, in any event, no more than 48 hours per week with at least one day off for every seven-day period; voluntary overtime paid at a premium rate and not to exceed 12 hours per week on a regular basis; overtime may be mandatory if part of a collective bargaining agreement.

8 *Compensation* – wages paid for a standard work week must meet the legal and industry standards and be sufficient to meet the basic need of workers and their families; no disciplinary deductions.

9 *Management systems* – facilities seeking to gain and maintain certification must go beyond simple compliance to integrate the standard into their management systems and practices.

Other internationally recognised standards include environmental standard ISO 14001, which is popular with the manufacturing sector, the GHG Protocol, and the Global Compact. Organisations, such as Business in the Community, have also developed their own reporting guidelines in addition to CR benchmarking indices. The group has also created recognised CR programmes such as Community Cares, which enables companies to regularly take part in local volunteer projects. In recent years they have focused their efforts on engaging the SME community, with the creation of the pioneering CommunityMark award programme, which officially acknowledges a company's societal contribution. International non-profit organisation the Ethical Trade Initiative[33] (ETI) offers its members a comprehensive reporting framework created around its own base code. The framework focuses on labour conditions, monitoring of company supply chain, complaint mechanisms, relationships with NGOs and trade unions, communication, and effectiveness of any corrective actions. Reports are then reviewed against assessment criteria, taking into account how long the company has been a member, the length of time it has been running an ethical monitoring programme, and the degree of year-on-year progress. Based on this assessment, each company will be categorised into one of five benchmarking indices.

It is important to remember, however, that CR reporting frameworks cannot be approached with a one-size-fits-all mentality. CR has many different interpretations, depending on the company, its size, industry sector, and geographical location. For example, a dotcom does not have the same environmental impact as a manufacturing complex, but it does consume energy. It can also be a costly discipline to implement, even though the end results will ultimately create value and save on costs, and therefore serves as a long-term strategy. Although it is easy to get 'bogged down' in the detail, it's as important to start measuring as it is to decide on what can be measured. CR reporting is an emerging concept for companies and stakeholders. Its development and progression needs time.

Case Study: What Good CR Means to Tesco

Over the past 12 years UK-based supermarket group Tesco has donated £21m to charity through its own foundation the Tesco Charity Trust and other schemes, and donated £77m in IT and communication technology to UK schools. The company also donates 1 per cent of pre-tax profits to charity.

Key performance indicators (KPIs) are set by the CR Committee. The company uses a Steering Wheel scorecard system, which is divided into four quads – people, customer, operations and finance. KPIs based on staff, customer and public opinion are then set within those quads. Management bonuses are based on the achievement of objectives, on a sliding scale. The CSR-devoted website is updated every two months and the company goes to great lengths to maintain total transparency in its trading and decision-making processes.

Essentially Tesco has divided its CR policies into three categories:

1 *Being a good employer* – Tesco makes it its policy to listen to all its staff. In 2002, it introduced a 'back to the shop floor' scheme for senior management. A wide number of training schemes are run, as well as an internal talent-spotting initiative. Its pension scheme, the Pension Builder, is based on career average earnings and not the traditional final end salary. As a result, the pension does not depend on stock market performance.

2 *Making a positive contribution to the community* – Tesco listens to the staff within each of its stores in an effort to understand the local issues. It also actively encourages a culture of CR throughout the organisation. In 2002, more than £1m was raised through collecting the old mobile phones and cartridges donated by staff.

3 *Reducing environmental impact* – In 2002, Tesco reduced its CO_2 emissions by 45,000 tonnes. In the Business in the Community environmental index it came 28th out of 186 companies, and third in its sector scoring more than 90 per cent. As well as being listed on both the FTSE4Good and Ethibel ethical investment indices, it operates an Ethical Trading Initiative, through which every buyer and technical manager is sent for ethical trading management training. The supermarket is a member of the Fairtrade Foundation, and has even set up its own Fairtrade banana programme. The chain has also set up a number of research facilities including the Tesco Organic Centre at Newcastle University and a food animal welfare centre, which tests the best environments for animal welfare. It discovered, for example, that chickens are happiest when roaming free in wooded areas. The chicken raised in these conditions is sold under Tesco's Finest brand.

Case Study: Johnson & Johnson

In 1982, Johnson & Johnson's popular painkiller Tylenol (acetaminophen) was deliberately contaminated with cyanide, killing seven people. At the time the drug, which represented around 15 per cent of Johnson's profits, was one of America's leading over-the-counter painkillers. As a result of the contamination, the company's capitalisation fell by $1bn. No one could have predicted that the same situation would repeat itself four years later – but it did. Johnson immediately ordered a nationwide recall, and set about developing tamperproof packaging. Only then would it re-release Tylenol onto the shelves.

The costs involved were extensive, but the company was rewarded for its quick and decisive action. Not only did it recover 70 per cent of the market share within six months, it continued to dominate the analgesic painkiller market.

The Future

There can be no doubt that CR in the future will have considerable impact on the 'true and fair view' of a company's financial performance. It has also been suggested that reporting will soon extend outside of the organisation and across the value chain; reflecting both the supplier and consumer impact of products and services.[34] Stakeholder focus will be on where an organisation is heading, not where it has been. The work of non-profit business institutions, such as Investors' Circle, the Global Reporting Initiative, Business in the Community, has undoubtedly achieved the attention and support of large organisations, but the SME community still needs to be effectively engaged. The benefits of CR are not just for the FTSE and Fortune 100.

Risks such as climate change will continue to register highly with stakeholders. In fact, factoring climate change has already become a core strategy principle for many energy producers and large manufacturers. According to the Coalition for Environmentally Responsible Economies (CERES), a company's 'response to threats and opportunities of climate change can have a material bearing on shareholder value'. Dow, General Motors, IBM, and Johnson & Johnson have all chosen to invest in renewable energies as a positive CSR benchmark. Almost 100 megawatts of renewable energy has been purchased through the Green Power Market Development Group, preventing 960 million pounds of carbon dioxide being emitted.[35]

Although progress has been made, there is still a distance to go. In a report by the Investor Responsibility Research Centre (IRRC), which provides impartial research to institutional investors with $5 trillion in assets, only half of the 20 global companies reviewed demonstrated sufficient compliance to realistically address climate change. The report, which included the five largest producers of greenhouse gases, and five large manufacturing companies, used a 14-point checklist to measure both corporate governance and CR compliance including materiality, executive payment, board oversight and emissions reports. Topping the list were BP and Shell with a maximum 14 points. ExxonMobil, General Electric and TXU only succeeded in addressing four. According to the IRRC, although most carbon-emitting companies were talking about global warming, many were failing to take the issue seriously, which was ultimately reflected in their reporting.

Case Study: Alcoa[36]

Alcoa is the world's leading producer of primary aluminium, fabricated aluminium and alumina, and is active in all major aspects of the industry. In addition to aluminium products and components, Alcoa also markets consumer brands including Reynolds Wrap® foils and plastic wraps, Alcoa® wheels, and Baco® household wraps. Among its other businesses are vinyl siding, closures, fastening systems, precision castings, and electrical distribution systems for cars and trucks. The company has 120,000 employees in 41 countries.

Alcoa's total shareholder return for 2003 was more than 71 per cent, meaning US$100 invested (with dividends reinvested) at the beginning of the year would be worth more than US$171 as of 31 December, 2003. In comparison, the Dow-Jones Industrial Average returned approximately 28 per cent during the same period. Since publishing its strategic environmental targets in 2000, Alcoa has reduced water use by 16 per cent, land-filled waste by 44 per cent and greenhouse gas emissions by 25 per cent (from 1990). Alcoa also recorded the best lost workday and total recordable injury rates in the company's history. The lost workday rate improved to 0.12 from 0.15 the previous year. The total recordable rate was 1.66, down from 2.22 in 2002. Its Sustainability Report is fully integrated into the alcoa.com website to increase user friendliness, promote further exploration of the extensive information contained on alcoa.com, and provide an opportunity to update relevant information throughout the year.

'Performance rather than talk is Alcoa's way of demonstrating progress toward a sustainable future. Through our 2020 strategic framework, we have established clear targets to support our vision of becoming the best company in the world.' Chairman and CEO, Alain Belda.

Notes

1 J. F. Keefe (2002) *Five Trends: The Rise of Corporate Reputation and CSR*, NewCircle Communications.

2 D. Grayson and A. Hodges (2004) *Corporate Social Opportunity: Seven Steps to Make Corporate Responsibility Work for Your Business*, Greenleaf Publishing, p. 111.

3 *The Ecologist*, May 2004, p. 14.

4 Smith, 2001 – CSR Europe.

5 Available online at: www.ibe.org.uk/DBEPsumm.htm

6 SAM Indexes GmBH (2003), Results of DJSI Review, see www.sustainability-indexes.com

7 Schmidt (2000), see www.socialfunds.com

8 Harvard University, see www.socialfunds.com

9 Available online at: www.co-operativebank.co.uk

10 Echo Research, CSR and the Financial Community: Friends or Foes (2004). Available online at www.echoresearch.com

11 Independently conducted research, source CSR Europe.

12 SRI: 'A Global Revolution' Russell Sparkes, 2002.

13 www.Greenbiz.com, a site created and operated by Green Business Network, a project of The National Environmental Education & Training Foundation, a 501(c)(3) nonprofit organisation based in Washington, DC.

14 European Business Campaign for Corporate Social Responsibility Excellence Report, 2002. Available online at: www.csrcampaign.org

15 Ibid.

16 Ibid.

17 Global Reporting Initiative website, see www.globalreporting.org

18 CSR Europe/Taylor Nelson Sofres 2001.

19 The United States–Asia Environmental Partnership (US–AEP) website, www.usaep.org

20 Available online at: www.Socialfunds.com

21 PwC (2002) 'Reputational Risk: Word of Mouth Now Has Global Reach', *Risky Business*, Issue 2a (Global Risk Management Solutions).

22 Ibid.

23 CSR Europe Excellence Report 2002.

24 The Corporate Citizenship Company (2003) *Good Companies, Better Employees*, ed. M. Tuffrey.

25 Arthur D. Little (2003), 'The Business Case for Corporate Responsibility'. Available online at: www.adl.com

26 Nicole Boyer and Global Business Network (2004) 'The Base of the Pyramid: Re-perceiving Business from the Bottom Up'. See www.gbn.com

27 Arthur D. Little (2003) 'Speaking the Same Language; Improving Communications between Companies and Investors on Corporate Responsiblity'. Available online at: www.adl.com

28 AccountAbility (2003) 'Redefining Materiality'. Available online at: www.accountability.org.uk

29 World Business Council for Sustainable Development (2002) *Sustainable Development Reporting – Striking the Balance*. Available online at: www.wbcsd.org

30 Available online at: www.wbcsd.org

31 Global Reporting Initiative website, www.globalreporting.org

32 www.sa-intl.org

33 www.eti.org.uk

34 World Business Council for Sustainable Development, *Sustainable Development Reporting*.

35 www.socialfunds.com

36 www.alcoa.com

CHAPTER 11

RISK MANAGEMENT

The Importance of Risk

Case Study: Bridgestone/Firestone and Ford

In August 2000, Japanese tyre manufacturer Bridgestone/ Firestone was forced to recall 6.5 million of its ATX, ATX II and Wilderness AT tyres after the models were blamed for thousands of accidents and 271 deaths in the USA. The tyres in question were fitted onto the popular SUV (sports utility vehicle), the Ford Explorer. Despite making the recall, Bridgestone blamed the vehicle's design, and Ford blamed the tyres. The fall-out temporarily ended a 95-year-long business relationship between the two companies. Although Bridgestone continued to sell tyres to Ford worldwide, it no longer supplied its car manufacturing plants. A few months later, however, the recall was widened to a further 3.5 million tyres.

Following legal action, Bridgestone was ordered to pay a $51.5m settlement related to the advertising and sale of tyres with high rates of tread separation. Ford was also forced to pay $51.5m when it faced legal action following allegations of 'deceptive trade practices' in connection with the faulty tyres. The action alleged that the company continued to use the tyres after it knew that they made the Ford Explorer more likely to roll over. Ford has spent around $2bn in replacement tyres.

For many senior executives the word 'risk' is associated with business failure, fraud, brand devaluation, and ultimately the destruction of shareholder value. Many companies have seen their share prices plummet because of an overly ambitious business strategy or, indeed, an under-developed one. But there is substantial evidence to suggest that if CEOs understand their organisation's risk profile, and put in place strategies and mechanisms to deal with them accordingly, they will generate superior shareholder returns year on year.

According to Puschaver and Eccles[1] risk can be broken down into three definitions:

1   *Risk as hazard* – resources are allocated to reduce the probability or impact of a negative event. This reflects a traditional defensive or non-opportunistic view of risk.
2   *Risk as uncertainty or variance* – controls are put in place to focus on the distribution of outcomes. Their purpose is to reduce the variance between anticipated outcomes and the actual results, reflecting a 'hedging your bets' approach to risk management.
3   *Risk as opportunity* – where direct actions achieve positive gains for a firm in this investment-focused approach. As such, a growth strategy is required due to the implicit relationship between risk and return. Therefore risk is an opportunity more proactive in nature.

Risk is therefore a key part of the business landscape and understanding its relationship to performance, conformance and returns to shareholders is a key competency. As such, risk is inextricably tied to governance and social responsibility. Enterprise Governance provides the necessary framework to not only manage risk successfully but optimise its potential.

A survey by CFO Europe and KPMG found that 26 per cent of organisations had established a Risk Management Committee in 2003, with 15 per cent of respondents saying that they were intending to do so in 2004.[2]

A survey of companies globally by the CODA Group found a striking difference between the USA and the UK regarding primary responsibility for risk management. The study showed that in the UK 43 per cent of businesses have given ultimate responsibility to the CFO but this figure rises to 81 per cent for US businesses. Only 19 per cent of the participants appointed had a dedicated risk director, but the UK led the way with 38 per cent of businesses having done so.[3]

Shareholder Value and Risk – Analysis and Determination

The determination of shareholder value through value analysis methodologies is already quite well developed and helps focus the risk management process on the value drivers that are key for managing threats and opportunities.

Shareholder value analysis provides an easy quantitative framework that can be used to evaluate the impact of possible risk scenarios. In most cases, risk impact will be related to the impact on future cash flow from operations, but the shareholder value model will show that other drivers like financial structure, taxation and market outlooks are also of importance. Likelihoods of risk scenarios could be supported by historical and bench-marking information. On the other hand, it could be assessed on a subjective basis to be able to predict the risks more reliably than historical data, certainly when new activities are commenced.

However, the area of managing risk is often not well understood by stakeholders. Work still has to be done on the relationship between the company risk profile and the common industry risk profile. In the future, the impact of risk management programmes will be determined by assessing the impact of risk management activities on the company risk profile. The shareholder value model will likely provide the framework for assessing this impact, which may be a more comprehensive way of assessing risk management activities than by quantifying impact and probability of each risk scenario. Assessing the changes in the probability distribution curve describing the possible future cash flow scenarios that are reflected in shareholder value calculation may do this. Information technology will facilitate better processing of the building blocks of shareholder value and generate further questions as more layers of the picture are revealed.

So What is Risk?

The sources of risk, and their magnitude, have changed dramatically over the past decade. Climate change, global health pandemics, terrorism, war, vulnerability of infrastructure, controversial technology, political upheaval, even obesity; are all new challenges to business and governments alike. These 'mega' risks are the product of globalisation; and not only to business, but to society and economies as a whole. There is the belief that mega risks only affect large multinational organisations. But the nature of globalisation means that even SMEs rely on global supply-chains and global markets thanks to the Internet and the growing adoption of e-commerce. Most of these problems are of such monumental significance, it is difficult for one party to accept responsibility. Changing the anticipated effects will also take time. Therefore mega risks are the responsibility of business, governments, and stakeholders alike.

Examples of Recent 'Mega' Risks

- Between 1990–99, the US Federal Emergency Management Agency (FEMA), spent $25.4bn on disasters and emergencies, compared to $3.9bn the previous decade; man-made or man-influenced catastrophes are said to be on the increase.
- The UK's BSE crisis is estimated to have cost £4.3bn; the costs were blamed on short-sighted decisions, and a loss of confidence in the UK meat market.
- The insured property loss following the terrorist attacks on 9/11 add up to more than $19bn; the financial loss exceeds damages caused by a natural disaster.
- World energy production rose from 6,600 to 9,352 million tonnes between 1980 and 2000 – an increase of 42 per cent. Future energy consumption is expected to increase by an additional 66 per cent by 2030; the mix of energy sources is expected to remain unchanged.
- By 2024, populations will remain static in developed countries; most of the world's population will be born in developing economies. Developed countries will also experience serious issues brought on by an ageing population.
- The market capitalisation of physical assets is reducing rapidly. Recent studies show that up to 75 per cent comes from intangibles.
- Water scarcity is already a major global problem; an estimated 2.3 billion people (41 per cent of the world's population) face severe water shortages. That number is expected to rise to 3.5 billion people by 2025.
- Viruses such as the MYDOOM virus, which affected two-thirds of the world's computer systems, demonstrate how vulnerable our connections are.

- In the past 20 years, AIDS has killed more than 21 million people in some of the world's poorest countries. Economic development has subsequently been seriously affected.[4]

Risk and Stakeholder Activism

Since 2001, investor relations with public companies have at best been strained. Senior executives, once revered for their business prowess and ability, are now having their actions and decisions scrutinised by stakeholders, legislators and institutional investors. Stakeholders are no longer content to let companies operate behind a corporate veil. Instead they are demanding transparency – and with an ever powerful voice. As the number of people adopting defined contribution retirement plans increases, so too does the interest in managerial decisions over corporate governance and CR issues that could ultimately reduce investor return. The California Public Employees' Retirement Systems,[5] one of the most powerful institutional investors in the USA, has not only succeeded in forcing board room changes, but regularly monitors corporate governance practices. Any company failing to reach acceptable standards is then named and shamed on its website as part of an annual governance index. Other fund managers have followed suit, including the Hermes UK Focus Fund, which lets CalPERS vote on Hermes shares in the US market and vice versa. Frankfurt-based Union Investment Gesellschaft has also created its own version of a name and shame index.

In 2004, the NYC Police Department, which has funds worth more than $150m, the NYC Fire Department, which holds funds worth more than $7m, and the New York City Teachers Retirement System, which holds more than $223m,[6] filed a series of shareholder proposals to giant ExxonMobil through New York City Comptroller William C. Thompson Jr. The proposals urged the company to implement renewable energy principles and to adopt a company-wide workplace human rights policy. A third proposal called for the implementation of the MacBride principles – a set of guidelines created by the Irish human rights advocate and a founder of Amnesty International Dr Sean MacBride, in order to create equal opportunity employment guidelines in Exxon's Northern Ireland operations. The proposals came on the back of an earlier demand to adopt policies that specifically barred discrimination based on sexual orientation made by the NYC Employees' Retirement System. The fund holds shares worth around $446m with ExxonMobil.

In France, the number of socially responsible investment funds has grown substantially over the past three years. According to the Novethic Indicator, a resource centre for SRI, French investors could choose from 108 funds by the end of 2003, as opposed to 80 in 2002 and 60 in 2001. The report showed that the total assets under management had risen to 4.4bn Euros compared to 2.5bn a year earlier. Much of this growth is being attributed to the decision by BNP Paribas Asset Management to switch retirement funds worth 550m Euros to SRI management, thereby creating a significant bond fund beating that of IDEAM (Credit Lyonnais) and AXA IM.

Risk and the e-Reputation Revolution

Organisations are quickly realising that investor power is growing in strength and is here to stay. Ensuring stakeholder value and brand sustainability needs enterprise-wide management and the correct technology to communicate timely, accurate information. But investor and stakeholder dissatisfaction is not always vented at annual general meetings (AGMs). The Internet has become a useful and far-reaching tool for the unhappy customer and shareholder. Although an increasing number of organisations are implementing systems to track their corporate and consumer reputation, many are failing to manage them properly.

The Internet offers an unhappy customer, employer or supplier the opportunity to vent his or her spleen to millions, and in turn encourage others to share their similarly miserable experiences. And there are plenty of examples to spur organisations into action. In 1997, disgruntled customer David Felton built a 'rogue' website to convey his unhappiness with US food chain Dunkin' Donuts. Despite advertising four different types of milk, the chain was unable to offer Mr Felton skimmed milk, and when he complained through the appropriate channels his complaint went unanswered. The site, www. dunkindonuts.com, attracted millions of hits and it was not long before other unhappy customers began posting their complaints. Dunkin' Donuts, furious at the existence of the website and aware of the lasting damage it could cause to its reputation, threatened to sue Mr Felton. But in something of a u turn, decided to buy the site from him instead. It later adapted the site as its own official corporate website.

Other websites imparting the same level of annoyance and dissatisfaction to an audience of millions include www. mcspotlight and www.yourcompanysucks. Some sites exist to 'leak' sensitive information to the detriment of employees, investors and the consumer. In order to identify the real value of communication a true understanding of stakeholder needs is essential, since traditional PR and marketing are no longer sustainable, as they tend to be defensive or reactive.

Risk and Legislation

Since 2001, a number of financial institutions have announced that they will be unable to honour pension and life insurance obligations because of poor stock market returns and global economic downturn.

As a result, millions of investors have lost their life savings and will either have to rely on a state pension or work beyond retirement age. In response, governments quickly drew up legislation that would offer investors better protection and require banks and insurers to significantly improve their risk assessment.

Basel II

Basel II looks at the risk profile of a financial institution. It requests banks to set aside enough capital to buffer the transpiration of major risks and also the cumulative materialisation of a whole risk category. The code incorporates all areas of risk including strategic, market, credit and operational risk, and takes into account the effectiveness of controls introduced by the bank.

As such, a prudent risk management strategy can turn around the regulatory pressure to promote improvements in measurement, processes and transparency, allowing banks to gain competitive advantage from the inevitable changes in capital standards.

Managing Risk

Enterprise risk management is interrelated with corporate governance by providing information to the board of directors on the most significant risks, and how they are being managed.

It interrelates with performance management by providing risk-adjusted measures and internal controls, which are an integral part of enterprise risk management.

(The Committee of Sponsoring Organisations of the Treadway Commission (COSO) 2003)

In recent years, risk management has moved from minimalist compliance issues, such as fiduciary responsibility, to increased value enhancement and sophistication in the form of improved returns to shareholders. This forward-looking strategic approach, sometimes referred to as enterprise risk management, reconciles the assurance requirements of the board and stakeholders, and the need to better integrate risk management in decision making activity at all levels.[7] As a result, organisations are better equipped to assess risk and therefore manage it effectively, creating risk optimisation, risk awareness and accountability.

Although finance professionals have historically been responsible for risk management, they no longer have the monopoly on identification and measurement of risk. Risk assessment today is everyone's responsibility. However, accountants cannot put their feet up just yet. Re-insurance companies and auditors are quickly moving into this space. For finance to reinvent itself, it will have to be conscious of the competition.

From Risk Minimisation to Risk Optimisation

Many companies are realising that to generate greater shareholder value they will have to take more risk. However, the move from traditional risk minimisation to risk optimisation carries its own set of challenges. Companies must be prepared to establish clear ownership and accountability for risk at all organisational levels. Figure 11.1 shows the risk management cycle.

Establish a risk management group and set goals

A risk management group should be established whose task it is to conduct reviews of the risks, which include the risk of fraud, faced by the business. The group will need to assess the risk appetite of the business (i.e. the level of risk the company is prepared to accept). It should then begin the process of understanding and assessing risk, prioritising, and developing a strategy to deal with the risks identified. The risk management group should be responsible for reviewing systems and

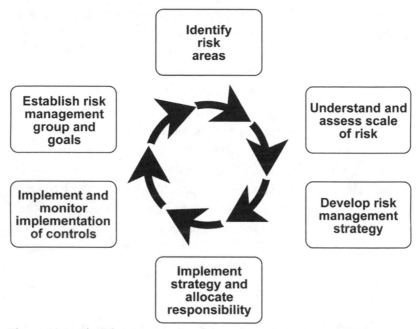

Figure 11.1. The risk management cycle.
Fraud Risk Management: A Guide to Good Practice, CIMA, London, 2001. Reproduced by permission of Chartered Institute of Management Accountants (CIMA).

procedures, identifying and assessing the risks, and introducing the controls that are best suited to the business unit.

Identify risk areas

Each risk in the overall risk model should be explored to identify how it potentially evolves through the organisation. It is important to ensure that the risk is carefully defined and explained to facilitate further analysis. The techniques of analysis include: workshops and interviews, brainstorming, questionnaires, process mapping, comparisons with other organisations, discussions with peers.

Understand and assess the scale of risk

Once risks have been identified, an assessment of possible impact and corresponding likelihood of occurrence should be made using consistent parameters that will enable the development of a prioritised risk analysis. In the planning stage, management should agree on the most appropriate definition and number of categories to be used when assessing both likelihood and impact. The assessment of the impact of the risk should not simply take account of the financial impact but should also consider the organisation's viability and reputation, and recognise the political and commercial sensitivities involved. The analysis should either be qualitative or quantitative, and should be consistent to allow comparisons. The qualitative approach usually involves grading risks in high, medium and low categories.

Impact

The assessment of the potential impact of a particular risk may be complicated by the fact that a range of possible outcomes may exist or that the risk may occur a number of times in a given period of time. Such complications should be anticipated and a consistent approach adopted which, for example, may seek to estimate a worst case scenario over, say, a 12-month time period.

Likelihood of occurrence

The likelihood of a risk occurring should be assessed on a gross, a net and a target basis. The gross basis assesses the inherent likelihood of the event occurring in the absence of any processes which the organisation may have in place to reduce that likelihood. The net basis assesses the likelihood, taking into account current conditions and processes to mitigate the chance of the event occurring. The target likelihood of a risk occurring reflects the risk appetite of the organisation. Where the net likelihood and the target likelihood for a particular risk differ, this would indicate the need to alter the risk profile accordingly.

Develop a risk management strategy

Once the risks have been identified and assessed, and the organisation's risk appetite has been set, strategies can be developed by the risk management group to deal with each risk that has been identified. Strategies could include ignoring small risks (but ensuring that they remain under cyclical review) contractual transfer of risk, risk avoidance, risk reduction via controls and procedures and transferring risks to insurers.

Implement the strategy and allocate responsibilities

The chosen strategy should be allocated and communicated to those responsible for implementation. For the plan to be effective, it is essential that responsibility for each specific action is assigned to the appropriate operational manager and that clear target dates are established for each action for the plan to be effective. It is also important to obtain the co-operation of those responsible for the strategy, by the use of means such as formal communication, seminars, action plans and adjustments to budgets.

Implement and monitor controls

The chosen strategy may require the implementation of new controls or the modification of existing controls. Businesses are dynamic and the controls that are in place will need to be monitored to assess whether or not they are succeeding in their objectives. The risk management group should also be empowered to monitor the effectiveness of the actions being taken in each specific area as these can be affected by internal and external factors, such as changes in the marketplace or the introduction of new computer systems.

Case Study: BOC[8]

Industrial gases giant BOC, which has three major lines of business, 18 business units and several specialist units, changed its perception of risk not because of poor performance but because it firmly believed that risk optimisation was a key driver of shareholder value.

In 2001, the company held a risk workshop for directors, which reviewed the value of future growth options and internal and external strategies, as well as overarching risks which might be faced by the existing business model. From this, the company produced an evaluative loop which identified the risks to the strategies and determined preferred risk treatments. From there the loop progressed through to the execution of the strategies, and the communication of the risk and risk treatments connected to a share price based firmly on the estimation of future earnings and an assessment of core competencies.

BOC then evaluated what its competitors were doing, what their future market entry strategies might be, and what their consolidation strategies could be. The predicted consequences were then evaluated.

The company also identified several other major risks to successfully implementing its risk strategy. These included the growth potential of Asia, its semi-conductor business, financial strategy, economics and organisational change.

Following this evaluation, the strategy was then given to the group's senior executives. Two-thirds of its six-monthly management workshop time was also given to the strategy. Since then there have been detailed strategic workshops and milestones, which can be monitored.

The company claims that its new risk management strategy has made it much more aware of what it needs to do in terms of acquisitions and the importance of collaboration with partners. The BOC Group now applies the principles to every project and every acquisition it undertakes.

Risk Management Technology

Robert Levine,[9] in an article on risk management technology, highlighted the importance of appropriate technology in support of Enterprise Governance. According to Levine, the first and most important technology requirement is flexibility. Organisations need the system to support enterprise-wide risk management across multiple geographies, business units, products and risk categories. Each of the traditional risk management cycle areas, including risk identification, prioritisation, analysis, communication and alleviation, needs to be supported by a range of functionality.

Emerging best practice suggests that the most effective way of achieving this is through an open, Internet standards-based data architecture using standards such as XML (eXtensible Mark-up Language) to allow the translation of content between systems.

Using standards-based approaches should facilitate interfaces from various source systems that may be running on legacy, and often proprietary operating systems. Such flexibility means a system design that can be easily modified to handle new regulatory requirements, new risk measurement techniques and advanced risk management processes.

Challenges in Implementing an Effective Risk Management Technology

The implementation of an enterprise-wide risk management solution requires organisations to clarify and review risk policies, and to harmonise conflicting policies within the organisation. For operational risk, such a collaborative environment will normally include functionality in the areas of risk identification, risk assessment (impact and probability of the risk actualising) and risk mitigation. By deploying collaborative risk management technologies organisations can move to greater control and self-assessment where line staff and managers play a front-line role in assessing their own operational risks.

According to Levine, under this approach individual departments test control procedures against an established template on a
regular basis, and also following certain pre-defined risk events.
They then rate their own level of compliance, develop action
plans to address gaps, and monitor progress. Next, auditors test
the validity of the self-assessment to ensure accuracy. Finally, key
performance indicators act as a management control by
quantifying and tracking the organisation's risk management
performance.

Effective Query and Reporting

The enterprise risk system should provide a robust *ad-hoc* inquiry
and reporting capability in addition to a suite of standard reports.
This means custom sorting, selection and calculation for risks
across various geographical or organisational lines, or for
individuals with different reporting needs.

Data Handling

Data handling is also a key factor in designing a risk system. The
solution must provide support not just for fast access to data for
real-time limit checking and exposure or limit updates, but also
must support the handling of historical data.

Organisational Factors

Levine suggests that the biggest challenge in implementing a
successful risk management system is the need to introduce
openness into a closed corporate culture. He warns that many
employees are reluctant to report risks because this would appear
to expose their own (or their department's) weaknesses. Also,
consistent risk policies, risk treatment and visible limits will
expose the activities of business units near and far to central risk

monitoring. This could be perceived as a loss of local office independence, and even a threat to local jobs as it becomes easier to manage risks centrally. These perceptions must be recognised during a system's implementation.

Internal Control

Internal control is a process not an end in itself.[10] In simple terms, corporate governance has to do with managing the risks of doing business, and thus protecting the stakeholders. Comprehensive, enterprise-wide risk management is the main purpose of corporate governance. Aside from the inherent risk implicit in the nature of business, a firm's risks can be identified with its systems, both manual and automated.

A corporation comprises many systems, two of which are the most significant: its operational system and its information system. The two systems create a mirror function. Operations are supported by information and at the same time, operations are a source of data from which information is derived. Risks emerge from operations, information systems or from the relationship between the two.

How to Gain Control

In order to gain the necessary operational control to avoid confrontation with stakeholders, directors need an integrated, automated platform that delivers a single point of control, as well as enforcing business rules and compliance with policies, across the organisation. Good corporate governance is about improving corporate performance, accountability and risk management and corporate control. Combined corporate performance management (CPM) and Risk Management and Corporate Control (RMCC) should ensure that information travels more quickly to the right people and that it is what they *need* to hear instead of just what they *want* to hear.

AMR Research's 2003 survey[11] of Fortune 1000 companies on Sarbanes–Oxley Act compliance revealed that 85 per cent of companies were planning changes to their IT systems to support compliance efforts. It estimates that around $2.5bn will be spent planning and executing SOX-related efforts. For most companies, however, SOX compliance requirements also present an opportunity to improve systems, processes, increase reliability and data security and enhance technology performance. For some time now, IT consultancy the Gartner Group has extolled the virtues of combining Planning, Measurement and Reporting in a single CPM framework. However, there is still a piece missing from this jigsaw – the area of RMCC. Planning applications help the management team decide on the key objectives that are worth pursuing; scorecard and measurement tools ensure efficient execution. RMCC is the next step – making sure that the execution of the plan does not compromise accounting standards, undermine ethical policies or breach codes of conduct. Overall, it ensures that the company does not lose out on major commercial opportunities.

The best way to embed risk policies thoroughly across the organisation is to combine policy communication with employees' daily routine, ensuring that risk management is comfortably aligned with managerial planning, culture and operation. This approach will enable the board to make management accountable for designing, implementing and monitoring the process of RMCC in a context of planning and execution. Bringing together RMCC and established CPM activities thus seems the obvious choice and it is increasingly becoming best practice across leading organisations.

However, the system will only yield the expected operational transparency and improved efficiency if its RMCC and CPM components are implemented with a high degree of automation and if they make it easy to capture qualitative and quantitative data related to the health and performance of both tangible and intangible assets. Non-automated processes, fragmented systems and hands-off attitudes by senior executives create loopholes that can leave the business exposed to a range of risks. Not least of these are human error, fraud, safety and environmental issues, as well as the possible impact of a damaged corporate reputation and brand value.

Case Study: AOL Time Warner

In 2000, Steve Case, CEO of America On Line (AOL) and Jerry Levin, CEO of Time Warner appeared on a New York stage to announce a merger between the two companies. Three years later, and the $112bn merger that created AOL Time Warner is widely regarded as a disaster. By 2001, AOL's business was in sharp decline as the number of new subscribers to its Internet services fell and advertising revenue dried up. Months later an investigation of AOL's accounts was begun by the SEC, and AOL Time Warner's share price fell by two-thirds. A year later both Case and Levin, who allegedly agreed to the deal without consulting any other board member, had lost their jobs.

At the beginning of 2004 the company's share price, still limping from devaluation, was 60 per cent up from its lowest point. However, the cost of regaining consumer confidence had been high. The company has been forced to sell half of Time Warner's highly successful channel Comedy Central to rival Viacom for $1.23bn, and Warner Music Group's DVD and CD manufacturing arm for $1.05bn. Other sales are expected. And in November 2003, the company finally renamed itself as Time Warner, dropping AOL from its name, if not from its history.

Notes

1 L. Puschaver and G. R. Eccles (1996) 'In pursuit of the upside: The new opportunity in risk management', *PW Review*, Dec.

2 Governance, Risk and Assurance survey, CFO Europe 2003.
3 CODA Group (2004) *Corporate Response to Governance Pressures – A Global Survey: Meeting the Challenge of Enterprise Governance*.
4 The World Business Council for Sustainable Development (2003) *Running the Risk: Risk and Sustainable Development – a Business Perspective*.
5 PwC Global Risk Management Solutions (2003) 'Corporate Governance: The Forces of Activism and Globalisation', *Risky Business*, Issue 2a.
6 CSR Wire February 2004.
7 Chartered Institute of Management Accountants (2004) *Enterprise Governance – Getting the Balance Right*, London: CIMA.
8 Financial Management Accounting Committee, IFAC (2002) 'Managing Risk to Enhance Stakeholder Value', November (www.IFAC.org)
9 R. Levine (2004) 'Risk management systems: understanding the need', *Information Systems Management*, vol. 21, no. 2.
10 V. Raval (2004) 'Resource Management and Corporate Governance: Information Strategy', *The Executive's Journal*, vol. 20, no. 2.
11 AMR (2003) 'Sarbanes-Oxley survey: Fortune 1000 will spend more than $2.5B in initial compliance', *AMR Research*, May 5, 2003.

CHAPTER 12

CONCLUSION: A STRATEGY FOR FINANCE PROFESSIONALS

Accounting, as perceived today, will go away. Less than 25 per cent of AICPA members actually provide traditional corporate accounting and auditing services. The majority now perform technology, management consulting and personal financial planning services. The profession is changing and evolving more into knowledge services.

(Leigh Knopf, director of strategic planning and change management of the American Institute of Certified Public Accountants (AICPA))

So far in this book we have focused on the systems and processes necessary for business to ensure good Enterprise Governance. However, the systems and processes you choose are only as good as the people implementing and overseeing them. Today's finance professional needs to communicate more than ever before, making relevant information accessible to the board and other decision-makers across the enterprise as well as to other stakeholders. They must recognise that success depends upon sharply defined, clearly communicated strategy, flawless execution, clear company values and a structure that promotes cooperation, communication and innovation.[1]

This chapter traces the changing role of the finance professional and focuses on the new skills they will need to meet the challenges of an evolving regulatory landscape and increased stakeholder scrutiny.

Management Accountancy – the Original Value-Added Function

Since the late 1990s, the finance department has been evolving from a back-office operation responsible for transactional processes and historical reporting, to a front-end function responsible for driving value creation and developing strategy. As such, the focus has shifted from sifting through historical data to the demanding arena of 'real-time finance'. Accountants, who have long been at their happiest when sat in front of a spreadsheet, will no longer spend much of their working time retrieving historical data for the dreaded month-end close, but collecting and analysing real-time data for decision support processes as planning and budgeting become continuous rather than fixed functions.

But finance professionals were already witnessing a gradual and gentle change to their role before Enron et al. accelerated the process and brought the profession sharply into stakeholder focus. Management accounting by its very own definition is designed to add value. Its purpose is to provide information for planning and control, cost management, strategic cost management and resource waste reduction. But its evolution from a technical activity in the pursuit of organisational objectives, to a distinctive dimension of the management process focused on organisational resource and managerial processes has taken more than 50 years.

Mark Adams, CFO of STA Travel

'Everybody within the group has to understand finance. This is very important to us especially as most of our managing directors have come up through the commercial end of the company, and therefore have not had any formal finance training.

'Our CEO expects to be able to talk to anyone within the organisation about finance, but it is all too easy to take it for granted that everyone is at that level.

'Around five years ago STA's finance department operated in the more traditional sense with the CFO managing the books. It was still very much a back office department and was not considered a key part of the business. That has changed dramatically following the implementation of our systems strategy.

'The finance function now has much more importance placed upon it, especially with the advent of real time technology. Control is gained through information. Up until now 80 per cent of our function has been pure processing, with 20 per cent value added analytics. We want to change the balance.

'Within the profession a lot of people simply keep their heads down and bury themselves in their work, not aware or interested in how they can add value to the business. In general, they do not have any commercial understanding. In fact, currently there are very few people who have both finance experience and business acumen. Before restructuring, the team had no responsibility or authority, nor were they expected to do anything other than what they were told to do. There were a number of employees, who despite intensive training and support, failed to alter their perspective in line with our vision. Although their skills remain valuable, the number of companies looking to employ those is getting smaller and will soon be restricted to private family-owned companies that need accountants to process the most basic financial regulation. They will not be looking for anyone to analyse financial data.'

The 1980s and 1990s

During the weak economic period of the late 1980s and early 1990s, the CFO was regarded as a cost-cutting wizard by the board. As trading conditions became more difficult, he was expected to wave a magic cost-cutting wand that would allow the company to remain financially watertight as it sailed turbulent economic waters. Board contact was still at the traditional minimum, and very few finance professionals were expected to demonstrate strategic capabilities or drive shareholder value. By the mid-1990s however, CFOs were increasingly being asked to provide substantial decision support on profitability improvement opportunities.[2] This newly fledged responsibility was temporarily grounded with the emergence of Enterprise Resource Planning (ERP) systems, together with Y2K-readiness paranoia. CFOs and finance directors soon found themselves overseeing complex, lengthy and costly system implementation with little time left over for strategy.

The New Millennium

A global sigh of relief was uttered as the world moved into the new millennium without a technological hitch despite the hype. But it was not all good news. By 2001, the dotcom boom ended with a resounding crash, turning the focus away from rapid growth and customer numbers and back to creating sustainable shareholder value. CFOs, now armed with data mining capabilities, resumed their emerging role as strategist and focused on analysing data that would help drive the business forward. Then, without warning, Enron collapsed, heralding a new regulatory dawn and the intensified scrutiny of financial reports and audits worldwide, as well as the domestic Generally Adopted Accounting Principles (GAAP) that guided them. As the drive for regulatory reform gained momentum, it became clear that the rapidly evolving role of corporate steward would fall into the CFO's domain. The impact of this, many believe, not only elevated the CFO to a co-executive position, but earned the role the recognition that many finance professionals claimed it had never fully received.

Following these changes, it could be argued that the finance professionals' traditional career path has eroded. Traditionally, promotion to senior finance positions reflected time served as an articled clerk and partner, or its equivalent, respectively. But increasingly, accounting qualifications and experience are no longer considered as the minimum requirement needed to run a finance department. In the USA, companies are already starting to employ non-finance professionals as CFOs, prioritising business acumen over accounting qualifications. Some observers have even gone as far to suggest that the CFO's increased commercial importance and business skills will lead to a greater number being promoted to the position of CEO. Fledgling finance professionals are therefore under pressure to develop and expand additional skills in MBA-related subjects such as strategy, forecasting and planning to scale the corporate ladder.

The Changing Role of the Finance Professional

The finance director is in a very, very important role in terms of ensuring that the information provided is objective and that there is proper financial control. Providing objective information can, from time to time, be very risky. If you go to your chief executive and say 'we need to make a profit warning', it is not what he wants to hear. Sometimes the messenger gets shot. For the messenger to be comfortable about producing independent information, he shouldn't have to worry about his personal circumstances. A one-year rolling contract, giving a year's compensation, means you can take a more objective view about the future including your own personal future and therefore you maintain that objectivity.

(CIMA chief executive, Charles Tilley)

Back in the 1970s, a finance director looking to change his place of work would avidly scan the *Financial Times* recruitment pages for suitable vacancies. The ideal candidate would be expected to have senior financial or management accountancy experience, as well as the 'maturity and gravitas' needed to fulfil the role. Knowledge of corporate governance and taxation legislation were previously not considered great priorities, nor were strategic thinking or the now obligatory 'personal attributes.'[3] Three decades later much has changed. Today's prospective finance directors or CFOs are expected to demonstrate strong leadership and communication skills, have generic IT systems knowledge, industry specific experience, and perhaps most importantly of all be commercially aware. Experience of regulatory compliance is paramount, especially for companies that fall under the jurisdiction of Sarbanes–Oxley, and any mergers and acquisition experience is highly prized. Research by auditors Deloitte and Bristol Business School to highlight the changing role of the finance director[4] revealed a dramatic reversal of skills that were desirable in the 1970s to skills essential in the late 1990s. The study, which compared job adverts for senior finance professionals over three decades, showed that while in the 1970s business acumen and leadership were not significant, they became increasingly so during the late 1980s and into the 1990s. The CFO's role therefore has seemingly evolved into a complex hybrid of strategist, corporate steward and management leader.

Other industry reports echo the profession's concerns. In a joint survey by CFO Research Services and Cap Gemini Ernst & Young, 60 per cent of respondents, all CFOs within Fortune 100 organisations, said their role in developing corporate strategy was a priority. But among the barriers to overcome in that ambition was convincing other business partners of the finance department's renewed importance. Only 25 per cent of those questioned said that they were viewed as a value-added function within their own organisation. The report also highlighted a lack of executive level support for CFOs over IT implementation, adoption or management practices in budgeting, forecasting and planning. Despite this, there are organisations, known as early adapters, who picked up the real-time baton early on and are now enjoying the performance benefits. American Express, which is currently working to a corporate manifesto of 'hands-free AP' now processes all its invoices through the web. It claims that the creation of three shared service centres in Phoenix, Arizona, Delhi, India, and Brighton in the UK, enabled it to produce financial reports across the group soon after 9/11.

Other professional accounting bodies are more positive about the changes being faced by the accounting profession. The International Chartered Institute of Accountants Australia (ICCA) not only predicts a dramatic change to role definition, but the working environment. It foresees a change in attitudes towards work and family issues with many finance professionals working from home, or 'hot-desking' to meet with project demands or even operating as consultants. But although all these changes have been gradual, they have left many finance professionals anxious over their ability to successfully fulfil their new role. According to further UK research by Deloitte in 2003, many finance professionals said that their jobs would become even more difficult over the next two years as new regulatory measures took hold and sustainability became the corporate by-word. Keeping up with regulatory changes was also cited as another key issue, especially as there had been only nine significant amendments to UK accountancy standards over the past 30 years compared to the numerous changes following Enron. Two-thirds of CFOs questioned said that they would have to spend more time at work, with one-third of respondents adding that they were seriously re-considering their careers.

The Challenges

> Most companies have very good skills for the business problems of tomorrow.
>
> (Anon)

Many finance professionals acknowledge that using spreadsheets to manage financial performance is a slow regimented process that fails to give insight into a company's health, wealth and future prospects. According to a CFO Research Services and Comshare joint survey[5] in 2003, which assessed what CFOs wanted from corporate performance management, only 11 per cent of 245 senior finance professionals working within major US companies were confident that spreadsheet-based procedures ensured the accuracy required for Sarbanes–Oxley-governed financial statements. Nearly 50 per cent said they were not confident using spreadsheet-based planning and budgeting. It is not hard to see why. Like a game of Chinese whispers, new versions of spreadsheets are sent back and forth, with much of the data re-keyed for each revision, thereby increasing the chance for human error. There is also a tendency for senior executives to spend much of the board meeting arguing over whose spreadsheet has the right numbers, when they could be agreeing strategy.

Regulatory compliance is not the CFOs' only concern. A sluggish global economy, the effects of terrorism and the so-called 'war on terror', including the Iraq conflict, have contributed to a general decline in domestic market conditions. Near-term sales and profits are still among some of the biggest challenges currently facing CFOs as lead times visibly shrink. But as the competitive environment gets tougher, so too are the demands on finance to provide decision support to the business. According to the CFO/Comshare report, 50 per cent of CFOs believed that their boards would demand better quality information in the near future, 43 per cent more detail, and 32 per cent increased frequency. Meanwhile, competing corporate priorities have led to redundancies within the finance department and dramatically reduced IT budgets. As a result the remaining finance workforce spends more time developing the numbers than developing actions that could ultimately improve market performance.

Barriers to Change

CFOs will have to overcome a number of barriers to evolve the finance department's function and improve performance management. Whatever the budget, size and type of organisation, or how well versed a CFO is in technical matters, technology should add value. According to CIMA, when selecting a good information system, the solution should:

- be defined by a company's profile, not the other way round;
- be focused on solving critical success factors rather than those that are merely desirable;
- have a flexible architecture to survive technological and business changes;
- be scaleable – offering key summary information down to detailed analysis;
- be integrated with the board's reporting process.

Beware Information Overload

As the finance department warms to its newly awarded strategic function and the demand for real-time data increases, CFOs will have to decide what to report and measure in order to identify leading indicators and key performance drivers. However, the temptation to include all the data available in the pursuit of detail will be great, even though accessing it may prove a little more challenging. Many companies find that having invested in complex business metrics, the information is buried deep within those metrics across the enterprise. Furthermore, if a company has failed to integrate its performance management systems into a single solution, the retrieval process could be slowed down even further (see Chapter 6). Finance professionals not only need to put more than numbers on the table, but have a real understanding of the business and added value processes behind it.

However, having the information processed and analysed is not enough to drive shareholder value. CIMA stresses that the need for 'clear information' and concise performance reports is as important as the data itself. The organisation encourages its members to ensure that all performance reports or *ad hoc* data are material, relevant, reliable, comparable and understandable. Therefore, CFOs preparing a monthly report should ensure that the report is:

- concise – just 10–20 pages should suffice;
- timely – board members should have time to digest it before meeting;
- readily understandable;
- focused – it must convey strategic and operational information clearly;
- clear – it should give an accurate picture of events;
- consistent;
- forward-looking – presents a view of the future with projections and scenarios for next month, next year or longer;
- easy to assimilate – by means of graphs, charts, colour-coding, clear headings and selective highlighting;
- to the point – supplementary information is annexed only if considered vital to a board's understanding of the report;

- comprehensive – allows the board to discharge its responsibilities to investors, suppliers, customers, employees and stakeholders.

Internal Resistance – The Importance of Communication

Although the business community has seemingly embraced the CFO's new corporate function, remnants of the traditional 'us and them' silo mentality still linger. According to a *Business Week* survey, which studied the views of corporate finance function of more than 500 medium to large enterprises, around 60 per cent of CEOs said they believed that the finance function was integrated with the business, compared to 38 per cent of CFOs. The study also showed that CEOs and CFOs disagreed over who was leading their firm's efforts to comply with new corporate governance rules and requirements. In the report almost half of CEOs said that they were leading the effort, whilst only 14 per cent of CFOs believed that the CEO was in the lead. Nearly 65 per cent of CFOs said that they were responsible for leading the company's compliance efforts.

Education, Education, Education

The International Federation of Accountants' Education Committee in its report *Continuing Professional Development (A Programme of Lifelong Learning and Continual Development of Professional Competence)* proposes a mandatory and voluntary international continual professional development (CPD) framework for the finance professional. The report identifies the importance of learning plans and competency maps which the IFAC, and a number of other professional bodies, have created. Through this framework, professional accountants are encouraged to review their current skills and competencies against a set target. The competency maps identify skill needs before identifying relevant learning activities. They also provide a list of key competencies for certain roles and career levels.

Recommended learning activities include:

- attending courses, seminars, and conferences;
- self-learning modules for new software, systems, procedures and techniques;
- publishing professional writing;
- participation on technical committees;
- formal study;
- speaking at finance-related events;
- writing technical articles;
- research;
- re-examination of formal testing.

The IFAC recommends that all learning activities should be measured in units to ensure desired CPD levels are reached. But a number of industry experts are calling for a complete reassessment of training programmes both in degree and refresher courses. In the USA, many universities such as Leonard N. Stern School of Business (New York University) are now offering double majors in accounting and IT.[6] Not only are students encouraged to take on part-time jobs, they are also required to do oral presentations and team projects in an effort to improve communication and interpersonal skills. Other education establishments including Chicago School of Business are customising internal training programmes to offer a wider spectrum of modules in pace with change and professional demands.

Achieving the Vision

To achieve better financial performance, finance professionals will have to reallocate resources to improve decision support and overall efficiency. Although the efficiency of transactional processes such as billing, time and expense, and fixed asset accounting, can be improved through IT they are finance functions that easily lend themselves to shared services or outsourcing.[7] Reporting and control processes, however, such as general ledger, closing, compliance reporting, require one central information control point to ensure high levels of integrity, effective compliance and most importantly 'one version of the truth'. Instead of outsourcing, financial professionals should consider standardising a chart of accounts, improving information retrieval, delivery and reporting, as well as consolidating any general ledgers. By their very nature, decision support processes including planning, budgeting, forecasting and cost accounting, utilise information to improve business performance and drive shareholder value. Therefore focus needs to be placed on implementing CPM tools that will improve management information capabilities.

But just as nature needs bio-diversity to create a stable environment, so too does the finance profession. The world of finance would not be able to sustain itself if each and every accountant chose to specialise in the same area of accountancy. There is still a place for the traditional 'bean counter' among the environmental accountants, finance analysts and CFOs. And although organisations will benefit from moving the finance function from the back seat to the driving wheel, their finances still need to be kept on track.

The Rewards

Increased remuneration is but one significant reward for the additional responsibilities and stresses. According to research by Robert Half International, salaries for US-based accountants are steadily rising, with entry pay packets for fresh-faced trainee graduates now advertised at the $30,000 mark. Women are also expected to receive better remuneration and career prospects against a historical background of poor rates of pay and promotion opportunities. More than half of America's accounting workforce is already female,[8] and that number is expected to rise over the next five years in-line with increased job flexibility and 'hot-desking'. Accountants will also have the opportunity to specialise in newly created roles as their profession becomes more diversified. Finance professionals who have long yearned to be involved at the 'sharp end' of the business will be able to pursue more strategic roles, or even make a move to consulting. Accountants with heightened IT skills will be called on to oversee integration or implementation projects such as web-based portals or CPM software, and those with analytical training could move into newly created specialised areas such as forensic accounting or specific finance analysis. The job will no longer be ring-fenced by a basic duty to count numbers.

Notes

1 N. Nohria, W. Joyce and B. Roberson (2003) 'What really works?' *Harvard Business Review*, July, vol. 81, no. 7, pp. 43–52.
2 Cap Gemini Ernst & Young and CFO Research Services 2003 report. *Finance Transformed: How Leading Companies are Succeeding*, Sept. 2003, London: CFO Publishing Corp.
3 R. Hussey and M. Sowinska (2000) *Changing Role of the Finance Director*, Deloitte/Bristol Business School.
4 Ibid.
5 Comshare and CFO Research Services 'CFO Survey' 2003.
6 'Next Generation Accountant: New Competencies, Converging Disciplines, Expanding Roles' Robert Half International, Inc. Available online at: www.nextgenaccountant.com
7 S. Lis (2002) 'The Changing Role of the Utility CFO – The Utilities Project Volume 2', IBM Global Services.
8 Department of Labor Women's Bureau, USA. Available online at: www.dol.gov/wb

INDEX